Britain Transformed

An Economic and Social History 1700-1914

Malcolm Falkus

Causeway Books

To M.C.

Causeway Press Ltd
PO Box 13
Ormskirk Lancs L39 5HP
© Malcolm Falkus 1987
1st Impression 1987, Reprinted 1990, 1992, 1994, 1997

British Library Cataloguing in Publication Data

Falkus, Malcolm
  Britain transformed : an economic and
  social history, 1700-1914.
  1. Great Britain — Social conditions
  I. Title
  941.07   HN385

  ISBN 0-946183-35-X

Typeset by WA Print Services, Manchester
Origination by Accrington Observer & Times
Printed and bound by The Alden Press, Oxford, England

Contents

(iv)

Acknowledgments

We are grateful to the following for permission to reproduce illustrations.

BBC Hulton Picture Library 50, 171, 173
Bedfordshire County Council 69
Bradford Art Galleries and Museums 153, 154
Bristol Museum and Art Gallery 23
Fotomas Index 176
Institute of Agricultural History 65, 184, 187
Mansell Collection 22, 62, 90, 93, 134, 145, 150 (bottom)
Mary Evans Picture Library 7, 9, 20, 31, 34, 35, 37, 38, 39,
        40, 41, 42, 56, 57, 76, 85, 92, 94, 132, 135 (top),
        137, 139, 150 (top), 157, 161, 188, 206, 207, 214,
        216, 220, 223, 224
Merseyside County Art Galleries 89
Merseyside Museum of Labour History 178
Science Museum 126
Sheffield City Libraries 121
Sheffield Museums Department 120
Victoria and Albert Museum 196, 197
Weidenfeld and Nicolson Ltd 209
Wellcome Institute Library, London 152
Wigan Record Office 111

Preface

No textbook in this subject can get it right. Economic and social history is so broad, its borders so ill-defined, examination syllabuses so all-encompassing, new research so continuous, that somewhere along the line the textbook virtues of comprehensiveness, simplicity, and up-to-dateness must, to some extent, fall by the wayside.

These are supply side problems. On the demand side too there are difficulties. The needs of pupils (and their teachers) vary; students come to the subject with different levels of background knowledge and experience; sometimes economic and social history is combined with a history course, sometimes with economics, sometimes it stands on its own.

Having both taught the subject at University level for many years and being Moderator of the London University GCE Examinations Boards for 'A' level and 'O' level Economic History, I am convinced that a clear gap exists among current textbooks. This book has been written to help fill the gap. There is a need for a book which will address the more complex parts of the subject found, for example, in A level syllabuses, yet which is written in simple and straightforward language. There is a need for a book which will say unequivocally where the results of present research stand, and, if no agreed conclusions are possible, say so. To say 'we do not know' is nothing to shy away from in economic history. There is a need for a book which will emphasise the questions asked by economic historians as much as the answers. This is not simply because examinations students must cope with questions; rather, it is because what defines the subject is more the questions asked than the answers provided. When students ask, as intelligent students always do, 'what **is** economic history', the best reply is that economic history consists of the questions economic historians ask and the approaches they use in answering those questions; the answers may well range over a number of related disciplines.

In short, this book is written to help sixth-formers and others understand something both about the evolution of Britain's economy and society and about the approach taken by economic and social historians in looking at the subject.

Students and texbook writers share a common problem: sorting out the general overview from the detail. The more we study a subject in depth the more rewarding and interesting it becomes, yet if every subject is treated in depth the poor sixth-former will promptly drown. For this reason I have included five short pieces at intervals in the book (at the close of Chapters 1,3,7,8 and 11) which might be thought of as answers to the kind of question so favoured by examiners who feel the need to cast questions at all corners of the syllabus: 'write on **one** of the following...'. The subjects have been chosen to represent the sort of topics most often asked about. The pieces are designed to show how an economic historian can approach such topics and treat them in a systematic way which manages to incorporate something about the economy and society generally.

Malcolm Falkus
June, 1987

Chapter 1
Eighteenth Century Economy and Society

Starting and terminal dates in social and economic history can never be followed rigidly. For convenience we may use the beginning or end of centuries or major wars to mark boundaries, but an economy never starts with a clean slate. The past always haunts the present, societies are stubborn, and social change normally gradual. Continuity rather than change is a theme which runs throughout British history. Indeed, not a few of the leading historical debates among scholars have been produced after one historian puts forward the significance of a particular event, or discovers a 'revolution'; others then point out how relatively unimportant this event was at the time, how its roots can be traced far back in history, and how its influence spreads only slowly.

So with the year 1700. It was not drastically different from 1699 or even — in the broad essentials and social and economic life — from the 1680s or the 1660s. Similarly, when Daniel Defoe, of *Robinson Crusoe* fame, made his celebrated *Tours* through England and Wales in the 1720s, the life he described would not have differed in fundamentals had he made his journeys ten or twenty years earlier or later.

However, to start a description of British social and economic history at the beginning of the eighteenth century is not simply a matter of convenience, for there are two reasons which make this period particularly appropriate. It is true that social and economic changes usually happen gradually rather than suddenly, and the further we go into the past, away from the present age of instant communications, global warfare, and massive technological advance, the truer this is. But some periods have always experienced more change than others, and the years around the 1700 mark one such period of change. Wherever we look we can find evidence that the economy was far from static: in the river improvement schemes of the 1690s, the financial innovations which led to the founding of the Bank of England in 1697, the introduction of new commodities from growing trade with distant parts (like coffee and cocoa in the 1680s), the spread of new crops and rotations in agriculture, the remarkable rebuilding of London after the Great Fire of 1666 ... and so on. There is no point in extending the list for the picture is clear: around the opening of the eighteenth century Britain's economy was on the move in a number of ways.

The second reason for starting around 1700 is to prick the bubble of the 'classic' industrial revolution. The once-fashionable view of a sudden transformation around the 1760s, with population, agriculture, and industry all advancing in step is now hopelessly out of date. The picture now is of a much more gradual evolution of economic activity with even the industrial changes of the years 1790-1820 less impressive than was once thought. A view from around 1700 enables us to get this more gradual pattern into a better perspective, and hence to understand the true nature of these changes we call the industrial revolution.

Was England Underdeveloped in 1700?

It is possible to present two quite contrasting views of the economy around 1700. One view likens pre-industrial Britain to a present-day underdeveloped country, pointing out that by today's standards the nation then was poor, predominantly agrarian, and little-urbanised. Most manufacturing industry was small-scale and carried on in the countryside using simple labour-intensive techniques of production. Like so many third world countries today, early modern Britain suffered from endemic poverty, itself largely the result of chronic underemployment. A sort of vicious poverty circle existed; techniques of production were primitive with the result that productivity, both in agriculture and industry, was low. Low productivity meant low average incomes (though some people, of course, were fabulously wealthy, just as in present-day poor countries). Low incomes meant low savings and so only limited capital investment which might have raised productive techniques. Under those circumstances population pressure was always to be feared, for rising numbers would quickly press on means of subsistence unless methods of increasing productivity could be found.

The comparison between pre-industrial Britain and today's less developed countries is an interesting one, and can be taken quite far. Phyllis Deane, for example, has calculated that England's average per capita national income around 1750 stood at £90 in the prices of the early 1960s. This would put England in 1750 roughly on a par with Brazil or Mexico in the early 1960s, and about three times richer than Nigeria at the same date. Mid-eighteenth century England, then, in terms of national income, ranks as a middling underdeveloped country by modern standards.

On the other hand we can present a different view. This view would point out quite simply that England was, in terms of average per capita national income, probably the richest country in the world in 1700. England was thus **relatively** an extremely advanced country. Wealth was manifest in many ways: London was possibly the largest city in the world, and increasing in wealth and numbers almost visibly; the tentacles of Britain's commerce were reaching ever further afield, in the Americas, Asia, and Africa; agricultural progress was such that by 1700 the countryside was normally able to produce an export surplus of grain; fine town and country houses were evidence both of mercantile and rural wealth; and foreign visitors to England were in no doubt that the ordinary Englishman was better clothed, better fed, and better housed than his continental counterpart. Britain's foreign trade in 1700 scarcely presented the picture of a backward country, for the nation had long been essentially an exporter of manufactured goods and an importer of raw materials and semi-processed products. At the end of the seventeenth century more than eighty per cent of Britain's domestically produced exports were manufactured commodities (most of them various sorts of woollen textiles).

To speak of England as an essentially agrarian nation in 1700, while true, should not lead us to underestimate the importance of manufactures. Much of the manufacturing was carried on in the countryside, in the cottages of agricultural labourers. Farming and manufacturing were not then separate activities as they are today, and both pursuits involved the entire family, the children as well as the parents. As far as can be judged, a surprisingly high proportion of Britain's domestically produced output consisted of manufactured commodities of one sort or another in the first half of the eighteenth century (i.e. before the classic industrial revolution). According to one estimate, less than half Britain's labour force was employed in agriculture in 1760 and agriculture was contributing little more than one-third to total national income. When we consider that a 'typical' backward country has perhaps 75 per cent of its labour force in agriculture and the primary sector contributes some two-thirds of national income, the relatively advanced nature of Britain's economy before 1760 becomes clear.

We should therefore be very careful never to attach to early modern Britain labels such as 'primitive', 'subsistence', 'self-sufficient', 'medieval', or 'feudal'. Defoe's *Tours* in the 1720s confirmed that England was already very much a national economy, with the twin magnets of London demand and foreign trade exercising an influence throughout the length and breadth of the land.

Everywhere a considerable proportion of agricultural produce was raised for the market, and the extent of regional specialisation both in agricultural and manufactured commodities was a feature Defoe remarked upon again and again: Norfolk turkeys, Cheshire cheese, Honiton lace, Sheffield cutlery, Norwich worsteds, and so on. Cash crops, wage labour, money as a medium of exchange, regional specialisation: these were the hallmarks of an economy where only the remotest border regions could still be called 'subsistence' or 'self-sufficient' with any degree of truth.

To serve this commercial economy a striking number of specialist institutions had arisen. Examples include banks, which were established in London in the second half of the seventeenth century while the Bank of England was set up in 1697. Another example is joint-stock company organisation, and by the end of the seventeenth century shares in some of these companies were being bought and sold at Lloyds Coffee House in Change Alley — an embryonic stock exchange. By 1700, too, insurance and mortgage markets had developed in London, while local organisations of trustees had emerged to improve harbours, docks, bridges, roads, paving and sewage.

Mirroring the complexity of the economy was the complexity of society. Far from the simple pyramid pattern which we might expect in a very backward country (with a small landed aristocracy at the top, a large poverty stricken peasantry at the base, and virtually no movement between the segments of society), the social hierarchy of early eighteenth century England had innumerable graduations with flexibility and mobility between different levels. Most striking, perhaps, was the existence of a substantial 'middle group', who included not only prosperous merchants, tenant farmers, bankers, lawyers, large merchant clothiers and other manufacturers, and brewery owners, but even craftsmen and shopkeepers whose enterprises had prospered and expanded.

In short, society and economy were neither static nor backward. Whatever useful insights might be gained by comparing Britain before the industrial revolution with a modern underdeveloped country, the comparison cannot be carried very far. For another reason, too, the comparison is inappropriate. This is that in 1700 no more advanced economy than Britain existed anywhere, whereas today many of the third world's problems arise simply because of the existence of advanced economies. It would take us far from the subject to discuss this point in detail, but the contrast is clear. We have only to think how difficult it is for the manufactured goods of poor countries to compete with those from the advanced, how underdeveloped countries are often unable to escape dependence on the export of one or two primary products, and how the more advanced segments of backward areas are often alien transplants, with foreign technology, foreign capital, foreign management, and with profits therefore flowing abroad. Contrast this with Britain in 1700. British woollen textiles had no serious rivals in European markets, British shipping was already at least as efficient as that of the Dutch, and Britain's technology and economic institutions had developed in response to the needs of the domestic economy. Britain was by no means universally dominant of course; French silks, Venetian glass, and Indian cotton goods, to mention only three, could not be approached in price or quality by British manufacturers. And Britain benefited much from foreign skills and technology, both in manufacturing and agriculture. But the point is that other countries, once Britain had decisively overtaken Dutch and French shipping, posed no threat. Britain belonged to a small elite of countries that was increasingly coming to dominate the then underdeveloped world, in India, the Caribbean, North America and elsewhere.

Population and Society in the Eighteenth Century

The first census of Britain's population was not taken until 1801, after which it was taken at ten year intervals. For the nineteenth century, therefore, we have an accurate guide to the numbers of inhabitants, and increasing detail about other matters, too, such as occupations. But for the eighteenth century we are dependent on estimates made both by contemporaries at the time and by the work of modern historians.

The 1801 census showed that about 9 million people were living in England and Wales and a further $1\frac{1}{2}$ million in Scotland. This was a very small total compared with today's figure of 55 million living in Great Britain. Yet in 1700 the population had been much smaller still, around 5 million in England and Wales and a further 1 million in Scotland. Questions we must ask, therefore, are why the population should grow in the eighteenth century, and when did the growth start.

Before this, though, we will look a little more closely at the sort of society which existed in England at the beginning of the eighteenth century. What did most people do for a living? Where did they live? Were they rich or poor? Of course, without censuses and other national statistics, we cannot answer these questions precisely. Indeed, one of the first lessons students of economic history have to learn is the limitations of the data at their disposal. Naturally, the further back into the past we go the less data we have and usually the more unreliable are the data which do exist.

With respect to England's social structure around 1700 we are fortunate to have some estimates made by an educated contemporary, Gregory King. King's assessments have generally been approved by modern historians, and recent research tends to confirm in broad outline the picture he painted.

Table 1.1 shows a simplified version of some of Gregory King's calculations made at the end of the eighteenth century.

Table 1.1 England and Wales in 1688: Gregory King's Estimates of Wealth and Social Structure

Group	No. of Families	% of Total	Average Income (£)
Landed Nobility	160	—	2800
Other Landowners	16,400	1.2	380
Professions and Clergy	46,000	3.3	101
Merchants and Shopkeepers	50,000	3.7	228
Artisans and Handicrafts	60,000	4.4	40
Farmers and Freeholders	330,000	24.3	45
Labourers and Outservants	364,000	26.8	15
Cottagers and Paupers	500,000	29.4	$6\frac{1}{2}$
Soldiers and Sailors	94,000	6.9	20
	1,460,560	100.0	18

We can see immediately from this table that agriculture was the basis of this society. Probably around 80 per cent of the population lived in the countryside, which means that only around 20 per cent lived in towns; and half of the population obtained their living directly from agriculture, although many, perhaps the majority, supplemented their agricultural earnings with some form of part-time manufacturing by-employment.

English society, then, was rural-based. The land provided most of the wealth and most of the jobs, and power and status were essentially bound up with the ownership of land. As the eighteenth century progressed this balance shifted, especially from the 1780s. By then the appearance of new industrial and commercial towns was producing new centres of wealth and influence. More and more people belonged to the industrial classes, and their lives became urban rather than rural centred. Nevertheless, the land continued to predominate. Not until about 1820 did industries employ a greater proportion of the workforce than agriculture, and not until 1850 did more people live in towns than in rural villages and hamlets. Moreover landowning continued to remain the basis of privilege and prestige well into the nineteenth century. In the eighteenth century rich merchants and bankers had sought to buy their

Family cottage labour in an attic in the eighteenth century.

way into 'society' by purchasing landed estates and country seats, as did wealthy industrialists in the subsequent century. Only gradually was the power and influence of the landed elite lessened.

According to Gregory King, there were just 160 families belonging to the hereditary nobility, and a further 40 or so non-noble families owned 10,000 acres each or more. The average income of these families approached £3000 a year at a time when more than half of all households were earning £15 a year or less. Wealth and land were thus monopolised by the few. In 1700 the top one per cent had more than one-eighth of the national income, while the latter two-thirds had less than 30 per cent of it. A few were fabulously wealthy. The Duke of Newcastle, for example, had lands in 13 counties, and his rents amounted to £32,000 a year.

The gap between rich and poor was obviously enormous, and it was virtually impossible for someone from the lowest ranks to climb very high. Of course, there were always the few exceptions. James Cook, the famous explorer and navigator, was the son of Cleveland labourer and entered the navy as an able seaman; the poet William Wordsworth was the son of a yeoman farmer; John Taylor, who founded Lloyds Bank and left a fortune of £200,000, began as an apprentice to a button manufacturer. But such extreme examples of social mobility are few and far between. Far more significant was the movement between relatively narrow bands of the social hierarchy which gave to English society a marked flexibility. Various factors were important in maintaining this flexibility. One was simply the existence of many strata of society, so that movement upwards (and downwards) was relatively easy. Another was the relative freedom of living and occupation enjoyed by eighteenth century Englishmen. By 1700 neither town guild regulations nor the attempts by poor law authorities to enforce settlement were of much practical effect in checking occupational or personal mobility. Above all, eighteenth century England saw a growing number of avenues of wealth developing outside the traditional confines of landowning and monopolistic trading.

Characteristics of Eighteenth Century Society

When Gregory King made his estimates of the division of incomes and occupations in the late seventeenth century he counted not by individuals but by families. Moreover, he included in 'families' the entire members of the household dependent on the head of the family. This would include even servants living in the household, so that the average household of the top nobility might consist of forty members, while that of the poorest would only be a husband, wife and their small children.

This reminds us that the family was the essential unit of social organisation and that society was divided into ranks rather than classes. The labourer or craftsman living in one of England's 15,000 parishes would feel himself part of a world which was centred on his parish, his master or manorial lord, and his family: there was as yet little sense of common cause with similar members in other areas. Divisions in society were vertical rather than horizontal. The horizontal division of the country into classes — working classes, labour aristocracy, middle classes and so on — emerged only slowly out of the industrial development of the late eighteenth and nineteenth centuries, and it is a process which has attracted much attention from historians.

Within pre-industrial society as well as in the process of industrialisation itself the **role of women** has often been neglected. This role is now being looked at afresh by social historians, and recent work suggests how significant their role was in eighteenth century society. The view that women were simply the bearers of men's children and looked after the house, and so played

Child labour was common well before the industrial revolution. These children are working in an eighteenth century rope factory.

little direct part in economic activity is far from the truth. Two points must be emphasised here. First, we now know that the average age at which women married in the early eighteenth century was high, perhaps 25 or more. Also, a significant proportion of women never married at all. Secondly, we have to take account of what might be called the 'family economy' of early modern England.

From the first point we can deduce that many females must have been available for full-time work well into their adult lives. The work they did depended on circumstances, but it would seem that generally women workers did lowly and poorly-paid jobs, such as domestic service. They also played a key role in manufacturing under the domestic system, some jobs, such as spinning on spinning-wheels, being very much a preserve of women. Marriage and child-bearing did not necessarily take women out of direct economic employment. The domestic system and the prevailing agricultural techniques were ideally suited to the 'family economy', with both women and children playing an essential part. Thus, at times of intense agricultural activity, like threshing and harvesting, the whole family would find work in the fields. In the long winter evenings various forms of other work could be undertaken, including industrial by-employment. Here, too, women and children had a key role to play, even the very young children doing light tasks. When Defoe in the 1720s visited the textile districts of the West Riding he recorded that 'hardly anything above four years old, but its tasks are sufficient to itself.'

By the standards of today, of course, the widespread use of child labour, especially children as young as four or five years of age, seems unthinkable. But we should remember that not only were many tasks both in the fields and cottage industry not particularly onerous, but that the earnings of women and children were often essential to keep the family income above starvation level. Gregory King thought that an average family of mother, father, and three children needed to earn around £40 a year without having recourse to poor relief or begging. Yet more than half of England's families earned less than this. Thus whatever the labour of working wives or even small children might bring in could make all the difference between abject poverty and an adequate existence. As Maxine Berg puts it, the labour of women and children 'closed the subsistence gap' of the family economy. Another important point is that England's population in 1700 was very young by present-day standards and was getting younger as the eighteenth century progressed. Today only about one in every five inhabitants in Britain is a child under fifteen; in 1815 the proportion was two in every five, and in 1700 about one in every three. So, if children had not worked, the burden of supporting them would necessarily have fallen on the adult population. This, at a time when techniques of production were limited and labour intensive, would have made poverty even more widespread.

The growth of industry and the spread of the factory system at the end of the eighteenth century was to bring some major changes in the employment of women and children. From the earliest factories until well into the second half of the nineteenth century the great majority of employees in the textile factories were women and children.

Appendix: Defoe's 'Tours' as a Source of Economic History

In the 1720s Daniel Defoe (1660-1731) made extensive journeys throughout England, and his descriptions were published in 1724-6 as *A Tour Through the Whole Island of Great Britain.*

The *Tours,* together with other of Daniel Defoe's writings, are a most valuable source for the economic historian. Defoe himself was an able writer and acute observer. What is especially useful is that Defoe toured many areas within a short space of time so that we can obtain a good comparative view of different regions. In Defoe's own words 'matters of antiquity are not my enquiry, but principally observations on the present state of things'. Defoe was particularly interested in the organisation of internal trade and distribution, matters which have left few records and are therefore often neglected. Defoe is therefore an important source of information about such matters as middlemen, fairs, markets, and roads.

Also, Defoe made his journeys well before the classic period of the industrial revolution but at a time when significant changes were taking place. Together with the works of Gregory King and a few others, Defoe's writings provide valuable information about pre-industrial England.

Defoe's *Tours* cannot be used uncritically. Defoe was a prolific writer, a journalist, pamphleteer and novelist, who possibly published more words than any other writer in the English language. Like any expert journalist, he had an eye for a good story and for the unusual rather than the typical. He was prone to exaggerate, and to use examples from the past when it suited his purpose. One example of exaggeration was his estimate of London's population. He thought London's population was $1\frac{1}{2}$ million at a time when it probably was no more than 600,000.

Historians must be careful, therefore, to allow for exaggeration and not to assume that what Defoe chose to record is necessarily typical. Historians must also avoid assuming that Defoe noted everything of importance; he neglected a great deal that was taking place in early eighteenth century England, and his descriptions of Wales, Scotland, and Northern England are only cursory. Above all he was interested in two aspects of the economy, the cloth industry (which he considered the basis of England's wealth and the source of future prosperity); and the distribution of goods to and from London. Both were important, but not as important as Defoe makes out. He says little about Birmingham or the metal goods industry growing there and little about the north-eastern coal industry.

Yet used sensibly Defoe's writing can yield much information about the economy of early eighteenth century England. Four major themes run throughout his *Tours*. First there was the high level of **commercialism** nearly everywhere. Again and again Defoe notes the existence of markets and fairs, where local traders and producers met to buy and sell the products of the area. England in the 1720s was obviously very far from being a backward economy; if pockets of self-sufficiency existed they were confined to the remotest parts of Scotland and Wales, and England was probably already, in Defoe's words, 'the most flourishing and opulent country in the world'.

Related to commercialism was a second theme, that of regional **specialisation** in agricultural products. Defoe used a great many examples of such specialisation, fruit and hops from Kent, turkeys and geese from Norfolk and Suffolk, cheese from Gloucestershire, cider from Devon. Hardly an area was without its particular specialism, which suggests, of course, a high level of commercial farming and inter-regional trade.

The main stimulus to specialisation was the pull of the London market, and this is the third great theme of the *Tours*. Throughout the country Defoe found regions producing for the London market, and as Earle writes 'hardly a page of the *Tour* passes by without a mention of some product of the particular locality which is destined to make the long journey to London'. Defoe commented that 'all the counties of England contribute something towards the subsistence of the great city', and that 'the neighbourhood of London...sucks the vitals of trade in this island to itself.' Thus Defoe described the droves of turkeys and geese, up to a thousand at a time, marched each year from Norfolk to London, and the cattle from Scotland being fattened and sold in East Anglia before making the final leg of the journey to the capital.

The fourth theme is the importance of the cloth industry. Defoe noted especially the concentration and specialisation in such areas as the West Riding of Yorkshire and the West Country. He thought the Leeds cloth market 'perhaps not to be equalled in the World', and drew an interesting comparison between the small 'working clothiers' of the West Riding, employing little capital and producing for the low quality domestic market, and the substantial West Country clothiers with large sums of capital tied up in raw materials and producing high quality cloths. Defoe also noted the importance of family labour in domestic industry, and wrote with approval of how young children, some as young as four or five years of age, helped their parents in the manufacture of cloth in the districts around Halifax.

Against the background of these major themes, Defoe paints a picture of flourishing internal trade, though with some depressed areas like Sudbury, in Suffolk, which he found 'very populous and very poor'. Most trade was carried on by means of markets and fairs, where again specialisation was in evidence. There were also some major general fairs, especially the great annual Sturbridge Fair, on Sturbridge Common, near Cambridge, thought by Defoe to be 'not the greatest in the whole nation, but in the world'.

Defoe found many of England's roads in a deplorable condition and he was enthusiastic about the recent development of turnpikes which he thought 'will lessen the rate of carriage, and so bring goods cheaper to market'. It was the growing use of roads, of course, which made their condition seem so inadequate, and it was the flourishing state of trade, much of it orientated towards London, which is among the most valuable insights Defoe's *Tours* has for economic historians.

Chapter 2
Population Change and Urbanisation

The Growth of Population

In 1700 Britain's population, England, Wales and Scotland, stood at around 5.5 million. In 1911, Great Britain had a population of 41 million, better fed, clothed and housed than their ancestors, and with greater life expectancy. In 1750, the average expectation of life at birth was just 36 years and by 1911 this had risen to 53 (today it is around 70). To maintain a growing population and rising standards of living was a great achievement, perhaps **the** great achievement of modern British economic history.

What caused the upsurge of population, when did it start, and what connection did it have with Britain's economic development?

Apart from migration into and out of a country (which in eighteenth and nineteenth century Britain was relatively unimportant) the rate at which a population grows is a combination of its birth rate and death rate. These rates are usually expressed as the ratio of the number of births or deaths in any year per 1000 of the total population. If the rates are the same the population will be stationary; if there is an excess of births the population will rise and vice-versa. The **rate** of population change will vary with changes in the birth and death rates. Therefore, the first question we must ask in order to establish the mechanism of population changes is what happened to birth and death rates.

For the nineteenth century the picture is fairly clear, for unlike the eighteenth century, historians have the help of the ten-year census, starting in 1801, and the official registration of births, deaths and marriages made compulsory in 1837. Table 2.1 shows that until the 1880s both birth rates and death rates were relatively high and stable; thereafter, both fell significantly.

The high death rates for much of the nineteenth century appear to be a puzzle, since we know that average living standards were improving for much

Table 2.1 Population Change in Great Britain, 1801-1911

Year	Population (millions)	Birth Rates (per 1000)	Death Rates (per 1000)
1801	10.7	34	25
1841	18.6	36	22
1881	29.8	35	21
1911	40.1	26	14

of the period and that there was a gradual spread of better medical knowledge and facilities, especially after 1850. The main causes of the high death rates were two. First there was a rapid growth of urbanisation in these years, much of it the result of internal migration. Mortality rates were always higher in the unhealthy environment of the towns than in the countryside, so that even if conditions in towns were improving (which they certainly were from the 1840s) the average national level of mortality could still rise. Secondly, the level of infant mortality (deaths of infants before they reached their first birthday) remained appallingly high throughout the nineteenth century and showed no tendency to fall until after 1900. Deaths of such infants were 154 per 1000 live births in 1840 and still 154 in 1900, having touched 162 in 1850. In other words of every seven babies born alive more than one died before reaching the age of one. After 1900 better medical care and nutrition helped produce a rapid decline in infant mortality. The figure was 105 in 1910 and 53 in 1938.

High death rates, both among adults and infants, in the nineteenth century should warn us against exaggerating the medical improvements of the period. Earlier historians laid considerable stress on the impact of better medicine and medical treatment. However, except for the effects of smallpox inoculation from the mid-eighteenth century, and Edward Jenner's new technique of vaccination against smallpox in the early nineteenth century, historians now give little credit to the medical profession for falling death rates. Earlier theories about the disappearance of certain killer diseases, like the plague, have also been largely discounted. Instead, historians now emphasise social factors, such as slowly improving standards of nutrition, less overcrowding in towns and greater cleanliness (thus controlling the spread of infectious diseases), purer water supplies, and so on. As we have seen death rates remained high before the 1880s, but without these social improvements we might have expected the rates to rise as urbanisation grew.

Birth rates began to decline from the 1880s for a number of reasons, the most significant of which were the spread of knowledge about methods of contraception and the growing cost of bringing up children. Family sizes were reduced first among the middle and upper classes, and only later did the working classes limit their families. This is probably because it was the middle-classes who were most able to acquire knowledge about contraceptive techniques and to afford them, and it was middle-class children who were staying at school longer and so costing more to raise. The decline in infant mortality (which occurred first among the better-off social groups) was a further reason for family limitation.

The relation, if any, between population and economic growth in nineteenth century Britain is difficult to determine. Older textbook writers were impressed by the growing population. Nowadays the tendency is rather to blame abundant cheap labour as a reason for Britain's slow adoption of capital-intensive technology, at least after the 1870s. Moreover it has recently been argued that France, **because** of its slow rate of population increase, was able to increase *per capita* living standards at least as successfully as Britain for most of the nineteenth century. But this is perhaps to view the matter the wrong way round. It is now clear that population growth in Britain accelerated before industrialisation became a dominant force. Without subsequent industrialisation Britain's fate may have been similar to Ireland's, where the disastrous famine of the 1840s led to mass emigration and a falling population. Ireland's demographic history was very different to that of Britain, and it cannot be discussed here in any detail. But it is a striking fact that in 1801 there was one Irish inhabitant for every two in England and Scotland. By 1911 there was one for every ten. And by this later date Ireland's total population had fallen to only 4.4 million from its peak of 8.2 million in 1841.

So far we have confined the discussion mainly to nineteenth century population change, but it is the eighteenth century which has given rise to most discussion and controversy. Attention has focussed on this period because historians are interested in a fundamental question: the relation between population change and economic development during the industrial revolution. Controversy has arisen because until recently the cause and timing of population changes were vigorously disputed.

The main sources of England's demographic history before 1801 are the registers kept by each parish of baptisms, burials, and marriages. These parish registers have proved a very unsatisfactory source of information; they were not always well-kept, they were often incomplete, and they exclude those like the dissenters and Catholics, who were outside the Church of England. Moreover apparent changes in baptisms or burials could be caused simply by internal migration into or out of a particular parish, rather than reflect real changes in the rates.

As a result, two quite contradictory explanations of eighteenth century population changes have been put forward. Until recently, the most widely accepted view was that growth was caused mainly by falling death rates, which in turn were usually ascribed to better medical facilities. The alternative view was that rising birth rates, rather than falling death rates, were responsible for the changes.

A new study by Wrigley and Schofield, published in 1981, has now settled many of the most controversial issues. Using the parish registers, but making painstaking family by family case-histories, the authors have been able to build up an accurate picture of the course and causes of demographic change in eighteenth century England. The growth of total population is given in Table 2.2.

Table 2.2 England's Population 1701-1821 (millions)

Year	Population (millions)	Year	Population (millions)
1701	5.1	1791	7.7
1731	5.3	1801	8.7
1751	5.8	1811	9.9
1781	7.0	1821	11.5

Contrary to what is sometimes suggested, England's population was on the increase for most of the first half of the eighteenth century, though at a slow rate. From the 1770s there was a steady acceleration in the rate of growth, and during the decade 1811-1821 the rate reached the high level of 1.5 per cent a year (a growth of 18 per cent in the decade).

This growth of population was due mainly to increases in the birth rate, though death rates were also falling. Roughly two-thirds of the growth in the eighteenth century population was due to rising birth rates, and only one-third to falling death rates. Fluctuations in birth and death rates were considerable, and until about 1740 there was no very obvious movement in the rates, either up or down. From this time, though, the level of birth rates rose from around 33 per thousand to about 40 per thousand in 1801. Death rates dropped, too, though less dramatically, from about 29 to 25 per thousand. As the gap between the rates widened, the rate of population growth increased.

Why were birth rates rising? The major reason was that the age at which women married fell, so that the number of children each woman might be expected to bear was increasing. In 1700 the average age at which women married was about 26½, while in 1800 it had come down to about 23½. At the same time the number of women never marrying at all fell from about one in six to about one in fourteen.

Why did the age at which women married tend to fall? The interesting point here is that the age of marriage in early modern England (and in other west European societies) tended to be governed by **economic** rather than by purely **biological** considerations. It is well established, for example, that at times of depressed economic conditions, when harvests were bad, couples delayed getting married and having children until better times returned. The implication is two-fold: that the late age of marriage around 1700 was a means by which society improved economic welfare, with consequent implications for capital accumulation and living standards; and that women got married younger in the eighteenth century when economic conditions were favourable. Contrary to Malthusian views there was no uncontrolled surge of population, but rather a deliberate response to improving economic conditions. Under these circumstances population growth can be a spur to economic development: growing population provides a larger workforce, and a larger population produces bigger markets and hence greater opportunities for specialisation and taking advantage of economies of scale. Population growth in the eighteenth century, therefore, should be viewed as a positive factor in economic development, rather than the depressive force feared by Malthus.

Urbanisation and the Role of London

The overall growth of population was accompanied by significant regional variations. Most important was the general faster rate of increase in the industrial counties than in rural areas, and the increase in urbanisation. Both these movements became more marked from the 1770s. Until this time, indeed, the largest provincial towns after London (which was always easily the largest city) were the old-established centres of Bristol and Norwich, but thereafter new industrial and commercial centres like Manchester, Leeds, and Liverpool soon outstripped them. Steadily and irreversibly Britain moved from a predominantly rural to a predominantly urban society. The 1851 census showed that for the first time more people were living in towns than in the countryside and the average Briton had become a town-dweller. In 1801 about one-third of the population lived in towns; in 1901 the proportion was over three-quarters.

The growth of factory towns in the north of England, with their novelty and their social problems, has tended to deflect the attention of the historian

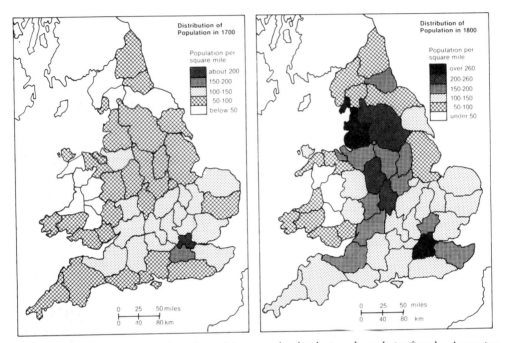

While total population grew in the eighteenth century, the distribution changed significantly. A growing proportion of England's population was concentrated in the growing industrial areas of the North and Midlands.

away from London. Yet in eighteenth century Britain, London was massively important, its influence felt far and wide. Recently historians have begun to reassess London's role, laying stress on the capital both as a centre for economic change and as a forcing-house for social change, with a growing group of middle-class merchants and professional people.

In the 1520s London's population had stood at about 75,000; easily the largest city, but only around 2 per cent of the population of England and Wales. By 1700, after a period of enormous growth in the seventeenth century, London (the City and its fast-growing suburbs) had around 575,000 inhabitants, or eleven per cent of the total population of the country. Growth continued. In 1750 the population stood at about 685,000, by 1801 nearly one million; and throughout the nineteenth century London continued to house around ten or eleven per cent of the entire population of England.

In the eighteenth century London was Europe's largest city, and possibly the largest city in the world (Asia contained some very large cities, but their size is uncertain). In 1700 London was just a little larger than Paris, Europe's second city. By 1800 London had grown to almost twice the size of Paris, despite the fact that France had a population three times the size of England.

Within England, no town could approach London in terms of size or influence, and the largest towns in Scotland, (Edinburgh and Glasgow) or Ireland, (Dublin) were minute by comparison. In 1750 Bristol and Edinburgh had populations of around 50,000, with Norwich next with some 35,000. Thus the urban hierarchy did not yet display either the very large provincial centres, or the northern industrial locations, which were later to become such a characteristic of industrial Britain.

How can we account for London's dominance? It was, of course, the nation's capital, and housed the court, parliament, and government administration. This in turn brought wealth, jobs, and — so important in eighteenth century England — patronage. London was also the centre of the leading professions, such as law and medicine, and was a major education centre with numerous famous schools and colleges (though no university until the nineteenth century).

London was also easily the nation's most important port, favoured geographically by its proximity to the continent, by its central location for internal trade and distribution, and by the great tidal River Thames. It is estimated that in 1700 one quarter of all London's jobs were connected directly or indirectly with shipping activity, and much of London's population was centred in the busy dock areas like Wapping and Rotherhithe.

The river was thus an essential part of London's prosperity. Docks, warehouses, commodity exchanges, and shipyards (including naval yards at Greenwich and Deptford) all served the nation's principal artery of foreign and domestic commerce. London's share of Britain's overseas trade remained considerable, and London continued to be a leading port throughout the nineteenth century. Although the rise of western ports like Liverpool and Glasgow meant a relative decline in London's importance in the eighteenth century, London contrived to control much of the trade with continental Europe, with the West Indies, and with India. This gave the capital a dominant place in the lucrative re-export trades, and warehouses stocked with commodities such as sugar, tobacco, tea and silks lined London's docks later to be resold to European markets. Overall London's share of total overseas trade fell from around three-quarters in 1700 to two-thirds in 1790 (though in absolute terms there was a huge expansion). The major change was the growth of exports from Liverpool and elsewhere; in 1790 London still took 70 per cent of all imports and sent 75 per cent of re-exports.

London was also a huge manufacturing centre, with a vast range of small craft and workshop industries and several major manufacturing enterprises. A trade directory published in 1747 listed 215 different occupations, and in 1792 the list had grown to 492. Some areas were highly specialised, like the

London's rapid growth was not without its critics as this illustration from 1827 shows.

jewellers and watchmakers of Clerkenwell or the tanners of Bermondsey. Among large enterprises were the silk mills at Spitalfields and some of the big breweries. However, the characteristic feature of London's manufacturing was its diverse and miscellaneous nature, ranging from ordinary everyday articles to hand-crafted luxuries (it is often forgotten that London produced some very fine quality goods which could stand comparison with those produced anywhere in Europe, for example, furniture, clocks, telescopes, and harpsichords).

By virtue of its size and wealth London was the centre of enormous building activity, and London's boundaries steadily expanded. By 1800 villages such as Kensington and Islington were being absorbed, while development north of the river was encouraged by Westminster Bridge (1750) and Blackfriars Bridge (1769) which supplemented what was hitherto London's only crossing at London Bridge.

The variety of London's services defy description. Some were connected with port activities, as we have seen; others with wholesaling and retailing, transport and distribution. London was a centre of fashion and entertainment for the wealthy, and the capital was noted for its theatre and concerts. The wealthier districts were the quarters of large numbers of servants (the Duke of Bedford kept a staff of 40 servants at his Bloomsbury residence even when he was in the country). The tens of thousands of city horses alone needed shoeing, grooming and feeding, and large numbers were employed in horse-related occupations such as saddlery and coach making.

What then was London's 'role' in eighteenth century Britain? Did this massive and expanding city make a positive contribution to economic development, or was its role a passive one, with the main changes taking place far away in the northern industrial areas?

London's role has certainly been neglected by historians. This is doubtless because the more spectacular changes were taking place elsewhere, while London's **relative** dominance was declining in the eighteenth century. Thus in 1700 perhaps 20 per cent of England's population lived in towns, but two-thirds of all these lived in London. In 1801 one-third of the population lived in towns, and of these only one-third now lived in London.

Yet historians have recently begun to reassess London's role, giving it much more prominence. Partly, no doubt, this reassessment is due to the realisation that Britain's economy was buoyant and developing long before the transformation of the industrial north. In this earlier phase of development London's prosperity played a major part. The most obvious feature of London's influence was its enormous consuming power. London's demand was felt throughout the country, as Defoe, in his celebrated *Tours* in the 1720s made clear. Defoe was prone to exaggerate, but the general point he makes is valid: 'This whole Kingdom, as well the People, as the Land, and even the Sea, in every Part of it, are employed to furnish Something, and I may add, the best of every Thing, to supply the City of London with Provisions.' This huge market encouraged regional specialisation and brought rising incomes and prosperity to provincial areas. Near London, the market gardens of Kent and Surrey sent fruit and fresh vegetables to Covent Garden market, from Cheshire came salt and cheese, while cattle for Smithfield came from as far afield as Wales and Scotland. London similarly drew raw materials and manufactured goods from all over the country. Particularly important was the great coal trade between London and the north-eastern coalfields.

London provided not only markets and wealth but also an example for the provinces. Many of the capital's fashions and improvements, the building of theatres, for example, or the provision of street lighting, were emulated later elsewhere.

From the last quarter of the eighteenth century came a general growth of urbanisation, with more and larger towns. In 1700 there were only 68 'towns' in England and Wales with populations in excess of 2,500. By 1801 there were 188. Moreover by 1801 fifteen towns were above 20,000; in 1700 only Bristol and Norwich, apart from London, had been as big as this. And by 1850 above half the population lived in urban areas, compared with one in five in

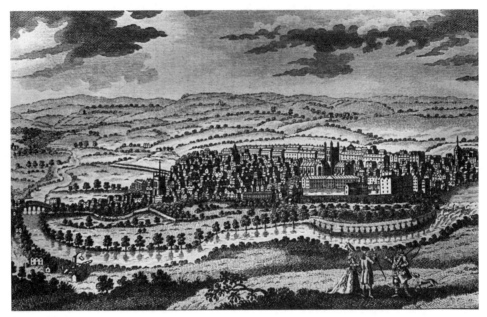

A view of Bath in 1752.

1700. In 1911 the proportion was nearly 80 per cent.

How do we account for urbanisation? Even before the industrial revolution, and continuing during it, there was slow but steady growth in many old provincial cities and market towns. Many were in the south of England, and others far from the burgeoning towns of the industrial north. Some towns grew with particular specialist functions. Bath became a fashionable spa resort early in the eighteenth century, while from the 1780s Brighton, patronized by the Prince of Wales (later George IV), became a favoured resort of the wealthy. Other spas and resort towns grew rapidly in the late eighteenth century, among them Tunbridge Wells and Scarborough, while the advent of the railways in the nineteenth century brought many more. Rather surprisingly, and usually overlooked, is the fact that spas and resorts grew faster in the first half of the nineteenth century than most of the northern towns. Some, like Brighton and Bath, maintained their appeal to the upper classes. Others, like Margate and Blackpool, became popular resorts for working class day-trippers (especially with the advent of the excursion train).

Ports were among some of the faster-growing towns. Here the major increases in the eighteenth century came in the west, where ports like Bristol, Liverpool (which overtook Bristol in population in the 1780s) and Glasgow benefited from the trans-Atlantic and the Irish trades. Newcastle and

Bristol, Broad Quay c. 1735. At this time Bristol was England's leading provincial city, its wealth based on the flourishing Atlantic trade with the West Indies and North America and on the slave trade between West Africa and the New World plantations.

Sunderland expanded as coal ports, while Hull developed as an important fishing and whaling port.

The distinction between ports and manufacturing towns cannot be drawn closely. Glasgow, Liverpool and Bristol, for example, all had important manufacturing sectors, some of them processing imported raw materials like sugar and tobacco.

Above all, though, the process of urbanisation was caused by the advent of industrial towns, especially those based on factory industry. Their significance was only partly because of the large numbers involved and the speed at which the towns grew; it was due also to the appearance of wholly new types of urban communities with new forms of social relations and social problems.

Overall, urban counties like Lancashire and Yorkshire experienced double the rate of population growth of the rural counties in the period 1770-1830. Large urban centres grew up in the textile regions of South Lancashire and Yorkshire's West Riding, in the coal and shipbuilding districts of the north-east, in the metal producing areas of the West Midlands, in the iron and coal districts of South Wales, and the Scottish Lowlands, a centre for shipbuilding, coal, iron, and textiles. Lancashire's population alone rose from around

Table 2.3 The Growth of Towns, 1801-1911 (000)

	1801	1851	1911
Greater London	1,117	2,685	7,256
Cotton Towns			
Manchester	75	303	714
Bolton	18	61	181
Preston	12	70	117
Woollen Towns			
Leeds	53	172	453
Bradford	13	104	288
Heavy Industry, etc.			
Glasgow	77	357	784
Middlesborough	—	8	105
Birmingham	71	233	526
Ports, etc.			
Newcastle	33	88	267
Liverpool	82	376	753
Resorts and Spa Towns			
Brighton	7	66	131
Bath	33	54	51
Blackpool	—	3	58
County Towns			
Exeter	17	33	49
York	17	36	82

318,000 in 1751 to over one million in 1821.

The statistics of urban growth show some amazing increases. In the early eighteenth century Liverpool's population stood at about 15,000, Manchester's 12,000 and Glasgow's 12,500. In 1851 Liverpool had 376,000, Manchester 303,000 (and Salford a further 63,000), and Glasgow 345,000. Some examples of urban growth are given in Table 2.3.

A striking feature of urbanisation was the growing numbers of very large towns. In 1801 no town other than London had a population above 100,000. In 1851 there were ten, and in 1911, 36. These 36 towns by 1911 contained nearly half Britain's total population. We may thus say that whereas in 1801 the representative Englishman was still a country-dweller, and in 1851 (just) a townsman, by 1911 he was fast becoming an inhabitant of a large city.

To explain the growth of industrial towns is not difficult, although why particular towns grew to the size they did when they did is a much more complicated question. Once the adaptation of the steam-engine to textile machinery allowed factories to locate away from rivers and streams, the way was open for the arrival of factory towns. Cheap coal now became the great attraction and all the leading new textile centres grew up either near coalfields or in places with easy access to coal. In other industrial areas, too, like the West Midlands, cheap coal was similarly important as well as the proximity of other resources like iron. Other factors included proximity to cheap transport, such as canals and later railways, and also access to ports. The role of agriculture, too, should not be neglected. Agriculture supported urbanisation in a number of ways. Urban populations relied on agriculture for food (until the 1870s the great bulk of Britain's food supplies were produced domestically), while agriculture supplied many basic raw materials. Growing agricultural productivity and production was an important factor in the growth of Britain's urban population.

Towns grew very largely by internal migration, especially before 1850 when urban death rates were higher than birth rates in many of the larger towns. Most of the migrants came from rural districts, attracted by the opportunities for higher wages and jobs in the fast-growing towns (though in some areas there was also a 'push' as rural conditions worsened for some as a result of the enclosure movement). Local studies show that long-distance migration was the exception. Towns mostly drew their migrants from villages in the surrounding districts, usually from within a 5 or 10 mile radius (the catchment area of the largest towns, especially London, was wider). In eighteenth century Sheffield, for example, apprentices in the cutlery trades were drawn from all over the country, but nearly one-half came from a radius of 5 to 10 miles and three-quarters from within 15 miles. Only one in 18 of these apprentices came from a distance further than 40 miles.

As we will see in the subsequent chapters the social impact of rapid urbanisation was one of the great problems with which nineteenth century administrators and reformers had to wrestle. It is worth emphasising the newness of these problems. No society before had ever had to cope with the challenge of industrial cities, which disrupted traditional family ties and redefined relationships between employers and employees. Not suprisingly, traditional institutions proved incapable of dealing with the new scale of urban growth. Ultimately the challenge was met, but not without strain, distress, and the appearance of horrifying social problems.

Chapter 3
Poverty, the Poor Law and Public Health

Poverty and the Poor Law

Poverty was a widespread and deep-seated phenomenon in pre-industrial Britain. The extent of poverty can only be guessed at, but Gregory King estimated that in 1688 more than half of the total population did not earn enough to sustain life. He thought that as many as 2.8 million out of a total population of 5.5 million were in this miserable condition, whole classes which he termed 'labouring people and out-servants', 'cottagers and paupers', 'common soldiers and sailors', and 'vagrants'. Evidently these people would, from time to time, be thrown on to private charity and various forms of public poor relief, while the numbers of people King classed as 'paupers' and 'cottagers' (squatters without land and without regular employment) were no less than 1.3 million, nearly one-quarter of the entire population.

Whatever we think of the quality of King's estimates, they reveal without any doubt the startling degree of poverty in late seventeenth century society. There is no reason to suppose that conditions improved markedly as the eighteenth century progressed, and any progress made before the 1760s was probably swallowed up thereafter by rapidly rising population. High prices of foodstuffs in the 1790s led to huge rises in the numbers seeking poor relief, and poverty became an increasing pre-occupation of the authorities by the turn of the century.

Why was poverty so widespread? Of course, there will always be groups in society who for one reason or another cannot support themselves and who need to rely on private or public charity if their families are unable to support them. They include very young orphans, the very old, handicapped and the infirm — the groups termed the 'deserving poor' in Tudor times because they could hardly be blamed for their predicament. The proportion of such unfortunate individuals must have been quite high in pre-industrial Britain.

Frequent visitations of killer and disabling diseases (although the plague never struck again on a large scale after the 1660s), the perils of childbirth, and rudimentary medical knowledge and practice, must have left large numbers of children without one or both parents, parents without children to support them in their old age, numerous individuals with handicaps and deformities resulting from illness, inadequate resetting of broken bones and so on.

However it was not these groups which troubled the authorities but the so-called 'able-bodied' poor. Gregory King's estimates show that many labourers and their families, 'cottagers', and others must sometimes, perhaps often, have sought charity and relief.

Why were there large numbers of able-bodied poor, people who were physically capable of working yet still needed relief? Many contemporaries, such as Defoe, thought these people were simply lazy, preferring to receive handouts than do an honest days work. The real situation was more complex. While some may indeed have preferred charity to work, the root of the problem lay in the nature of Britain's pre-industrial economy. This root was not unemployment (as in modern industrial societies) but **underemployment.** The vast majority of the population were directly or indirectly involved in agricultural occupations. Agriculture was essentially seasonal and could not provide employment for all throughout the year. There were times of peak demand, like harvesting or threshing, but at other times there was insufficient work and enforced idleness. If agriculture could be carried on with some form of by-employment, such as domestic spinning or weaving, or fishing, earnings might be sufficient. But otherwise the prevailing low levels of farming techniques and low agricultural earnings meant that resort to parish relief was always a possibility. Bad harvests, which raised food prices and reduced the amount of work available, forced some of those whose principal earnings came from wage labour to seek relief. Enclosures added to the growing proportions who were dependent on wage labour and hence were vulnerable to the effects of poor harvests. Another factor tending to increase poverty was the rapidly increasing population after the 1760s. The whole economy scarcely grew faster than the rate of population growth between 1760 and 1820, during a period when the population of England and Wales doubled, adding some six million to the total. Moreover those years also saw substantial immigration into England from Scotland and Ireland, whose populations were also mounting rapidly.

One side of the coin of the 'poverty problem' was thus the great numbers who were too poor to sustain existence without some form of help from private charities or the poor law. If industrialisation ultimately brought improvement to the lot of the average worker, as it probably did after 1820, and certainly improved conditions for particular groups of workers, it also brought deterioration for some sections of the workforce. Groups like the handloom cotton weavers, who were displaced by machines from the mid-1820s, or linen workers who were unable to compete with the cheaper products of cotton factories, were among the losers. And even the factory workforce, and others whose labour was in increasing demand like coal miners, suffered from periodic bouts of unemployment as the trade cycle became a regular feature of economic life.

The other side of the coin was the mounting expenditure by poor law authorities on relief. To the middle and upper classes, who paid the poor rates, this was the essence of the 'problem'. Pressure to reform the poor law came not only from those who wished to see a more humane treatment of the poor, but from those who wanted to spend less. As poor law expenditure rose, especially during the period of war between 1793 and 1815, agitation for reform increased. Although the peak level of national poor law expenditure in 1818 was not reached again until 1871 (when the country was much wealthier and more populous) the average levels of the 1820s and 1830s remained high. (See Table 3.1).

Table 3.1 Expenditure on Poor Relief in England and Wales, 1750-1832

Year	Expenditure (£000)
1750	700
1785	2000
1803	4300
1818	7900
1825	5800
1832	7000

The general pattern of expenditure on poor relief shows steady growth from the 1750s, as population grew, with very rapid increases during the war years and post-war recession. Levels were lower, though still relatively high in the 1820s, and in the early 1830s the total started to mount once more. Poor law rates were levied and spent locally, not nationally, and expenditure was naturally not spread evenly but tended to be concentrated in 'difficult' areas such as the depressed rural southern claylands after 1815, where no large towns with alternative industrial employment existed.

The Old Poor Law

Throughout the seventeenth and eighteenth centuries, and lasting until

1834, the principles of poor relief in England remained those enshrined in the great Tudor Acts of 1597 and 1601 and in the Act of Settlement of 1662. Above all the 1601 Act had determined that the 'impotent poor', the old, handicapped, child orphans, and so on were entitled to relief; that those who could do so should be set to work; and that pauper children old enough should be apprenticed in some trade. The administration was to be at local, parish level, with each of the 15,000 parishes appointing unpaid overseers of the poor, the appointments being made each year by parish vestries or by local JPs. Money for relief, too, was to come from the parish, from a poor rate levied on the better-off, the property owners. This money was to be used to give directly to the impotent poor, or to purchase tools, materials, and perhaps erect a building where others could work.

The poor law legislation of 1601 was no sudden development, but had evolved gradually from a variety of practices and precedents in the sixteenth century. Such was the case, too, with the 1662 Act of Settlement.

It should be stressed also that the system of publicly given poor relief which developed in England was unique. No continental country had organised relief in this manner, while neither Scotland nor Ireland had a poor law until the nineteenth century. In these countries the relief of the poor was left to private charity, although in Scotland the kirk (Church) came to levy contributions from its members in a way which more or less amounted to a compulsory rate.

The Tudor poor law was probably meant to do no more than supplement existing charitable alms giving. Legislation tended to follow periods of extreme dearth and hardship (as in the 1590s) when resources of alms givers were lowest and when the threat of public disorder from food rioting (a constant nightmare for Tudor governments) was greatest. Well into the seventeenth century private charity continued to provide more for the relief of the poor than did publicly provided parish relief. Only from about the Civil War period in the mid-seventeenth century did public relief became dominant.

Yet an important principle had been established which was only gradually realised. As long as poor relief rested on individual charity the interests of givers and receivers were assumed to be the same. One path to heaven lay through charitable giving: the more given the greater the ultimate rewards to the giver. It was in the interests of the rich to endow almshouses, schools, and hospitals. They would receive their rewards in the next life, the poor in this one. But once poor relief was collected not as charity but as a compulsory rate, the situation changed. It was in the interests of ratepayers to pay as little as possible, by restricting the numbers given relief and by limiting the rate levied. Moreover, the inhabitants of one parish could now compare their situation directly with another parish, and the more heavily burdened could put pressure on their authorities to lower the rates.

The poor rate was levied by the parishes, and each parish was naturally reluctant to give relief to outsiders. Hence the 1662 Act of Settlement, which was itself the culmination of a long series of similar piecemeal enactments. This Act made the parish overseers responsible only for those paupers 'settled' in their parish. Outsiders should be returned to their own parishes for relief.

The Act of Settlement was a much disliked corollary to the Poor Law. There were many harrowing cases of flint-hearted overseers moving destitute cripples, children, and pregnant women from parish to parish. Pregnant women were especially vulnerable since birth in a parish gave the baby 'settlement' there. But historians have tended to exaggerate the importance of the Act. It was never applied strictly everywhere, and could hardly be so with overseers unpaid, and often overworked, incompetent, or corrupt. The claim that the Act reduced internal migration in England seems improbable, except on a very limited scale. The Poor Law authorities were little concerned with the able-bodied genuinely seeking work. London and other towns were able to expand by inward migration while each year waves of migrant workers, some from as far afield as Scotland and Ireland, arrived at harvest time in the grain, hop, and orchard regions of England.

The operation of the Old Poor Law enhanced the powers of the local authorities, especially the JPs and magistrates. Prior to the Civil War there were some attempts by parliament to exercise some control over the administration of poor relief, but thereafter the matter was left almost entirely to local authorities. The consequences were two-fold. The influence of the landed gentry became all-important (they were, or appointed, the justices and magistrates), and they tended to represent the interests of those who paid the poor rates. Secondly, the actual operation of the Poor Law became a hotch-potch of diverse measures and customs which varied considerably from parish to parish. Some parishes erected workhouses in which paupers were set to work. Others built separate institutions for the aged and infirm or for pauper children. In some, all groups of paupers were lumped together in one building. Elsewhere there were no separate buildings and all paupers were given 'outdoor relief'. We cannot, therefore, truly speak of a poor law 'system' at all in the eighteenth and early nineteenth centuries.

During the long period of the Old Poor Law between 1601 and 1834 there were several attempts at reforms. By 1700 there was a growing feeling that the able-bodied poor, the 'undeserving', should only be granted relief within a workhouse, as several parishes were doing already. An Act of 1722

The Old Poor Law: A workhouse in Marylebone, London c. 1809

(Knatchbull's Act) made it easier for parishes to set up workhouses, and authorised the justices to withold relief from those who refused to enter.

The idea that the able-bodied poor were to blame for their predicament and that they should be obliged to work in a workhouse failed to get to grips with the real problem — low productivity and underemployment. From the 1760s, as we have seen, poor rates began to rise and the workhouses were filled. A softer attitude to the problems of the poor was reflected in an Act promoted in 1782 by Thomas Gilbert. This Act provided for unions of parishes to set up institutions for the non-able-bodied poor, with those who were able to work given employment near their own homes or given outdoor relief. A few years later, in 1796, the workhouse test of 1722 was removed, and justices were ordered to provide relief for 'industrious poor persons' near their own homes. In any event, the soaring wartime prices after 1793, with consequent destitution among certain sections of the community, would have overburdened the existing workhouses and forced the spread of outdoor relief.

The form of outdoor relief which attracted most attention was the Speenhamland system. This was the system adopted in 1795 by the Berkshire justices at the village of Speenhamland and which spread rapidly to many counties, especially in the south of England. The background was the rising prices, destitution and disturbances in the early 1790s (a dangerous combination in view of the revolutionary turmoil in France). Bad harvests were the immediate cause of the problem, and the authorities were anxious to avoid general wage increases in case it should be difficult to lower them again when normal times returned. The scheme adopted in Speenhamland was to supplement wages from the rates on a sliding scale, the scale to vary with the price of bread and the size of the family. The higher the price of bread, and the larger the family, the more relief would be given.

The Speenhamland system, and the many variants of it, provided a stop-gap measure to stave off mass destitution during the unusually bad harvests and other abnormal circumstances of the war period. It should be stressed also that the system provided relief for employers as well as the poor, since wages were kept down. From 1815, though, there was increasing dissatisfaction with the growth of poor law expenditure, and the Speenhamland system became the focal point of attack.

The attack on the Old Poor Law was led by 'political economists' such as Thomas Malthus, David Ricardo, and Nassau Senior. They argued that the Speenhamland-type allowance system encouraged rising poor rates, since the idle would have no incentive to work; rising prices would be covered by more relief, and the relief would be given in the paupers' own homes. The subsidy to employers, which 'topped-up' wages out of rates, was also criticised.

Particularly influential were the writings of the Reverend Thomas Malthus. He predicted that rapidly rising population would soon outstrip food production, publishing his analysis in his famous *Essay on Population* in 1798. Malthus argued that there was a direct link between an allowance system, like Speenhamland, and uncontrolled population growth. This was because subsidising large pauper families out of the rates, in line with the size of their families, would simply encourage even larger families.

A strong case against the existing poor law was just what the rate payers wanted to hear. They were paying to support the able-bodied in idleness, which was bad for the economy, bad for the ratepayers and bad for the paupers since they were encouraged in idleness, drunkeness, and in having irresponsibly large families.

In 1817 and 1824, two Parliamentary Commissions examined the poor law question. They agreed on the evils of the existing system, but offered no real alternative. However, in 1830 a series of agricultural uprisings, rioting, rick burning and machine smashing, took place largely in the southern counties where Speenhamland prevailed. The connection between poverty and the allowance system seemed clear, and Parliament, fearful of more unrest, appointed a Royal Commission on the Poor Laws in 1832 to examine the question once more and to suggest an alternative. The Commission sat and heard evidence between 1832 and 1834, and in 1834 published its influential report which became the basis of the 1834 New Poor Law.

The New Poor Law

The Commission's Report noted that under the present system very little work was actually provided by parishes in workhouses. There were four principal ways in which relief to the able-bodied was given: by paying rent for cottages, by paying money (especially supplementing wages according to the price of bread), by spreading available work among the poor (which effectively subsidised wages) and by creating employment with projects financed out of the rates. All these methods, argued the Commissioners, encouraged idleness and rising poor rates.

The Commission made a number of proposals, all of which were immediately accepted and incorporated in the 1834 Act. First, no outdoor relief should be given to the able-bodied, and the Speenhamland-type allowance system should be abolished. Second, all relief should be given in workhouses, where all those able to work should be obliged to do so. Thirdly, no attempt should be made to distinguish between the deserving and the undeserving poor — the problem which had dogged authorities since 1601. Instead, the solution was both simple and ingenious. Conditions in the workhouses were to be worse than those of the lowest independent labourer, so that no one who could work would be likely to opt for relief in a workhouse. This principle was known as 'less eligibility', since workhouse conditions were to be 'less eligible' than outside.

The workhouses were to be built and administered through Poor Law Unions, formed by groups of parishes. The Unions would elect Poor Law Guardians and appoint full time parish officers. The entire system was to be financed by local poor rates, but overall expenditure was expected to fall since less people would be likely to seek relief (and, in fact, expenditure did fall substantially after 1834).

The Commission's final principle was to set up a new central body of Poor Law Commissioners in order to keep central control of operations in the country and prevent slackness and local variations. The body was to be independent of parliament, in the hope that this would preserve its independence and impartiality, although in the event the three Commissioners were replaced in 1847 by a President of the Poor Law Board sitting in parliament.

The work of the Commission was strongly influenced by the theories of the

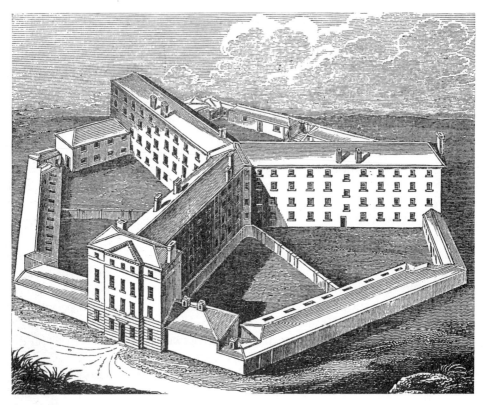

The New Poor Law: Abingdon workhouse in 1836.

political economists and especially by the **Utilitarian** philosophy of Jeremy Bentham (1748-1832) and his followers. Bentham had argued in 1776 that all institutions should be judged on whether they promoted 'the greatest happiness for the greatest number'; if not, the institution should go. Bentham was quite prepared to see some form of central or state control, if this was necessary to achieve the 'greatest good' for the majority. Edwin Chadwick was a disciple of Bentham, and he was one of the most influential voices in the drafting of the Commission's Report (Chadwick became a Commissioner in 1833). Utilitarian principles can be seen in the proposal for 'less eligibility' (since despite the inevitable cases of real hardship and distress, the majority were supposed to benefit from the system), and for a central body to control the operation of the poor laws.

The New Poor Law of 1834 has attracted much criticism, both from contemporaries and from historians. Among contemporaries, the Tory squires were unhappy with the new central authority and the lessening of the powers

The New Poor Law dormitory for paupers in Marylebone in 1857. Note the strong religious emphasis typical of the times.

of local county justices and magistrates which it implied. Radicals like William Cobbett mounted scathing attacks on the rigours of the harsh workhouses and on the principle of less eligibility.

More recently, historians have questioned the evidence and the findings of the Commissioners, not simply their conclusions. Detailed studies have shown that poor rates were not necessarily highest in the counties where the Speenhamland system prevailed, a fact which was glossed over in the Commissioner's Report. Recent studies show that the root cause of poverty where poor rates were highest (whether Speenhamland areas or not) was the lack of alternative employment outside agriculture. Thus in Lancashire and Yorkshire rural wages were high and poor rates low because expanding industrial opportunities gave rise to higher demand for labour. By contrast, some of the agricultural southern counties in the 1820s suffered from low wages and declining employment (for example, in places where threshing machines were introduced). Malthus's claim that high birth rates and the Speenhamland system were connected has also been proved false. The highest birth rates were in the most prosperous areas, such as Lancashire, where poor rates were low. Moreover, the Report of the Commission ignored the facts both that total poor law expenditure had declined from its 1818 peak and that the Speenhamland allowance system was already disappearing in several regions by 1834.

A further important criticism of the 1834 Report is that it virtually ignored the question of poverty in industrial areas. Here the problem was not one of low wages, the allowance system, or supposed idleness, but unemployment.

In the event the operation of the 1834 Act was less drastic than its critics feared. The first 5 years were spent organising the system in the southern counties, and only after 1840 did it spread to the North. As far as the 'impotent poor' (the aged, young and sick) were concerned, the aged, young, and sick, the 1834 Act made little difference. They continued to be given outdoor relief as before (indeed only one page in the 372 page Report by the Commissioners dealt with the problems of the helpless poor). It has also recently been suggested that the operations of the new workhouses were not as severe as earlier critics have maintained. Examples of cruelty and brutality in particular workhouses were exceptions to a general picture of well regulated and reasonably humane institutions.

The Public Health Movement

The dreadful conditions which appeared in Britain's new industrial towns eventually gave rise to pressure for reform. Reluctantly, and only after revelations of the extent of the problem and the growing awareness of a connection between filth and the spread of disease, the government passed the first Public Health Act in 1848. The growth of government intervention in social matters is significant. Together with factory reform, public health legislation marked a major breach in the doctrine of 'laissez-faire' and led the way towards still more social legislation in the second half of the century.

Poor conditions, which were naturally at their worst in the largest and fastest-growing towns, were caused by the related problems of bad housing, overcrowding, inadequate sanitation, and contamination of water supplies. The inevitable results were very high death rates, particularly among infants, and especially in the working-class slum areas of the big towns. Overcrowding and bad sanitation encouraged the spread of infectious diseases, and polluted water was another cause of high death rates. Middle-class reformers were

Slums existed in all industrial towns in the mid-nineteenth century. As many as ten or more might live in a single room. This illustration of a room in Back Queen Street, Deansgate, Manchester, dates from 1862.

shocked by the housing conditions in which so many of the poor had to live, and they were shocked, too, by other manifestations of degrading living conditions: crime, drunkenness, prostitution, and — particularly important to many reformers — general ignorance about religion and lack of church attendance.

Overcrowding and poor housing were caused by a number of factors. Most important was simply the speed at which towns grew, fast outstripping the housing and other facilities available. The fastest **rates** of town growth occurred in the first twenty or thirty years of the nineteenth century. In the two decades between 1811 and 1831 the populations of Manchester, Liverpool and Glasgow all doubled. Towns grew by migration, most of the migrants coming from rural areas. Life-styles appropriate to the country were not necessarily suitable for towns. In the countryside the lack of a privy, or of any means of rubbish disposal, might be unimportant; but in towns the effects of rotting rubbish and excrement could be devastating.

Another problem was that towns grew unplanned and unregulated. Existing forms of town government were simply inadequate to cope with what were often completely new situations. Often urban agglomerations grew up where

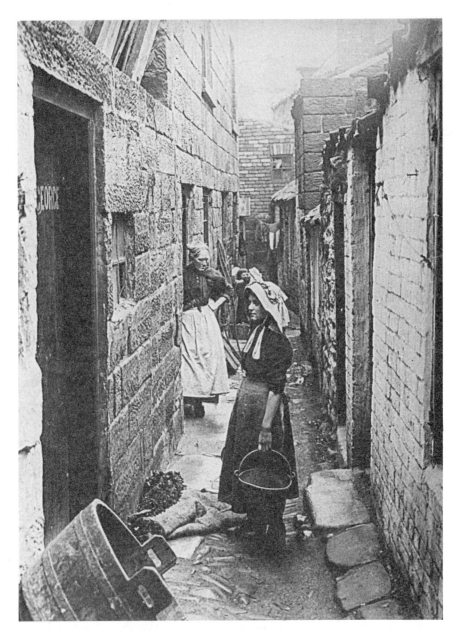

During the nineteenth century, squalid 'back-to-back' houses were put up in many northern industrial areas. This picture shows such houses at Staithes, Yorkshire, at the end of the century.

The late eighteenth century saw many towns making improvements such as paving, street lighting and water supplies. This picture shows the re-paving of Edinburgh High Street in 1785. But such improvements were usually confined to the better-off districts.

no existing town authority existed at all. Factory owners or speculative builders hastily erected ill-built houses to which the factory labourers and their families flocked. Naturally it was in the interests of the owners and builders to build as cheaply as possible, and the result was often rows of small back-to-back houses fronting on to a courtyard with a single exit and with a single cess-pool or open sewer for sanitation which characterised many northern towns. It was particularly unfortunate that in the Napoleonic War period, when demand for houses was growing rapidly, the cost of timber rose to unprecedented levels. The best quality wood was taken for naval purposes, and houses built in this period were frequently of very shoddy quality.

A major problem was the connection between poor housing and poverty. It was naturally in the poorest areas that overcrowding was worst, for the high urban rents and the need to live near the workplace (especially where employment was casual, as in the docks) encouraged multiple occupations of single rooms. Sometimes as many as ten would share one room, sleeping in

Although most of the better-off areas of towns had piped water supplies to houses by the 1860s, many slum dwellers usually had to collect water from stand pipes, as here at Bethnal Green in 1863.

shifts. Unfortunately it was just in the poorest areas that early nineteenth century town government was weakest; since 'improvements' were paid for out of the rates, and since rates were paid by the better-off property owners, it was naturally in these wealthier districts that such amenities as paved streets, rubbish disposal, pure water-supplies, lighting and policing were generally to be found.

The movement for improved public health gained ground only slowly. Apathy, hostility to higher taxes and rates, and the laissez-faire doctrine, which objected to state interference on principle, all stood in the way of progress. Only gradually, as the evils of the fast-growing towns became more visible, and as the revelations of social reformers began to have an impact on public opinion, did the movement gather strength. In the 1820s Dr. Southwood Smith was among those who drew attention to the connection between poverty, bad sanitation, and disease. His work at the London Fever Hospital after 1824 convinced him of the need for sanitary reform.

The first of the great cholera epidemics, in 1831-2 hastened awareness. This epidemic was of considerable importance for two reasons. First it was a particularly horrible disease and a great many of those who caught it died.

A COURT FOR KING CHOLERA.

The caption to this 1852 *Punch* cartoon speaks for itself. Public awareness of the connection between squalor and disease was spreading.

Secondly, although the cholera outbreaks were worst in the poorest areas, all classes were affected. Of the 32,000 deaths, over one-third were in London. Although not understanding how cholera spread, the middle and upper classes were brought face to face with the consequences of urban epidemics. A second and even more virulent outbreak of cholera occurred in 1848-9 when perhaps 80,000 people died. Only in 1849 did Dr. John Snow show empirically the connection between water supply and cholera, and only many years later was the connection proved. Nonetheless, after 1850 the various measures of sanitary reform and other improvements (including better water supplies) ensured that the later cholera visitations in 1853 and 1866 were much milder.

Following the 1831-2 cholera outbreak a further landmark in sanitary reform came in 1838 with a report on the causes of an epidemic in east London. This survey was commissioned by the Poor Law Commissioners, or rather by Edwin Chadwick (1800-90), the Secretary to the Commissioners.

This famous *Punch* illustration in 1858, titled 'The Silent Highwayman' is a striking comment on London's polluted water supplies.

Chadwick appointed Southwood Smith and two other doctors, James Kay (afterwards Sir James Kay-Shuttleworth, famous for his pioneer work in education), and Neil Arnott. Kay had already published an important enquiry into working conditions in Manchester cotton factories in 1832. The 1838 report was significant because it drew attention to the connection between insanitary conditions, disease, and pauperism. Since paupers were relieved out of the rates, Chadwick was able to argue that sanitary reform would actually save rate-payers money by reducing the number of paupers to be relieved. This argument won many middle-class supporters for the public health movement.

The 1838 report was confined to London. In 1839 Chadwick decided to make a nationwide survey and the result was the immensely influential *Report on the Sanitary Condition of the Labouring Population,* published in 1842. This brought before the public the full horrors of slum conditions, the overcrowding, the filth-ridden streets, the damp and squalid conditions in which so many lived — and died. Indeed, it was shown in 1843 that a child born of upper class parents in rural counties could expect to live on average to the age of 52; if born to a Liverpool labouring family its life expectancy was 15 years.

Chadwick's 1842 Report was followed by a Royal Commission on the Health of Towns. This Commission drew attention to the inadequate water supplies in most large towns, and also to the weakness of local administration and their inability to improve matters. As a result of the Commissioner's Report (1844-5), parliament at last passed the first Public Health Act in 1848. Under this Act local authorities could set up Local Boards of Health with powers of water supply, sewage disposal, and so on. A General Board of Health was also established with loose powers of control over the Local Boards.

The 1848 Act was important symbolically but its immediate effects were limited. The main problem was that the provisions of the Act were mostly permissive; there was no compulsion on local authorities to adopt them. Thus not until 1872 did it become compulsory to appoint Medical Officers of Health.

Improvements were piecemeal, often the results of local efforts by devoted individuals. But steadily after about 1850 there were perceptible improvements in most areas, and urban death rates began to fall significantly. Among individual pioneers one of the greatest and most able was Dr. John Simon, appointed Medical Officer of Health for the City of London in 1848. He became principal medical adviser to the government in 1855, and did much to influence opinion in favour of stronger government initiative. In 1868 a Royal Sanitary Commission was appointed which led in 1871 to the setting up of a central Local Government Board (with Simon its Chief Medical Officer). This was followed by two Public Health Acts in 1872 and 1875, the second being one of the major pieces of Victorian social legislation. Under this Act a uniform system of public health administration was established for the whole country, bringing together all the various pieces of legislation into one major consolidated Act, and ensuring powerful central control by the Local Government Board.

Appendix: The 'Mob' and riots before 1815

Throughout the eighteenth century and well into the nineteenth 'the Crowd' or 'the Mob', as it was often called, was a feared feature of Britain's social life. Mob riots and disturbances were common, though their causes were various. There were, for example, riots against increases in the price of bread, protests against enclosures, destruction of toll-gates on turnpike roads, destruction of machinery which threatened to create unemployment, and riots against employers who tried to lower wages. To these strictly economic protests were added those with political, social, or religious overtones (often enough the same disturbance was a medley of motives and grievances). People rioted in favour of parliamentary reform and they protested against Catholic Emancipation; there were even uprisings against the introduction of the new Gregorian Calendar in September 1752. The rioters nearly always belonged to the poorer social classes and were led by common people. Those who rioted most frequently included weavers, agricultural labourers, and apprentices. Not unnaturally, the authorities feared such disorder, and they normally dealt savagely with the ringleaders of disturbances.

The frequency and gravity of eighteenth century riots is not fully known. Probably serious riots were not common for much of the period, although in the war period after 1793 there was a marked increase. Between 1793 and 1815 there were well over 700 full-scale riots, nearly half of which were protests against high food prices. Impressment for military service was another common cause of rioting at this time. In 1811-12 there occurred a series of outbreaks of machine-breaking known as the Luddite riots, so called because the rioters issued threatening letters and proclamations in the name of 'King Ludd' or 'Ned Ludd'.

Earlier historians have made the mistake of treating 'the Mob' rather as contemporaries themselves did: as bands of ignorant people stirred up irrationally by forces they could not control and did not understand, fed by rumour-mongers and led by fanatics. Breaking machines or destroying turnpikes seems as futile and unprogressive as Don Quixote tilting at windmills, while to protest against rising bread prices was in effect to riot against a bad harvest: similarly pointless. Crowd control was therefore essentially a problem of law and order, a question of rounding up the ringleaders and persuading the unruly rioters that their grievances would be listened to.

More recently, however, historians have looked more closely and more sympathetically at 'the Crowd' and have tried to penetrate the sometimes opaque language of the crowd leaders, (which was often, for example, couched in the evangelical religious terms of the time) in order to understand what the mobs were really saying. The principal point to emerge is that there was a common theme to a great many of the riots. This theme was the presence of a strong sense of social justice often rooted in traditional customs. When something happened to outrage this sense of justice, uprisings could follow. The historian E.P.Thompson has stressed two important concepts here. One is the idea of the 'moral economy' of the poor : the existence of a framework within society where everybody from the richest to the poorest had their own niche and their own part to perform. According to Thompson 'An outrage to these moral assumptions, quite as much as actual deprivation, was the usual occasion for direct action'. The second concept is 'legitimation': the rioters' belief that their action was legitimate because they were simply claiming traditional rights. They believed that their actions would be endorsed by the authorities (like the county Justices of the Peace or the landowners) since they were upholding the prevailing order. Thus we do not often find uprisings against authority as such, but against newcomers, middlemen, changed customs and so on.

Why did men resort to violence and riot? We must remember that the opportunities for other forms of protest were extremely limited. Elections were corrupt and the right of voting before 1832 was confined to only about 3 per cent of the total adult population. Even after the 1832 Reform Act the proportion rose only to about 7 per cent. Common folk had no way of expressing their protests through the ballot box. The law, too, was expensive and corrupt, and was operated by, and very much in the interests of, the ruling groups. At the same time the eighteenth and early nineteenth centuries, especially from about 1780, saw momentous changes which threatened existing social patterns and relationships.

The regulated worlds of traditional village life and corporate towns were steadily disappearing before the rising industrial towns, the turnpikes and enclosures and other changes, the rising tide of private property, the game laws, and the increasing numbers of middlemen of all kinds whose dealings threatened the established direct customary bargaining between producer and consumer. Riots were therefore often a reflection of deep social changes, and not simply spontaneous outbreaks in response to hunger or agitator-led envy or superstition.

Chapter 4
Eighteenth Century Internal Trade and Transport

Efficient and cheap transport is a necessary part of economic development. This is why economic historians pay so much attention to the many improvements which took place in transport and communications during the eighteenth and nineteenth centuries.

Transport improvements can take many forms, but it is particularly useful to distinguish between those which **cheapen** transport and those which **speed up** deliveries. The former is normally of greatest significance in the transport of bulky, cheap, non-perishable commodities. Coal and grain are the most obvious examples, and others include salt, timber, and china clay. For very valuable goods however where transport costs are only a low proportion of value, speed and reliability might be more important than cost of transport. The same is true of perishable commodities like milk or fruit. Generally speaking, then, transport improvements which resulted in greater speed were of significance in the transport of these more expensive goods and also of passenger traffic.

Better transport, whether resulting in lower costs, greater speed, or both, is significant for a number of reasons. Improved transport and communications can widen the market for products and extend the sources of supply for consumers. This in turn promotes regional specialisation and economies of scale. The transport of people and mail is also important both for economic and social reasons. Workers can seek jobs in growing areas, centres of tourism and recreation can develop, firms can receive orders by letter, and so on. Also, the provision of transport services can be considered as an industry, or rather several industries, in its own right. This was most clearly the case with the railway development in the nineteenth century, for the railways directly employed thousands of workers as drivers, guards, porters, station-masters, or ticket-collectors and thousands more in the engine workshops. The actual construction of railways also meant vast numbers of jobs and huge sums of capital expenditure. Railways needed materials for their construction and maintenance (iron, coal, timber, and others). In short, as an industry in itself, and quite apart from any effect from the transport services provided, the railways became a significant element in the Victorian economy. And what was true of the railways was true also, though less dramatically, of other forms of transport — roads, canals, rivers, and coastal and long-distance shipping.

As final general points we should stress also the various specialist skills and developments in the capital market which went hand in hand with transport developments. As regards the first, of special significance was the growth of **civil engineering,** which was involved in the cutting of canal and railways, for example, the building of bridges and tunnels, or the laying of roads; and **mechanical engineering,** especially the growth of the locomotive industry in the Victorian years. These developments helped create a class of skilled engineers whose skills both stimulated other sectors of the economy and laid the basis of British engineering enterprise in distant lands. The second point about the capital market is simply this: in pre-industrial England and later, in the railway age, necessary investments in transport were usually well beyond the financial means of individuals. Moreover, transport interests tended to require a high proportion of fixed capital (capital tied up for many years before profits accumulated sufficient to repay it). Thus, whether we consider river navigation improvements, canals, roads, or railways, we always find some financial institution created to facilitate borrowing money for capital expenditure. In the case of river and road improvements these were normally **trusts,** where groups of local trustees formed a body to borrow money on the security of fees and tolls. In the case of canals and railways the institution was a **joint-stock company,** incorporated by Act of Parliament, and empowered to raise money through the issue of shares. The significant point is this: that outside these transport developments there were very few areas of enterprise needing such large capital sums. In the eighteenth century, for example, joint-stock company organisation was more or less confined to the great trading companies like the East India Company, a few insurance companies, and the canal companies. Transport improvements therefore played a pioneer role in the mobilisation of capital and the development of financial institutions.

Internal Trade

The main stimulus for transport improvements came from the growth of internal trade, that is, trade between different regions of Britain. There can be no doubt that by 1700 internal trade was highly developed. When Defoe made his tours in the 1720s he stressed the great regional specialisations to be found everywhere. Some were based on favourable resource endowments such as the development of the coal industries of the Newcastle area, or of tin in Cornwall, or lead in Derbyshire. Sometimes other factors, like available labour supply, ease of transport, or entrepreneurial initiative played their part. Thus arose the woollens of the West Riding, the mixed cotton fabrics of Lancashire, the metal industries of the West Midlands, and the multitudes of agricultural specialisms such as cheeses, fruit, hops, and turkeys.

The main stimulus to growing internal trade came from London, which both from its size and prosperity exercised a dominating influence over regions far from its immediate vicinity. Defoe emphasised this again and again: 'the neighbourhood of London ... sucks the vitals of trade in this island to itself'. To a far lesser degree, though nevertheless significant, were regional centres like Bristol, Norwich, Newcastle, Birmingham, and Liverpool, or the Scottish towns of Glasgow and Edinburgh. These too exercised a considerable influence on the surrounding districts, encouraging specialisation and large-scale production.

How was internal trade organised in the eighteenth century? Most goods reached consumers through markets rather than shops. There were in England some 700 market towns each with their weekly or bi-weekly market where buyers and sellers would come together. Markets in the larger provincial towns would be held every day. Much trading also was done by itinerant hawkers and pedlars who travelled from village to village. Only in the centres of larger towns were found specialised shops, although by the late eighteenth century glass-fronted shops in the fashionable parts of London, with attractive window displays well lit by oil lamps on winter evenings, were becoming increasingly common.

London's huge markets, such as Smithfield for meat, Billingsgate for fish, and Covent Garden for vegetables, were the sources of the bulk of the capital's supplies, though there were many lesser markets. In the eighteenth century meat usually came on the hoof, driven from the Scottish Highlands, Wales and the north of England, fattening itself on the journey through the Midlands or East Anglia, and so reaching Smithfield. Between 1700 and 1800 the number of sheep arriving at Smithfield increased from half to three-quarters of a million, the numbers of cattle from 25,000 to 100,000. Turkeys too, mostly from Norfolk and Suffolk, were driven to London, sometimes as many as two thousand at a time.

As well as regular markets a great deal of trading was still done at various fairs, horse fairs, goose fairs, and general fairs. Many small villages held annual fairs (there were 180 in Somerset in the early eighteenth century, though only

39 market towns). Some fairs were of far more than local significance. Defoe in the 1720s described the great Sturbridge Fair held annually near Cambridge. This fair Defoe described as 'not only the greatest in the nation, but in the world'. Dealers came from far and wide, from London, the North, the Midlands, as well as East Anglia. From London there were 'goldsmiths, toyshops, brasiers, turners, milleners, haberdashers, hatters, mercers, drapers, pewtrers, china-warehouses'; from the north came Yorkshire cloth and Manchester fustians; and in addition there were wine, groceries, iron goods, wool, hops, and many other commodities. The Sturbridge Fair was large because of its central location between London in the South, the rich cloth centres of East Anglia and the West, the iron goods of the Midlands, the textiles of Lancashire and Yorkshire, and the agricultural goods of all these regions. There were other important fairs, too, even though they could not match Sturbridge.

By the second half of the eighteenth century fairs were everywhere in decline. Growing urbanisation and industrialisation necessitated regular, year-round, trading, and this was made possible by improved transport and communications.

Road Improvements in the Eighteenth Century

The main developments in road transportation during the eighteenth century were (a) the growth of turnpike trusts, and (b) improved methods of road making and road surfacing. But we should take care not to exaggerate either of these developments. In 1836, when the number of roads maintained by turnpike trusts reached its peak of nearly 22,000 miles, some 106,000 miles remained under parish control. And relatively few even of the turnpiked roads had been improved by the methods we associate with Metcalf, Macadam, or Telford. In 1815 it is estimated that less than 1,000 miles of highway had been improved in this manner.

Turnpike trusts (the term derives from the erection of toll gates, called turnpikes) developed in the seventeenth century because of dissatisfaction with existing methods of road maintenance. Under a Tudor law of 1555 the burden of repairing roads had been placed on the parish, most parishioners having to provide a certain number of days work each year (usually six from 1563) or equipment. Already in the mid-seventeenth century some parishes were substituting highway rates for the compulsory 'statute labour'. Then, in 1663, came the first turnpike trust, set up to maintain a busy section of road near Ware in Hertfordshire. This was an isolated example, and was probably short-lived. Not until the 1690s did other turnpike trusts appear, and then

A turnpike gate, c. 1802

there was a period of slow development until the burst of activity which followed 1750.

Turnpike trusts were not companies. They did not issue shares or attract speculative investment. They were bodies of individuals, invariably local men, who formed themselves into boards of trustees. Each trust would then apply for an Act of Parliament, establishing the body for a period of time (usually 21 years, but always renewed), empowering the trustees to repair, maintain and extend a given section of road. Most of the trusts managed sections of roads ten to twenty miles in length running through several parishes. The money for repairs came from tolls levied on users, who had to pass by the toll house (at the turnpike). Sometimes trusts borrowed money, again usually raised from local farmers and traders, and interest was paid from the tolls.

From 1750 the expansion of the turnpike system was rapid. At that date there were some 143 miles of highway. By 1770 there were more than 500 trusts and nearly 15,000 miles turnpiked in England and Wales. And in 1836 more than 1,000 trusts maintained 22,000 miles of turnpiked roads. In

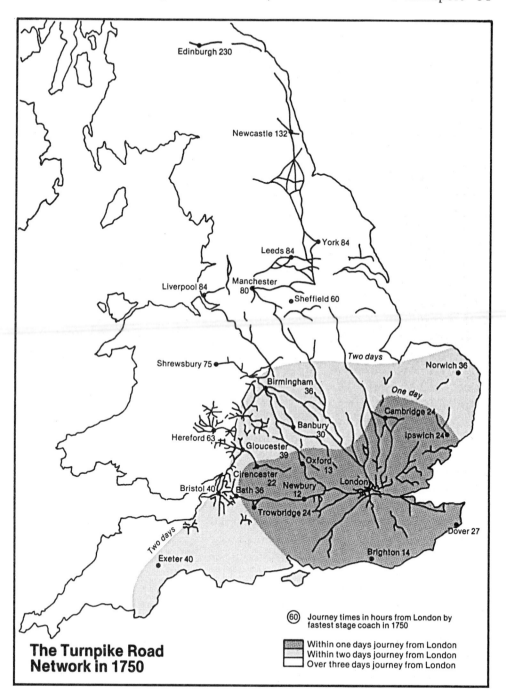

Edinburgh 230

Newcastle 132

Leeds 84   York 84

Liverpool 84   Manchester
                        80   Sheffield 60

Shrewsbury 75   *Two days*   Norwich 36

                    Birmingham
                        36   *One day*

                                    Banbury   Cambridge 24
                                        30
Hereford 63   Ipswich 24

            Gloucester
                39   Oxford
                            13
        Cirencester   London
                22   Newbury
Bristol 40   Bath 36   12
                    Trowbridge 24   Dover 27

Two days   Brighton 14

    Exeter 40

⑥⓪ Journey times in hours from London by
      fastest stage coach in 1750

      Within one days journey from London
      Within two days journey from London
      Over three days journey from London

**The Turnpike Road
Network in 1750**

Scotland, too, turnpike trusts had been set up to maintain many miles of road in the lowlands, while about 1,000 miles of military road were built in the central highlands in the eighteenth century, and several hundred more built after 1803 by the Commission for Highland Roads.

Strictly speaking, there was no turnpike 'system' in Britain, for each turnpike was purely the result of individual initiative, nearly always springing from local demands and local individuals. Earlier historians were very critical of the turnpikes, emphasising their administrative weaknesses and the apparently haphazard way in which they evolved. However, recent work has shown that far from being developed haphazardly, the vast majority were established on the main trunk routes and hence came in response to the demands of growing traffic. First came connections with London, and later some of the major routes serving other important towns were turnpiked. Already by 1750 trunk roads connecting London with such important towns as Manchester, Birmingham, Bristol, York and Dover had all been turnpiked. The turnpiking of the Great North Road was virtually complete as far as Berwick. In the 1750s came another 184 new turnpike trusts (more than the total existing in 1750) and between 1761 and 1772 a further 205 were established. These extended the turnpiking of roads to neglected areas in the West Country, the East Midlands, and the growing industrial districts of Lancashire and Yorkshire. By the end of the Napoleonic War period (by which time the bulk of canal construction was also over) Britain had a national network of serviceable roads extending to most parts of the country.

Although turnpiking a road did not, by itself, guarantee improved road conditions, and there were many instances of appalling roads in the hands of the trusts, nonetheless, the turnpike movement did bring about a marked improvement in the quality of roads. Before the advent of the turnpikes the authorities had tried to stem the damage done to parish roads by regulating the size of wagons and the width of wheels on carts. But this restrictive policy was doomed to failure at a time when internal trade was growing significantly. Turnpike trusts, despite the tolls they charged, probably reduced the cost of road transport because of the time they cut from journeys and the greater

Table 4.1 Journey Time By Stage Coach from London
(average number of hours)

To:	1700	1750	1800
Norwich	50	40	19
Bath	50	40	16
Edinburgh	256	150	60
Manchester	90	65	33

reliability they introduced into services. In 1740 there was only one stagecoach a day between London and Birmingham; by 1763 there were 30 a day. Moreover, the journey time had been cut from two days in 1740 to 19 hours by the 1780s. Some idea of the progressive decline in journey times, very largely as a result of turnpiking, can be seen in Table 4.1.

Allied to the development of turnpike trusts were improved methods of road building techniques. The three most famous road engineers of the period were John Metcalf (1717-1810), John Loudon Macadam (1745-1836), and Thomas Telford (1757-1834). Metcalf, blind from the age of six, built three miles of road for a Yorkshire trust in 1765 and went on to construct a further 180 miles of road, mainly in Yorkshire and Lancashire, before 1792. At one time Metcalf employed some 400 men. His techniques were sound and efficient (in essence, indeed, they were similar to those used by the Romans). He covered a solid foundation of stone blocks with stone chippings, ramming the chippings hard and adding a camber to help drainage. The methods of Telford and Macadam were variants of this technique, Telford, for example, laying two layers of three inch stones, covering these with seven inches of broken stones and one inch of gravel. Apart from the use of the steam roller in the 1860s, these methods of 'metalled road' construction remained little changed until the twentieth century.

Telford was far more than a road builder. He was an accomplished architect and civil engineer, building canals, bridges, harbours, churches and houses. He was the son of a Scottish shepherd and apprenticed to a stonemason. Among his notable achievements were the Menai Bridge, opened in 1826, the Caledonian Canal in Scotland, and the Gotha Canal in Sweden. Telford was appointed Surveyor of Public Works for Shropshire in 1787 (then one of the centres of industrial growth), and there he constructed 42 bridges before 1796. Later, after 1802, Telford superintended the building of 920 miles of government-financed roads in the Scottish Highlands and a further 184 miles in the Lowlands. He also build over 1000 bridges in Scotland. After 1815 he reconstructed and rebuilt the London to Holyhead road, a project which included the Menai Straits Bridge and the Conway suspension bridge.

Macadam's principal contribution to roadmaking was to employ sound principles with economy. Like Telford, Macadam was a Scot, but unlike Telford he was essentially an entrepreneur rather than a technician. He seems to have popularised rather than invented the method of using small broken stones rather than expensive large stone blocks for foundations, a method known as 'macadamising'. Nevertheless, from 1815, when he was appointed General Surveyor of the Bristol Turnpike, his ideas were quickly adopted. By

1823 he was advising thirty-two trusts, and his three sons were working for a further eighty-five.

Rivers and Canals

Water-borne traffic, pre-eminently suited to the transport of cheap bulky goods, was a significant element in the movement of freight in early modern Britain. Coastal traffic was already well developed and organised before 1700, with London, for example, receiving goods like coal from the North East, grain from Norfolk, hops from Kent, stone from the West Country. The London coal trade was particularly important because of the huge tonnages involved, and hence the need for coal ships and barges and merchant seaman. In the seventeenth and eighteenth century the tonnage of coal shipped from the north-east along the coast nearly always exceeded the total tonnage of England's imports each year. In 1700 London used an estimated 800,000 tons of coal, in 1750 about $1\frac{1}{2}$ million tons, and in 1790 around $2\frac{1}{2}$ million tons.

Supplementing the coastal trade was river navigation. In terms of tonnage, rivers in 1700 carried about one-fifth the traffic of the coastal trade, but the two were of course complementary, with goods sent by sea often distributed inland by river, and vice versa.

Preceding the canal age, which commenced around 1760, came a period of river improvement which greatly extended the mileage of navigable rivers in England and enabled bigger barges to be used over greater distances. Such improvements were undertaken in a variety of ways. Sometimes wealthy individuals, or groups of individuals, were authorised by parliament to carry out improvements and to charge tolls to users. In other cases trusts were established by Act of Parliament, empowered to borrow money on the credit of toll charges. And some of the later schemes, such as the Don Navigation, were carried out by a form of joint-stock company with a small number of shares which could be bought and sold: a forerunner of the canal companies.

The main bursts of river improvement schemes came in the 1690s and again between 1719-21, although not all the projects authorised in these years were started, and many took years to complete. In all, the length of navigable rivers in England grew from around 685 miles at the middle of the seventeenth century to 960 miles in 1700 and to 1160 miles by 1725. By this latter period river navigation was increasingly being extended to the northern industrialising districts. For example, the Aire and Calder Navigation brought water transport to Leeds and Wakefield in the 1720s, the Mersey and Irwell Navigation linked Manchester in the 1730s, the Weaver Navigation linked the Cheshire saltfield also in the 1730s, while in 1751 the Don Navigation improved communication in the Sheffield district. Nevertheless, the limits of river improvement were soon reached. Despite widening, deepening, the introduction of locks, and the cutting of awkward bends in the course of rivers, river navigation remained a slow and often uncertain means of transport. The competing demands of millers for the flow of water, the seasonal reductions in the flow of water, and, above all, the physical limitation of the actual location of the rivers all put pressure for some better means of transport for bulky goods. Even in 1750 many important regions like Birmingham, the Staffordshire Potteries, and the South Wales valleys had no navigable water transport.

The solution was canal construction. Significantly, the earliest canals were built for the carriage of coal: significant because this reflects both the need for better ways of transporting cheap bulk products, and the growing significance of coal in the economy. Canal investment marked a distinct shift in the economic centre of gravity of the country towards the coalfields and the industrialising areas. The first canals were in south west Lancashire, where both coal and salt (from north Cheshire) provided the main traffic. The earliest was the ten mile Sankey Brook Navigation which was built to link the coalfields around St Helens with the Mersey. The canal was constructed between 1754 and 1757, largely with capital supplied by Cheshire salt merchants. It resulted in cheaper coal in Liverpool and also attracted industries to the St Helens district.

Of greater significance was the opening in 1761 of a seven mile canal which was later extended a further 35 miles and became known as the Bridgewater Canal. This canal was started by Francis Egerton, the third (and last) Duke of Bridgewater. The wealthy young Duke (he was born in 1736 and died in 1803, inheriting his estates when a boy of twelve and still only in his mid-twenties when he commenced his famous canal project) owned coalmines at Worsley, but the seven mile land journey to Manchester made his coal too expensive to find a ready market. As a result he promoted an Act of Parliament in 1759 and engaged James Brindley to undertake the construction. The completion of the canal in 1761 resulted in the price of coal in Manchester being reduced by about half.

The significance of this small canal, which may be said to have begun the Canal Age, lay in several factors. First, it was an outstanding success, producing enormous profits for the Duke of Bridgewater, and clearly demonstrating to others the potential which canal investment possessed. The Duke himself was wealthy enough, and his initial project small enough, for a single individual to raise the necessary finance. But later canals were financed by companies, raising money through the issues of shares, and paying

Bridgewater Canal around 1793, showing the Barton Aqueduct over the River Irwell.

dividends to shareholders. A further significance of the project was that in the Duke of Bridgewater and James Brindley (1716-72) it brought together two of the outstanding figures in the early canal era. The Duke was a major canal entrepreneur who was prepared to give Brindley his chance and act on his advice. The Bridgewater Canal is reputed to have cost the Duke some £200,000 of his own money, and to have brought £80,000 a year in revenue. It provides an example of the important link between agricultural wealth and industrial enterprise, often found in the eighteenth century, and also of the fruitful partnership which could arise between capitalist entrepreneurs and brilliant engineers.

Brindley's first canal project for the Duke was a major engineering feat; it involved carrying the canal over the River Irwell by means of an aqueduct, which many experts considered impossible. Brindley had been apprenticed to a Cheshire millwright, and his engineering skills were largely self-taught and acquired through practical experience. As well as his work for the Duke he was involved in a vast range of canal projects. Before his death in 1772 Brindley had planned and mostly completed some 365 miles of canals,

Manchester-Leeds Canal running side by side with the railway at Littleborough, c. 1850.

including the important Grand Trunk Canal. This canal, built between 1766 and 1778, linked the Mersey and the Bridgewater Canal with the River Trent, serving the Staffordshire pottery districts as well. Other Brindley canals included the Staffordshire and Worcester (1766), and the Oxford and Chesterfield (1769). Brindley's canals involved not simply major engineering achievements, such as the 3,000 yard tunnel to carry the Trent and Mersey Canal under Harecastle Hill. He also had to train his workmen in new tasks, thus creating a group of 'navigators', or 'navvies', whose skills were used not only for other canal projects but, later, for railways.

With the success of the Bridgewater Canal and other early canals, the number of projects increased. In this first phase of canal construction in the 1760s and 1770s a number of major projects were started but remained unfinished. From the 1780s until the end of the war period in 1815 there was considerable canal construction, especially during the 'canal mania' of the 1790s. From 1792-5 alone there were 51 Canal Acts passed by parliament, authorising expenditure of £7½ million. This second phase of development attracted investment not just from local sources, which had been a feature of the early canals, but nationwide (although local investment predominated

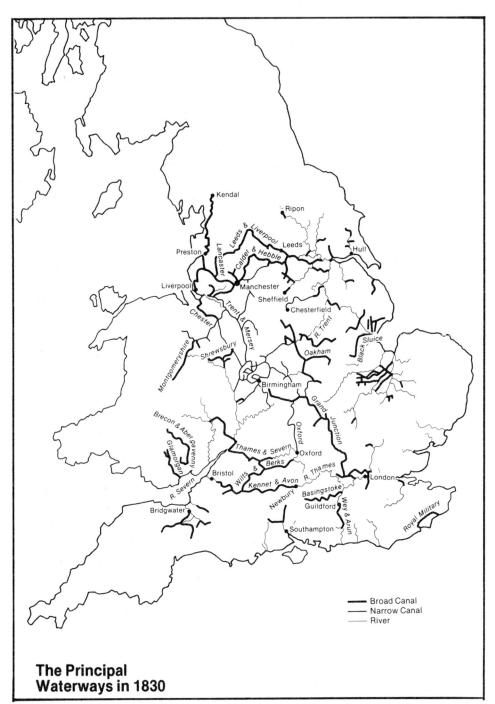

**The Principal
Waterways in 1830**

always). The spur to the 'mania' came from the profitability of the earlier schemes and from the opportunities for grain movements prompted during the war period. Two points may be emphasised by this later spurt of canal construction. First, the canals increasingly aided the movement of agricultural goods as well as industrial. The first canals had been built largely for the coal trade; later canals were more broadly based. Secondly, the later canals provided some fundamental 'cross' links, and so enabled a much greater flow of long distance traffic than the mileages involved suggest. Most important was the Grand Junction, which provided through communication between London's docklands and the West Midlands, and so linked London and Birmingham with the industrial districts of Lancashire and Yorkshire.

What was the significance of the canals to the British economy? First and foremost they provided a significantly cheaper and better means of transporting bulky goods, especially coal, just when demands were growing rapidly with the rise of industrialisation. Also, they brought water-borne transport to areas like the Potteries and Midlands which had hitherto been ill-served by existing navigable waterways. In this way canals both cheapened transport and widened the area served. In 1777 a ton of freight between Liverpool and the Potteries cost £2.10s. by road and 13s.4d. by canal. Thirdly, canals brought prosperity to particular towns and ports. The linking of Liverpool and Manchester, for example, with coal districts greatly stimulated the cotton textile trade once this became based on steam power, and hence could benefit from cheap coal. Fourthly, the canals helped provide in some areas a cross-country alternative to the long coastal route. For example, the linking of Leeds and Liverpool put Lancashire textiles in direct communication by inland waterways with Hull, from where they could reach northern Europe. Also, canals were a major form of investment, canals being the only fields of enterprise where joint - stock company organisation was widely adopted. In all, by 1830 (after which time the growth of railways soon put an end to new canal construction) some £20 million had been invested in canals. This was not a large sum by the standards of the railways, but it was a very considerable amount by the standards of the pre-railway age. Finally, we should stress again the importance of the canals in the training of civil engineers and navvies. Brindley, Smeaton, Rennie and Telford were the most famous of the engineers, whose constructions included locks, tunnels, and aqueducts.

Chapter 5
Agriculture and The Agricultural Revolution

We have underlined on several occasions that agriculture was in 1700 and remained in 1800, easily the most important sector of economic activity. Agriculture provided most of the jobs, the largest proportion of national income and wealth, and the foundation of social prestige and influence. Not until around 1820 did the value of industrial output exceed that of agriculture and were more people employed in industry than in agriculture. And only after 1850 did the majority of England's population become urban dwellers (and even later in Scotland and Ireland). Even in 1870 about one-fifth of all those in employment worked in agriculture.

Of course, although throughout the eighteenth and nineteenth centuries agriculture declined **relatively** compared to industry and services (like transport and retailing), the total output of agriculture continued to expand **absolutely** for nearly all this period, only contracting after about 1875. This expanding output was accompanied most of the time by growing numbers of agricultural workers, and there was no significant fall in those working in agriculture until after 1850. Indeed, apart from one or two Scottish exceptions, no county in Britain actually lost population before 1850, although naturally industrial regions expanded more rapidly than rural ones.

Eighteenth century agriculture provided all the basic foodstuffs for Britain's population. Bread was the staple diet, made from the main grains — wheat, barley, oats or rye. Of these, wheat was always the most important, and bread made from wheat flour became almost universal in southern England and East Anglia by 1760, although bread made from other grains remained common elsewhere for much longer. Bread was supplemented by a variety of other foods, such as peas, beans, potatoes (which were becoming more common in the late eighteenth century, especially in Ireland), cheese and meat. But regular meat eating, outside special occasions or the odd rabbit, was probably not common among ordinary folk. The main drink, beer, was also made from grain, as was whisky and gin.

Agriculture was important not only as a source of food and drink, but as a supplier of many principal raw materials, wood, flax, timber, hides, tallow, oils, straw thatch, and many others. Agriculture also had to supply animal fodder, not only for farm animals but for urban horses.

It is worth at this stage stressing a significant point about agriculture in this period. Most of the main agricultural products were bulky and therefore expensive to carry over long distances, especially by land. For this reason, international trade in such products was very limited, and became substantial only when harvests failed. Even then, because supplies could only be drawn from Europe, harvest failures often affected most of the main producing regions at the same time. During the second half of the nineteenth century all this changed. Then, the opening of new lands and the development of efficient, cheap steamshipping allowed vast quantities of bulky agricultural products to be traded over long distances. But in the eighteenth century this was not possible. Not surprisingly, therefore, such international trade as existed in agricultural foods was either short distance (such as the export of East Anglian barley to the Low Countries) or of goods with a very high value in relation to their bulk. The exotic imports from the Far East, coffee, tea, spices, and pepper fall into this category, as do sugar and tobacco from the Caribbean.

Because international trade in basic agricultural commodities was limited and expensive, it is clear than any increased demand for agricultural products in Britain had to be met from home supplies. If people work in industry and towns rather than in agriculture, then they must buy their food. If agriculture cannot produce the necessary surplus then it is impossible to sustain a large industrialised population (and the same is true of the supply of raw materials to industry). In eighteenth century Britain there **was** industrialisation and urbanisation, population **was** growing (especially after 1760), and average incomes **were** rising. These factors all raised demand for agricultural goods; the question is, how was agriculture able to respond?

An Agricultural Revolution?

Historians used to speak of an 'agricultural revolution' taking place in the second half of the eighteenth century. This revolution was supposed to be largely the work of a few great landowners, who introduced a number of improved farming techniques to their farms. These included new crops, like turnips and clover, new rotations (especially the famous Norfolk four course rotation), and new machines (like the seed drill), better fertilisers, and

Many new forms of agricultural machinery were introduced during the eighteenth century. The illustration of ploughs here comes from the 1740s.

improved breeds of sheep and cattle. These innovations, it was once supposed, were stimulated by the rapid spread of enclosures which freed the countryside from a pattern of inefficient and antiquated open fields to one of highly productive enclosed fields. At the same time there was a movement towards large estates, with the decline of small landowners. This again prompted greater productivity, and, together with the impact of enclosures which dispossessed many who had lived on the land, provided a labour force to swell the growing industrial towns.

Our view of eighteenth century agricultural change is now very different. The idea that any 'revolution' or sudden change occurred is unacceptable. At one extreme Kerridge has suggested an 'agricultural revolution' in the sixteenth and seventeenth centuries rather than in the eighteenth. Other writers, like Chambers and Mingay, point out that the changes of the eighteenth century took a long time to penetrate all areas and they suggest a terminal date of 1880 for the agricultural revolution. Not very revolutionary! And Thompson talks of a 'second agricultural revolution' in the middle years of the nineteenth century, when farms became more like industrial businesses, buying raw material (animal fodder and artificial fertilisers, for example), and selling the 'manufactured' product.

Slow change, diffusion, regional variations: these are the hallmarks of agrarian change in industrialising Britain.

In another significant way our ideas are changing. There is no doubt that between, say, 1660 and 1800 agricultural productivity increased markedly. The output per acre increased, both because crop yields increased and because land was being put to better use. But, it appears, most of the improvements came **before** 1760, not afterwards. There are a number of indicators of this, but one of the most significant is the behaviour of prices. Between the late seventeenth century and the 1750s the general trend of agricultural prices was downwards, markedly so in the 1720s and 1730s. This was because output grew faster than demand, although demand was certainly increasing. In this period Britain was able to become a major exporter of grain (and cheap grain is one explanation given for the 'gin craze' which swept London in the 1720s). A succession of good harvests was partly responsible, but so was rising productivity which stemmed from improvements. After the 1750s, however, and even more so at the very end of the eighteenth century, agricultural prices began to rise. Although agricultural improvements continued, rising demand now started to outstrip supply; the exportable surplus had disappeared by the 1770s and Britain became a net grain importer on a small scale even in years of average harvest.

This revised version of agricultural change carries several important implications. First, the 'role' of agriculture during the period of rapid industrial growth at the end of the eighteenth century was not so positive as once thought. Supply was not matching demand and agricultural productivity was growing only slowly if at all. Secondly, it follows from this that the rapid growth of enclosures after 1760, which we will discuss later, could not have had the dramatic effect on agricultural performance which was once thought. Thirdly, we must emphasise the key developments which took place prior to 1760 and even prior to 1700. Perhaps the traditional open field system was not so backward and impervious to improvement as once thought.

The New Techniques

The most important improvement in agriculture was the spread of **new**

fodder crops which enhanced the fertility of the soil. These crops were of two sorts, so-called 'artificial grasses' and roots. The former included clover, sanfoin, rye-grass and lucerne, and their nitrogen-fixing properties built up the fertility of light soils, such as found in East Anglia, so that grain crops could be grown. Since the crops also provided animal fodder the manure from the animals also improved soil fertility. The root crops (of which turnips were the most important until largely replaced by swedes late in the eighteenth century) also provided fodder for animals which in turn raised soil fertility.

These fodder crops were important because they permitted the growth of both arable and livestock production. On light soils new rotations replaced waste or rough grazing. The Norfolk rotation normally had four successive courses, wheat, turnips, barley and clover, so doing away with the need for a period of fallow in which arable land could recuperate. On heavier soils, as in the Midlands, the fodder crops allowed the spread of mixed farming, with breadgrains, fodder crops, and livestock all linked in a pattern which maximised the value of the land.

By 1700 both the new grasses and root crops had made considerable headway, especially in the southern half of England. Both crops were introduced from the Low Countries, where farming techniques were highly advanced, turnips in the late sixteenth century and leguminous grasses around 1620. The grasses spread more rapidly than the root crops, the latter being unsuited to the heavy clay soils of the Midlands, but by the end of the seventeenth century turnip cultivation as a field crop was well established in Norfolk and Suffolk. Defoe in the 1720s described these counties as 'remarkable for being the first where the feeding and fattening of cattle, both sheep as well as black cattle with turnips, was first practised ... from whence the practice is spread over most of the east and south parts of England.'

In addition to the action of the leguminous grasses and animal manure there were other methods of improving soil fertility which spread slowly from the seventeenth century or earlier. **Marling** became widely used in the eighteenth century, the 'marl' (a type of clay) being quarried and spread on light sandy and clay soils to raise fertility. **Liming** was another method, and by 1800 most villages had lime kilns for the purpose. During the seventeenth century the practice of flooding meadows adjacent to rivers spread from the West Country to many parts of southern England and the Midlands; the **water meadows** then produced rich pasture for animals.

Another source of improvement was **selective breeding** to produce better quality sheep and cattle. The most famous exponent was Robert Bakewell (1725-95) who pioneered modern breeding on his estate at Dishley in Leicestershire. Bakewell bred both sheep and cows, aiming specifically to

Sheep-shearing on the Duke of Bedford's estate at Woburn, c. 1811.

maximise the wool, meat, or milk. There were other notable breeders too, like George Culley in Northumberland (1753-1813) who improved Bakewell's Leicester sheep, or John Ellman, who developed the famous Sussex Southdowns. Whereas Bakewell favoured longhorn cattle, the Colling brothers in Durham favoured shorthorns, and their breeds quickly became popular both for milk and beef.

There is no doubt that the major improvements in selective animal breeding took place in the second half of the eighteenth century inspired by the work of improvers like Bakewell. Here, then, the traditional story of the 'agricultural revolution' does seem acceptable. But in other cases the influence of the great improving landlords has been exaggerated. We know, for example, that the most famous of all progressive landlords, Thomas Coke (1750-1842) of Holkham in Norfolk was neither the pioneer of the new rotations which was once thought, nor were his improvements so financially successful. Similarly, Lord 'Turnip' Townshend (1674-1738) certainly did not introduce the turnip into Norfolk rotations; the turnip was already common as a field crop when he was born. Although a number of large landowners did undoubtedly play a part in popularising new methods, it appears that a much more significant role was played by the large tenants and independent farmers. This in turn raises a key point. The uniquely English structure of landholding, with large estates, substantial tenant farmers, and agricultural labourers, was well suited to the introduction of improvements. This three-tier pattern (which contrasts with the large estate-peasant structure found on the continent) was flexible and adaptable. Capital for improvements could come both from the estate owners and the large tenant farmers, while the latter were likely to be a class who were interested in profits and who had the expertise to introduce appropriate methods.

Were Open Fields Inefficient?

At one time in the high middle-ages, a large part of the land (though by no means all) lay in what is called 'open' fields rather than being parcelled into smaller units and 'enclosed' by hedges or ditches. Gradually over the centuries the areas under open fields declined. Sometimes, as in the early sixteenth century, this was because land was enclosed in order to change its use from arable crops to more profitable sheep for wool. Sometimes small enclosures, or closes, were carved out of open fields to provide grazing for animals, or so that some special crops could be grown. Sometimes enclosure was carried out to provide smaller individual farms rather than the communal system which characterised the open fields. Sometimes too wasteland beyond the open fields was enclosed and cultivated by enterprising landowners.

Just as the reasons for enclosure varied so did the methods. In some parts of the country enclosure was piecemeal, with various irregularly shaped fields being carved out of the predominantly open fields. In other parts, especially in the seventeenth century, general enclosure was the prevailing method. Here an entire open field could be broken into enclosed parcels, by agreement among the various landowners. We call both these methods 'enclosure by agreement'. Although there are unfortunately few records by which we can trace the progress of this movement it does seem as if enclosure by agreement, especially in the seventeenth century, was much more common than once thought.

But although by 1700 a great deal of land had been enclosed, much still remained in open fields. The commonly accepted figure that half the arable land in England and Wales (nearly all Scotland remained unenclosed) was under open fields may be too high. But certainly much land was still open in 1700; much of it lay in a large triangle stretching roughly from the Humber area in the north east to the Avon in the West Midlands and the Thames in the south; and most of this land was relatively fertile and densely populated.

What was the open field system? Its essence was strip-farming. Each cultivator would own or lease his land in strips scattered in the large open fields. Each village community might have two, three, or more open fields attached to it, and there would also be some essential common land ('wasteland') as well.

The prevalent form of open field farming, especially in the Midlands counties, was the division of land into three large fields. One field would always be fallow, with no crops on it (though animals might graze on the rough grass). This was because after a few years under grains (wheat, barley, oats or rye) the soil loses its fertility unless measures are taken to restore it. A period of fallow was therefore essential if reasonable yields were to be maintained. On the other two fields crops would be grown, normally a spring sown crop on one, and a winter one sown on the other.

There were enormous variations within this 'typical' arrangement, but cutting the system down to its bare essentials we can emphasise three basic features. First, strip cultivation meant communal farming. Since an entire field was planted with one crop all activities such as sowing and harvesting had to be done at the same time. There was little opportunity for variation and experiment. Second, the basic social unit of organisation was the village community, the members of whom would farm their strips, while the common wasteland also belonged to the village. Third, the basis of cultivation was the farming of cereal crops. Few animals could be kept under such a system, and so open field villages were characteristic of the arable areas of the South and Midlands, while the pasture areas of the West were generally long enclosed.

Historians often write of the inefficiencies of the open fields, and it is easy to compile a long list of weaknesses. One, already mentioned, was the difficulty of introducing new crops into the open fields or experimenting with different rotations. Another was the practice of leaving one-third or even one-half of all land fallow. A further source of inefficiency was the necessity for each village to maintain commons and wastes. Such land was essential to the traditional village economy for many reasons. It was a place where villagers could graze their pigs and goats, hunt for rabbits and game birds, fish in the ponds, and gather fuel. The landless might build cottages and live on the common land, and wastes might make the difference between subsistence and starvation.

The methods used by open field farmers could also be wasteful. Such drawbacks included the time which could be spent trekking between widely-scattered strips; the valuable land wasted in the necessary paths and tracks among the fields and strips; the bad practices of some farmers which could affect others, like the spread of weeds or plant diseases; the damage to crops which could be caused by unfenced animals trampling the crops; the small-scale nature of farming operations which limited economies of scale (which might come from larger horse-teams for ploughs, or better machinery); mixing of animals together so that selective breeding was impossible.

But the list of **possible** inefficiencies in the open-field system, which is almost endless, should not lead us to conclude that they all occurred all the time. In fact historians have often been too critical of the open-field system. We now know that some open-field farming was by no means so static and inflexible as once supposed. Small enclosures from the open fields could be made where animals could be kept, so improving the productivity of the arable fields, allowing controlled breeding, and keeping cattle from wandering among the crops. New crops and rotations were sometimes introduced within traditional cropping patterns. The wasteful paths and inefficiently sized and shaped strips were frequently reduced by **consolidation** and **engrossment.** Consolidation was the gathering together of adjacent strips to form more compact units, and such an arrangement could benefit both parties making the exchange. Engrossment was the process where some farmers extended their holdings at the expense of their less fortunate neighbours (who in turn might become wage labourers).

Thus, even within the open fields there could emerge a varied pattern of landholdings with both substantial cultivators and compact holdings, small enclosures for animals or special crops, and landless wage labourers. Even the dispersed strips may not have been so inefficient as sometimes suggested. A farmer who held widely scattered strips had a sort of insurance against localised crop failures, pests and diseases which might affect a particular area.

Changes in Organisation

As well as new agricultural techniques the eighteenth century also saw major changes in organisation which facilitated the adoption of new methods of farming. The principal changes were two: the gradual rise in the size of estates and farms, and the acceleration of the enclosure movement.

Earlier views that there was a dramatic rise of great estates and large farms in the eighteenth century, with small 'yeoman' owners being squeezed out, have been revised. Throughout the eighteenth century small units predominated. Even in 1851, nearly two-thirds of all farmers who had holdings of more than five acres had less than 100 acres. There was certainly **some** increase in estate and farm size, but it was gradual and incomplete. In 1700 it has been established that the great landowners, with estates of more than 10,000 acres, owned about 18 per cent of England's arable land. In 1800 the proportion had risen to around 25 per cent. Smallholders, with less than 300 acres, saw their share fall from around one-third to one-fifth of the total, though they remained a very numerous group. In the middle came the county

Enclosure surveyors at work in the late eighteenth century.

families and 'squirearchy' with holdings varying from a few hundred to a few thousand acres.

As we have noted earlier, the normal pattern of English farming organisation was for the estate owner to lease his land to tenants. During the eighteenth century there was a tendency for farm sizes to increase, for the numbers of substantial and wealthy tenant farmers to rise, and for leases to become shorter. The number of large farms, say of 300 to 500 acres, rose while there was a gradual decline in the number of smaller farms.

Slow as these changes were, they were significant. The landlord-tenant relationship brought the benefit of flexibility to English agriculture. The large tenant farmer had the money to invest in good quality livestock and to farm his land efficiently. He had the **working capital** to buy machines and other farm equipment. The large landowner, on the other hand, provided the **fixed capital** necessary for farm buildings, barns, drainage schemes, and so on. Many of the most progressive landowners, like the Walpoles, Cokes, and Townshends, let their land on leases which insisted on the introduction of new improvements, like particular rotations or methods of farming. And shorter leases encouraged this process.

Larger farms and substantial tenant farmers were thus powerful factors in the progressiveness of England's agriculture. We should note that the trend towards larger units long preceded the acceleration of enclosures after 1760, and had been occurring since 1660 at least. Why were estates and farms getting bigger? As mentioned already, as the possibility of getting more rents from improved husbandry increased, so the great landowners sought to let their lands to larger tenants who could implement the improvements. Changes in land law in the second half of the seventeenth century also encouraged large units. The growth of **entail** and **strict settlement** made it difficult for the owners of large estates to sell their land, and they were obliged to pass on their holdings intact to their heirs (usually to the eldest son). This ensured that great family estates would be passed from generation to generation, immune from the occasional spendthrift or incompetent owner. A related factor was the growth of the land mortgage market, which also developed in the late seventeenth century. By mortgaging their lands, landowners could borrow money in order to maintain, improve, and enlarge their estates.

Large holdings were also stimulated by land taxes (first introduced in the 1690s) and by the low agricultural prices which prevailed after 1680, with marked falls between 1730 and 1750. The pressure of higher taxes and lower prices forced landowners and farmers to become more businesslike and efficient, while the unfortunate (often the smaller farmers without the means of investing in improvements) were obliged to sell. An active land market therefore encouraged the growth of larger units, a movement which was also being fostered through enclosures by agreement.

In some parts of England, for example in the clay lands of the Midlands and South, where there was a switch from arable to mixed pasture farming, the decline of small owners and tenants was quite substantial. Elsewhere the movement was often less noticeable or even in the opposite direction. Recent research by local historians confirms the fact that small owners and small tenants were still widespread at the end of the eighteenth century; indeed their numbers may not in total have been very different in 1800 from those in 1700. Only after 1815 was there a marked decline in the numbers of small farmers.

How do we explain the survival of so many small owners and cultivators? Of course tradition, custom, long leases, and the continued backwardness of some of the remoter regions of Britain were contributing factors. But historians now realise that some forces were at work which actually encouraged the small farmer, just as others were stimulating larger holdings. It was therefore quite possible to find even in the same county (Wiltshire is an example) one region where small farms were prospering and on the increase, while elsewhere there was growing concentration in the hands of a few large individuals.

Three main factors seem to have encouraged small farmers in the eighteenth century. Specialisation for urban markets, helped by transport improvements, meant that a variety of small farms could prosper by producing such goods as fruit, vegetables, hops and dairy products. The market gardens of Kent, producing for the London market, are an example of this. Secondly, the active land market could produce small farms as well as big. Sometimes small parcels of land came on the market as a result of enclosures. Also, wealthy merchants and industrialists were often on the lookout for a minor country seat with a small home farm and a few tenants. Finally, the war years of 1793-1815 saw exceptional conditions with rapidly rising food prices and the extension of cultivation on the marginal lands. In these years even the smallest and most inefficient farmer, if he could survive the enclosure movement, was able to prosper.

Enclosures, together with larger holdings, were the two principal developments in farming organisation. Both were related to the spread of the new techniques of farming, for both on enclosed and larger lands the innovations could be more readily and efficiently applied. Not necessarily, of course. Small farms could be efficient and open fields innovative, as we have seen. And an enclosed farm could be run inefficiently with antiquated methods. But the **tendency** for enclosures and improvements to go hand in hand cannot be denied.

We do not know how much enclosures accelerated during the eighteenth century because we have few records of enclosures by agreement, which probably were widespread at the beginning of the period. We do have information about **parliamentary enclosures,** however; that is, enclosures which were awarded by act of parliament. The great advantage of parliamentary enclosures to the landowners was that, unlike enclosures by agreement, not everyone had to consent. Enclosures by agreement were arranged privately by all the commoners holding land; acting as a village body, they appointed surveyors and commissioners to plan and allot the new consolidated holdings. These agreements were then normally confirmed by the Court of Chancery or Court of the Exchequer.

Enclosure by act of parliament, on the other hand, required agreement from owners holding three-quarters of the land (who might be one or two individuals) and the recipient of the tithes. Parliament would then appoint commissioners to survey the land and make the awards on the basis of existing legal titles to land. The enclosures were binding on the minority who might object in vain to the proposals of the commissioners.

Enclosure certainly benefited the larger landowners, who were able to increase their holdings at the expense of those who could not establish a legal title to the land they farmed. They also benefited from the more compact holdings. Not surprisingly therefore, in nearly every case the major petitioner for an enclosure act was the principal landowner.

The drawback with enclosure by act of parliament was its expense. The process was cumbersome and lengthy. First came the petition (and any counter-petition); then came the appointment of commissioners (three, five, or seven as a rule), who were usually experienced land surveyors or agents. The commissioners then had to decide who had claims on the land (including common rights) in order to apportion the land. Often new roads had to be provided for, giving access to isolated farms. The whole process might take five or six years from petition to enclosure, with expensive legal and parliamentary fees along the way. An enclosure could well cost several thousand pounds: the average cost in the late eighteenth century was about 28 shillings an acre, but could reach £5 an acre or more. And then came the expenses of the enclosure itself; the hedges and ditches, erection of new barns and other buildings and the introduction of whatever improvements might accompany the enclosures.

The expense of enclosures meant that they were undertaken mainly when farming was prosperous and prices were rising. The owners of enclosed land could draw up new leases with tenants, and if times were good the rentals could be increased. Agricultural prices were generally low in the first half of the eighteenth century: they rose significantly in the 1750s and continued increasing steadily (except for the inevitable harvest swings) until the dramatic inflation of the war years between 1793 and 1815. Around 1750 wheat prices were under 30 shillings a quarter, and they generally averaged in the range of 25s to 35s in the late 1740s and early 1750s. It was in this period that England's grain exports reached their peak. But then, as population started to increase more quickly, grain prices began to rise and the export surplus disappeared. From 1766 Britain ceased to be a net grain exporter, even having to import significant amounts at times of bad harvest. By the late 1780s wheat prices were between 45 shillings and 60 shillings a quarter, representing something like a two-thirds increase over the levels of mid-century. Then, in the war years, came a period of quite exceptional prices, marked by unprecedented peak prices in particular years: 90 shillings in 1795, 114 shillings in 1800, 120 shillings in 1801, 126 shillings in 1812. In only six years between 1793 and 1815 did average wheat prices fall below 65 shillings a quarter.

The increases for wheat were matched by those for the other main cereals.

Meat prices, too, rose from the mid-1760s, though not so steeply as grain; then, like grain, they shot up after 1793, averaging about 100 per cent more in the period 1793-1815 than they had done in the 1780s.

The response was a spate of parliamentary enclosure largely corresponding with the rising price levels. Prior to 1750 only 64 Acts of Parliament were passed for enclosing land from the open fields. Between 1750 and 1850 roughly 3000 such Acts were passed, some 800 occurring between 1760 and 1780 and well over 1000 between 1793 and 1815. By around 1820 the process of enclosing open field land had left little such land unenclosed; thereafter most of the enclosures were of wastes and commons. In all, in the century after 1750 some 7 million acres were enclosed, about 4½ million from open fields and 2½ million from wastes and commons. As we have seen already, most of the open fields land remaining in 1700 (about one half of all arable land) was concentrated in the Midlands counties, so usually it was here that the impact of the parliamentary enclosure movement was felt. Between 1750 and 1815 about half the agricultural land in Leicestershire, Oxfordshire and Bedfordshire was enclosed, and one-third of Warwickshire.

What was the impact of the parliamentary enclosure movement? We must be very careful not to exaggerate the impact. First, as we noticed already, enclosures did not necessarily lead to improvements, nor were open fields impervious to innovation. The older view that enclosures were largely responsible for agricultural improvements is now not accepted. Nevertheless, local studies have shown that where open fields and enclosed land existed together, the greater productivity increases tended to occur on the enclosed farms. Thus there was a tendency for enclosures to be associated with improvements (possibly because the enclosing landlords were more enterprising and profit-seeking rather than any inherent reasons in the land itself). Secondly, although there was undeniably a major acceleration of enclosures after the 1760s, the 'silent enclosures' of an earlier age had certainly accounted for considerable inroads into the three-field system. One historian has even suggested that the seventeenth century saw twice as much enclosure as the eighteenth century, though this seems unlikely.

Thirdly, earlier historians exaggerated the social consequences of enclosures. The Hammonds, for example, wrote of the depopulating effects of enclosures, with rapacious landlords driving the peasantry from the land into the towns, and of the disappearance of the small cultivator, now swallowed by great magnates. Small owners and tenants did not disappear, as we know, and in some places their numbers increased. The notable decline in the post-1815 depression years occurred **after** the peak of the enclosure movement. The work of the enclosure commissioners seems to have been carried out impartially, with those who held legal titles to land and commons being compensated with appropriate-sized holdings. Villages were not depopulated by enclosures, nor were rural folk driven by destitution to the towns. Enclosures themselves involved a great deal of work in hedging and ditching, while if enclosures were made from land whose use did not require much labour, like pasture, into labour-intensive cultivation, like cereal farming, then demand for labour would actually rise. Chambers and Mingay suggest that on balance most enclosures in the eighteenth century were probably made for converting pasture land into arable land (though this was certainly not the case in many parts of the Midlands). We know that rural populations everywhere were rising in the century after 1750, and that no English county actually lost population in this century. Thus any idea of a rural exodus has to be dismissed.

Nevertheless, there were very real losers from the enclosures. These were those who could provide no clear title or lease to their land, usually the poorest members of the village community such as the customary tenants, small cottagers, squatters on the common land, and so on. For such individuals and their families the loss of common rights could be devastating. Arthur Young, who in the 1770s had been an enthusiastic propagandist for enclosures, had by 1800 changed his mind. He thought that 'by nineteen Enclosure Acts out of twenty, the poor are injured, in some grossly injured'; the poor might well say 'all I know is I had a cow, and an Act of Parliament has taken it from me'. Arthur Young may have exaggerated the scale but not the existence of the problem; in countless parishes cottagers who had hitherto had perhaps some land or at any rate some grazing rights on the commons now had none, and such families now became dependent only on labouring for their more fortunate neighbours, or upon parish poor relief.

In 1815 the long period of rising agricultural prices came to an end, to be replaced by a sharp depression and then a lengthy time of re-adjustment to the new circumstances of supply and demand. Adjustment was helped by the passing of the Corn Law in 1815, a protective measure designed to keep grain prices high. The Corn Law, inspired by the still dominant landowning interest, forbade wheat imports if prices were below 80 shillings a quarter. In the 1820s Huskisson took steps to modify the Corn Laws, but it was not until 1846 (by which time demand had risen and there was no longer any threat of large grain surpluses from European suppliers) that they were finally repealed. At this stage agriculture, more productive and boosted by the railways, was on the eve of a new golden age.

Chapter 6
The Industrial Revolution, Causes and Consequences

An Industrial Revolution?

Economic historians commonly pose such questions as 'was there an industrial revolution?', 'what were the causes of the industrial revolution?', 'why was England the first nation in the world to industrialise?', and so on. Such questions are deceptively simple. There are no simple answers, and, unfortunately, economic historians are still not agreed on many basic issues. The best the student can do is to try to understand the problems which arise in trying to answer these questions and to pinpoint the reasons for controversy.

Let us start by noting that two quite separate points often arise when we talk about the industrial revolution. One is the definition, or **concept,** of the industrial revolution we have in mind. What do we mean by an 'industrial revolution?'. The second point concerns the actual data, or **facts,** which economic historians use as evidence, for here again, there are several areas of controversy.

Can we define an industrial revolution? Broadly speaking economic historians have used the term in two distinct senses: short-term acceleration or long-term structural change. The first approach looks for a particular period when the economy began to move faster. The second approach takes a broader view and says that if, after a certain length of time, the economy has been transformed, then a revolution has taken place.

Those who focus on short-term acceleration have used two approaches. The first seeks to find out what was happening to the entire economy, and hence looks at aggregate data like national income, or national income per head (which is the usual measure of **economic growth**). The best known version of this view was put forward in the 1960s by Rostow. Rostow used the term 'take-off' rather than industrial revolution, and he suggested that economic

Arkwright's Mill at Cromford, Derby, built in 1771; Britain's first spinning factory using water-powered machinery.

growth 'took-off' in Britain in the 1780s, and that by the very beginning of the nineteenth century the nation was already launched on a path of high growth in which rising incomes produced more savings and investment which in turn sustained high growth rates. Rostow was particularly impressed with the performance of the cotton textile industry, which he termed a 'leading sector', spearheading the entire economy on to a new level of growth.

Many other economic historians, although not necessarily agreeing with Rostow's dates, or his emphasis on textiles, nevertheless agree that the significant point is the onset of sustained economic growth. In the writings of such distinguished scholars as Kuznets and North, we can find the idea that Britain was the first country in the world to experience sustained economic growth, and that the process started sometime after 1760 and was finally launched by, say, 1830.

The second variant of short-term acceleration looks not at the whole economy but at just the **industrial** sector. If we define an industrial revolution as a marked acceleration in the rate of growth of industrial production, then we need to look at an index of industrial output and see when a significant change took place.

Historians who understand the industrial revolution as a process of long-term structural change take a different view. They argue that the economy was fundamentally different in, say, 1850 (or some other convenient date) from what it had been in 1760 (or, again, some other date), and assess the changes as 'revolutionary'. This approach makes a great deal of sense, for it is obvious that Britain in 1850 had evolved a wholly new form of society and economy, whatever the actual rates of growth to get there. Britain had become the first country to be predominantly industrial and predominantly urban, with all the economic and social consequences which flowed from this. The structural transformation from a basically agrarian economy, with pre-industrial characteristics such as the domestic system and low levels of technology, to a basically industrial modern economy can surely be called 'revolutionary'. The consequences not only for Britain but for the rest of the world were profound, for many of the results of Britain's development (for example, the steam engine and the railway) later affected countries everywhere.

Our view of the industrial revolution, then, depends partly on how we choose to define it. But what support do statistical data and other facts give to the different approaches? It cannot be stressed often enough that until the second half of the nineteenth century the basis for aggregate data about the economy is very slender. A great deal of pioneering work has been undertaken by such scholars as Deane and Cole, yet much remains doubtful and controversial.

Table 6.1 presents two sets of estimates for the growth of national income between 1700 and 1831.

Table 6.1 Annual Growth Rates of National Income in England and Wales 1700-1831

	I	II
1700-1760	0.66	0.69
1760-1780	0.65	0.70
1780-1801	2.06	1.32
1801-1831	3.06	1.97

Column I shows the estimates of Deane and Cole, published in the 1960s. We can see a long period of slow, steady growth, lasting until the 1780s. Then comes a sudden jump, with growth rates trebling to reach more than 2 per cent per annum, followed by an even higher growth rate of more than 3 per cent. Annual growth rates of 2 to 3 per cent annually, sustained over a long period, are impressively high (especially for a country like Britain around 1800, unable to import advanced technology from abroad in contrast to all later developing countries). Column I tends to support Rostow's hypothesis of a take-off in the 1780s, although if we were to divide these figures by population growth rates, which were rising quickly, to get estimates of per capita income, the acceleration would look less dramatic.

The picture shown in column II is different. The estimates here are by Crafts, published in 1985. They show less acceleration after 1780, and considerably lower growth rates anyway.   .

Now look at Table 6.2, which gives estimates for the industrial sector only (mining and manufacturing). Again, there are two sets of figures, by Deane and Cole (column I) and Crafts (column II).

Table 6.2 The Growth of Industrial Production in Britain (% per annum)

	I	II
1700-1760	0.98	0.69
1760-1780	0.49	0.70
1780-1801	3.43	1.32
1801-1831	3.97	2.32

Once again Crafts' recent estimates show nothing like the dramatic acceleration of industrial growth shown by Deane and Cole. Nor do they show the high absolute rates of growth; over the period 1780-1831 Crafts' figures show a rate of less than half that given by Deane and Cole. If we are to believe Crafts, the 'industrial revolution', interpreted as a marked acceleration in the rate of industrial growth, has virtually disappeared. Instead we get much slower growth, increasing steadily from the middle of the eighteenth century until about the 1820s. Only from this period does Crafts find a definite upturn both in the rate of industrial growth and in the growth of per capita national income.

In Tables 6.1 and 6.2 we have given estimates from two well-known studies. But both views, that of fast growth and that of slow growth, find support from other historians. When Deane and Cole suggested an acceleration of growth in the 1780s they were confirming what was already widely accepted, and had been supported by Ashton, Nef, and many others. Hartwell and Hobsbawm are other well-known economic historians, who, though differing in their interpretation of the industrial revolution, nevertheless agree on an upturn of industrial growth after 1780. The 'slow growth' view, on the other hand, has found increasing numbers of adherents in recent years. Harley suggests that high industrial growth rates of three per cent or more a year were not achieved until the 1840s, and McCloskey also accepts a more moderate view of industrial development. Fores, noting how widely interpretations of the period differ, even writes of 'the myth of the British industrial revolution'.

How can such diverging views arise? The main problem lies in the difficulty of constructing satisfactory index numbers either for total national output or for industrial growth. Even if we knew exactly how different sectors of the economy performed (and we do not), it would still be impossible to calculate a single series of index numbers which would adequately and unambiguously show growth rates over a long period. The 'slow growth' view of the industrial revolution focuses on two issues. First, Crafts and others suggest that the initial starting point at the beginning of the industrial revolution period (say, in 1760) was higher than others have thought. From a higher starting point, subsequent growth rates will obviously be slower. Secondly, the 'slow growth' view has challenged the index of industrial production calculated by the economic historian Hoffmann in the 1930s and used by most scholars subsequently. The Hoffmann index, it is claimed, exaggerates the acceleration of industrial growth after 1780 by giving too much weight to the fast-growing industries like cotton textiles. Since it took a long time for the new industries to become important in the economy we should pay more attention to the traditional, but slower-growing, sectors.

It is not really sensible to reach a dogmatic conclusion about the merits of 'fast' or 'slow' growth. The issues are not yet resolved, and in any case some of the problems are more statistical than historical. Nevertheless, earlier views almost certainly exaggerated the acceleration of economic activity after 1780, although recent revisions probably go too far in the opposite direction. From all that we now know about pre-1780, or pre-1750, economic development, it certainly seems reasonable to suppose less dramatic growth rates thereafter. The spread of agricultural improvements before 1700, for example, is consistent with a higher starting point by the mid-eighteenth century. Again, earlier writers may have underestimated the amount of industrial output produced before 1750 by rural workers. Furthermore, the impact of the great changes we associate most with the industrial revolution, the spread of steam power, the growth of cotton textiles, the production of puddled iron, and so on, significant as they were within their own sectors or regions, cannot quickly have had a dramatic impact upon the entire economy. Nevertheless, even if we modify Hoffmann's index to take account of the critics, some upturn of industrial growth remains. It seems premature to discard the notion of an industrial revolution based on this upturn, even if the highest growth rates did not appear for another three or four decades.

To use the term 'revolution' to describe the structural transformation of the British economy also seems well justified. Beyond dispute, Britain by 1850 was an urban industrial economy, with modern factories, modern forms of business organisation, and significantly higher per capita incomes than a century before. Of course, it can always be argued that the changes were slow and incomplete. To some it seems strange to talk of a 'revolution' lasting three-quarters of a century or more. Clapham long ago emphasised how narrowly based were the 'new' innovations; how even in 1830 only cotton-spinning had undergone a complete technical revolution and become a mechanised factory industry. Musson is correct to point out that 'in most industries there was no technical revolution in the century before 1850,' and that 'the typical worker in the mid-nineteenth century was not a machine operator in a factory but still a traditional craftsman or labourer or domestic servant'.

Nevertheless by 1850 Britain **was** predominantly urbanised and industrialised, even if many industries and urban services were traditional and unmechanised. This was a social transformation of sufficient significance to deserve the label 'revolutionary'. Moreover, and this point is often overlooked, part of the significance of the industrial revolution lay just in its narrowness. It was this concentration and specialisation in a narrow range of products which gave the British industrial revolution its special character: its regional pattern, its export orientation, its factory towns, its dependence on coal and steam technology. To point out how much remained outside this narrow dynamic sector is thus to miss a fundamental aspect of the process of change.

Living Standards and the Industrial Revolution

The debate over whether working class living standards rose or fell during the period of Britain's rapid industrialisation has been both vigorous and inconclusive. On the one side have been ranged the 'pessimists', historians like Hobsbawm, who have argued that conditions deteriorated for most workers between the 1760s and the 1840s. On the other side are the 'optimists', Hartwell and others, who maintain that living standards significantly improved.

Before we examine the debate in any detail, it is helpful to understand just why the subject has proved so controversial and elusive. Obviously the topic itself is important: how living standards, dietary standards, health, and so on changed over time, and what caused these changes, is one of the key economic and social questions with which we have to deal. Yet both measuring the changes and attributing the causes has proved extremely difficult.

One problem is that there is no adequate measure of 'living standards', nor any general agreement on what aspects the term should cover. Historians have mostly used two indicators, average real wages and the 'quality of life'. Both raise difficulties. Real wages are money wages adjusted for price changes. Unfortunately, for the period in question data on money wages are unsatisfactory and tend to be drawn from statistics for southern districts (whereas it was in the North that most industrial development was taking place). Price statistics are also inadequate, and the series we have usually fail to reflect regional variations and sometimes omit important commodities. At best, real wage indices are only guides to average trends, which may not reflect the real conditions of particular regions or particular groups of workers. Neither do they show family earnings, yet an adult man's wages would normally be supplemented by the earnings of his children and perhaps his wife. A true picture of living standards would have to take account of these family earnings, yet the wage data we have tell us little about them.

The problem with estimating the 'quality of life' is that so many of the features we might wish to include, such as smoky or unsanitary living and working conditions, or the new rigours of factory discipline, defy numerical accounting. We may feel that the squalid conditions in the industrial towns would make necessary the payment of higher wages in order to compensate workers for the poor environment. But this raises the difficulty that if wages in the factory towns were higher than elsewhere (which was, in fact, the case), at least part of the difference simply reflects the wretched conditions of the towns.

An additional complication to the debate has been that different writers have examined different time-spans. Some have looked at changes over the whole century 1750-1850; others have looked at shorter periods, 1790-1830, 1780-1840, and so on. Depending on the time-span chosen and the sort of data used we can get very different answers.

A further problem has been the ideological commitment which some historians have brought to the debate. Marxist historians, like Hobsbawm, are fierce critics of capitalism and capitalists. They expect to find that during industrialisation the workers suffered at the expense of the employers, and it is difficult to avoid the conclusion that they sometimes **start** with their conclusions, and then seek evidence to support them. This is equally true of some 'liberal' historians who allow their belief in the ultimate benefits of the capitalist system to colour their view of early industrialisation, and to argue that living conditions **must** have improved. Although there are exceptions, left-wing and Marxist historians tend to be pessimists, and right-wing 'liberal' historians tend to be optimists.

Even if we knew what was happening to living standards it would still be difficult to attribute causes. The question we really wish to answer is this; what impact did industrialisation have on living standards? But unfortunately industrialisation was not the only factor operating on living standards. In the period 1793-1815, for example, we have other factors such as a series of very bad harvests, the dislocation caused by the wars, mounting population growth, and rapid urbanisation (not all due to industrial growth). All these factors, on the face of it, would operate to depress living conditions, so that even if we find that living standards deteriorated it would not necessarily follow that the cause was due to industrial growth. Even after 1815, when peace returned, and harvest failures occurred less frequently, rapid population growth still continued. From this time, though, it does become easier to relate changes in living standards to industrial development, and certainly by around the 1840s there is no question that industrialisation was the main cause of changes in the standard of living.

A sensible way of approaching the standard of living debate is to narrow down the areas of agreement and disagreement. Note first that nothing has been said so far about living standards before 1750, and, indeed, very little research work has been done on this period. Given, though, the prevailing low level of population growth in the first half of the eighteenth century, the definite improvements in agricultural productivity in the period, and the generally falling levels of food prices for much of the time, it would be surprising if general living standards were not slowly improving. This would certainly be the conclusion of historians like John and Eversley, who have both argued that the growing home market was a potent source of demand for industrial products. Eversley has stressed the importance of growing home consumption until the 1770s. Evidence of rising home demand, and hence of better standards of living, is stronger for the industrialising areas of the Midlands and North then it is of London and the South.

At the other end of the time period, there is again little dispute about the general movement of living standards after the 1840s. Chaloner showed long ago that the term 'hungry forties' is really quite inappropriate for most of the country, although the history of Ireland, with its catastrophic famine in 1845-6, when the potato crop failed, was different. Generally though, from the trough of the deep depression in 1842, there is clear evidence of improvement in average real wages. The improvement continued slowly until the 1870s, and then advanced rapidly in the last quarter of the nineteenth century as prices fell sharply. At the same time many indicators of the 'quality of life', such as the factory and urban environment, also show gradual improvement. Towns were getting healthier, and after the 1860s there were no longer any major outbreaks of cholera. Hours of work, a very important factor in living standards, gradually fell too, whereas in the early nineteenth century they may actually have increased in the industrial towns. Although we cannot generalise from one occupational group, Table 6.3 gives an indication of how the average working hours in the coal industry fell between 1842 and 1913.

Table 6.3 Average Weekly Hours Worked by Unskilled Underground Coalminers, 1842-1913

Year	Hours worked per week
1842	65
1850	59
1860	58
1870	55
1880	51
1890	48
1905	47
1913	43

Debate, then, has largely focused on the period from approximately 1780 to the early 1840s, years of the classic industrial revolution. On one point all would agree: these were years of more pronounced change and fluctuations than had ever been known before or were to be experienced again until the First World War. The war years, 1793-1815, were times of exceptionally high food prices which sometimes reached famine levels. Obviously at these times wage earners, whether urban or rural, northern or southern, were bound to suffer. Then there were cyclical downturns, with years like 1815, 1819, 1832 and 1842 seeing widespread unemployment, especially in the textile areas. Moreover the fortunes of different groups of workers fluctuated and diverged as never before. The demands set in train by the industrial revolution without question benefited certain groups, who included skilled engineers and some factory trades like fine cotton spinning. An 'aristocracy of labour', earning perhaps 30 shillings a week or more, when the average was half that, emerged during these years. Many groups of workers, of course, earned much less than this even in the growing industries. These included the women and children, who dominated the textile labour force. Nevertheless, the contributions of many of these workers to family earnings probably meant that working-class textile families tended to improve their real earnings.

Groups of workers whose real wages and living standards deteriorated over much of the period 1780-1840 included agricultural labourers, especially in the populous southern districts where alternative factory labour opportunities did not push rural wages up. Other groups to suffer were those made redundant by the new machinery. The early advances in cotton spinning had at first brought prosperity to handloom weavers, but the rapid spread of efficient power looms in the 1820s spelled disaster for them. Their struggle to compete with factory output was unequal. From peak earnings of about 23 shillings a week in 1805 their average earnings were only 6 shillings by 1831. Handloom weavers were not the only sufferers from technological change. Workers in the linen industry suffered from competition with cheap cottons; machinery replaced the work of framework knitters, wool combers, and many others; the well organised coaching trade, with its attendant services centred on inns or staging posts ultimately, like the canals, lost out to the railways.

Clearly it is unsatisfactory to attempt to balance the gainers and losers by striking some kind of average of real wages, yet there is no other way of reaching an overall picture. If we do make such a calculation, however, two points emerge. First, the statistics lend support to the pessimists' case before about 1820 and thereafter to the optimists' case. Secondly, prices tended to fluctuate more than money wages, so that it was the former which tended to exert the greatest influence on movement of real wages. This was especially the case during the war period, 1793-1815, when rapidly rising prices eroded any gain from increased money wages, and for most workers these years saw generally depressed living standards. Table 6.4 gives an illustration of this point.

Table 6.4 Price and Wage Movements (% change), 1790-1850

Years	Money wages	Price changes	Real wages
1740-1815	+ 63.1	+ 74.1	− 11.0
1815-1825	− 10.6	− 29.3	+ 18.7
1825-1850	+ 9.8	− 19.4	+ 29.2

A recent study by Lindert and Williamson confirms the view that a marked upturn in real wages occurred not from the 1840s, as was once thought, but as early as 1820. They calculate that average real wages hardly rose at all between 1781 and 1819, falling in the war years and remaining depressed during the post-war slump. These post-war years were also years of high unemployment, another important factor to take into account in assessing living standards. But after 1819 real wages rose sharply, just about doubling by 1850.

The 'quality of life' is difficult to measure. From the late eighteenth century there were various urban improvements such as better paving, lighting, water supply, and policing. Pall Mall was the first street in the world to be lit by gas lamps in 1807. From 1815 street lighting by gas spread to provincial towns.

Yet if, on balance, real wages were on the increase after 1820, other evidence is less supportive of the optimists' case. Some regional studies, for example of Glasgow, Bath and London, show little improvement before the 1840s. Also figures for working-class consumption show that some basic commodities such as tea and sugar did not increase at all until after 1840. Sugar consumption, for example, remained at around 18 lbs per head between 1800 and 1845, and then jumped to 30 lbs in the 1850s and 68 lbs by the 1870s. Meat consumption by the working classes seems to have declined between the 1780s and the 1840s.

Evidence on the 'quality of life' must also support the pessimists' case before the 1840s. There were obvious evils, like the appalling conditions in the fast-growing factory towns and the exploitation of child labour (there were some five thousand boys and even some girls between the ages of 5 and 10 working underground in the coalmines in 1841). Less obvious deterioration included the loss of independence experienced by factory workers, subject now to strict time-keeping, the factory hooter, and the need to keep the machinery turning. Factory labourers, the pessimists suggest, suffered a loss of status as their lives and livelihood became determined by factors outside their own control. Periodic bouts of unemployment were a feature of industrial work from the beginning of the nineteenth century. Family ties were also changed by the industrial revolution as factories destroyed the family economies which had been part and parcel of the domestic system.

Yet for all the qualifications we should make about changes in the environment and qualitative changes in living conditions, it is doubtful whether the view that for the majority of workers living standards were improving from the 1820s can be seriously challenged. We should certainly avoid the mistake of thinking of pre-industrial conditions as idyllic. Under the domestic system hours of work could be as long, or longer, than in the factories, and child labour was common and arduous.

If the average worker was getting better off after 1820 there were much sharper gains both for particular groups of workers and for the middle classes. Lindert and Williamson estimate that real wages for skilled workers quadrupled between 1815 and 1850 while those for unskilled workers less than doubled. This underlines the appearance of a clear aristocracy of labour in these years. Moreover total real per capita income in Britain was growing faster than real wages, so that the share going to profits, rents and investment was relatively increasing. Recent work confirms the view that income distribution was becoming increasingly unequal during the first half of the nineteenth century.

A final point, often ignored by pessimists, is the consequences of rapidly growing population. In England and Wales there were seven million more mouths to feed in 1841 than there had been in 1801. Even had real wages not improved in these years, to sustain this rapid growth without substantial deterioration was itself a considerable achievement. Some idea of the sort of Malthusian crisis that might have affected a non-industrial England can perhaps be seen in the tragic experience of agricultural Ireland. In Ireland, too, there was rapid population growth in the opening decades of the nineteenth century, and population had reached over 8 million by 1845. But the consequences of the potato famine of 1845-7, starvation and emigration, resulted in an absolute fall of 4 million people by 1914.

Finance and Organisation of Industry

How were the industries and other enterprises of the period financed? Here it is useful to distinguish between those businesses — the vast majority, including nearly all manufacturing and mining — which required relatively little capital at the outset, and those few like the canals and railways which required large outlays before any returns were forthcoming. Where capital needs were not large, an industrial entrepreneur or a partnership would raise the necessary money (possibly through savings, or borrowings from friends and family) and start the enterprise. Especially in the early stages of the industrial revolution the cost of fixed capital (the land, buildings, machinery and so on) was normally small, perhaps only a few hundred pounds. The working capital, to pay for raw materials and wages, would sometimes come from local banks, or from credit from suppliers, or perhaps by delaying payments of wages until goods could be produced and sold. How did such firms grow bigger? The usual path to expansion lay in re-investing ('ploughing back') profits in new plant and equipment. In this way the individual family firm, with carefully managed accounts and often rather frugal lifestyles for the owners in order to maximise profits for re-investment, became characteristic of the industrial revolution.

For canals, railways, gas and water companies, some of the larger trading companies, and a very few industrial concerns before 1850, the sources of finance had to be larger and wider. Here the solution was the joint-stock company, where the company sold shares either to a small group of partners or to the general public. Public companies required an act of parliament, which was expensive, but a great advantage of such an act was that it could grant **limited liability** to the shareholders. Without this provision a shareholder might, if the enterprise went bankrupt, lose not only the amount he had invested in his shares, but also be liable for the enterprise's debts from his personal funds.

A major consequence of the growth of railways was to popularise share investment and encourage the formation of limited liability companies. An Act of 1844 made the formation of companies cheaper and simpler, while further Acts of 1856 and 1862 made limited liability possible for all ordinary companies (the provision was extended to banks in 1858).

The appearance of joint-stock companies with limited liability from the middle of the nineteenth century was potentially significant, for much wider sources of public savings could be tapped. But there was no rush to take advantage of such limited liability. The tradition of the family-owned firm with complete control over the undertaking remained strong, and as late as 1885 only about 10 per cent of companies had been limited under the 1862 Act. Nevertheless, from about this time the numbers of limited companies grew rapidly, and the rise of large firms with ownership divorced from management (as in the case of Courtaulds from the 1890s) became more characteristic of the industrial landscape. Banks, too, began to take advantage of limited liability provisions, especially after the failure of the (unlimited) City of Glasgow Bank in 1878.

Chapter 7
The Growth of the Basic Industries

Steam Power

Of all the technical innovations during the industrial revolution period, James Watt's famous steam engine, first patented in 1769, may be said to be the most fundamental. It was fundamental for several reasons. First, steam power could be applied to a wide range of different industries, raising efficiency and productivity and lowering costs over an extensive area of the economy. By 1800 steam power was being used to drive textile machinery, drain mines, provide power for malt, sugar and flour mills, and drive brewery and pottery machines. By 1850 the area of application had extended dramatically, and by this latter date steam-driven railways were well established and long distance steam-driven ocean shipping was developing rapidly.

Secondly, steam engines for the first time gave industrialists a power source independent of the muscle-power of men or animals, or of the vagaries of the weather as in the case of waterwheels and windmills. Machinery could now be driven constantly, all the year round, day and night if necessary. Industries could locate in more favourable places, now no longer dependent on fast-flowing streams to drive waterwheels. Thus the steam engine allowed the development of large factory towns, such as occurred in the textile towns of south Lancashire.

Thirdly, steam engines were expensive, required considerable capital investment (a steam engine in 1800 could cost over £1,000, apart from the buildings and other machinery), and were obviously most economical when they could be used to drive as much machinery as possible. The steam engines thus promoted large-scale factory production and the concentration of workers in large enterprises employing perhaps several hundred workers (the largest Manchester cotton mills in 1815 were employing around 1,000 workers).

Fourthly, the manufacture of steam engines for workshops, factories and

Pithead of a coalmine with steam winding gear (a Newcomen engine), c. 1820.

railways, produced a significant new industry, one of the few in the industrial revolution to be based on the application of science to industry. The manufacturers and designers of steam engines and the components which went into them led to the creation of a skilled workforce of mechanical engineers and metal workers. The firm of Boulton and Watt, for example, one of the country's leading manufacturers of steam engines before 1815, produced a stream of skilled workmen whose talents spread far and wide, to locomotive design and construction, gas apparatus, waterworks, metal working of all kinds, as so on.

The steam engine itself had a long history. The first successful machine to be operated by steam power was patented by Thomas Savery in 1698. Savery's engine used both atmospheric and steam power, and was first developed for pumping water from the tin mines of Devon and Cornwall. Savery's engine was cumbersome and inefficient, and a great improvement was made by Thomas Newcomen about 1705. His 'atmospheric engine' was also developed for draining West Country mines and used the principle of a piston being driven in a cylinder. The force came from atmospheric pressure on the piston, steam being used in the cylinder to create a vacuum (by being condensed with cold water), so drawing the piston down.

The Newcomen engine became widely adopted in mines during the

Matthew Boulton's famous factory at Soho, Birmingham, around the 1750s. Boulton later went into partnership with James Watt.

eighteenth century, especially in the coal fields since the process of alternately heating and cooling the cylinder was extremely wasteful of fuel. Perhaps two thousand Newcomen engines were built during the course of the eighteenth century, but until the 1780s the fact that they could only produce an up-and-down motion restricted their application almost entirely to draining mines.

It was the fuel problem which James Watt was first able to solve. After several years of experiments, Watt produced a successful alternative, and in 1769 he took out a patent for his innovation. His patent introduced the principle of a separate condenser for which steam from the main cylinder could be drawn and the main cylinder itself kept permanently hot. This cut the cost of fuel enormously, by two-thirds to three-quarters.

Watt was a brilliant engineer, employed as an instrument maker at Glasgow University. Although he had solved a theoretical problem with Newcomen engines, more was needed before his engine could become a practical success. It was necessary to combine Watt's engineering talents with practical business and manufacturing expertise. Watt first went into partnership in Scotland with John Roebuck, a coal and iron entrepreneur, and with Roebuck he produced his earliest engines. Upon Roebuck's bankruptcy in 1773, Matthew Boulton, a far-sighted and scientifically-inclined Birmingham metal manufacturer, offered Watt a partnership. So began in 1774 the partnership of Boulton and Watt, at Soho, near Birmingham, the most famous firm in the history of engineering. Watt provided the engineering designs, Boulton the capital and business skills. In 1775 Watt was able to extend his patent for a further 25 years, so that until 1800 steam engines on Watt's separate condenser principle could only be manufactured by, or under licence from, Boulton and Watt (the firm itself did not, in fact, manufacture the engines until 1795).

The weakness of Watt's early engines, like the Newcomen engines, was that they supplied only a pumping motion. Watt's engine was soon adopted throughout the mining areas of Devon and Cornwall, but made slower progress in the coalfields where fuel was cheaper. Both Newcomen and Watt engines were also used to drive waterwheels, pumping the water driving the wheels back again so that the waterwheels could be used throughout the year.

Only in the early 1780s was Watt able to develop a rotative engine, and it was this which really ushered in the steam age. The key inventions were the **sun and planet motion,** patented in 1781, and **parallel motion,** patented in 1784. Together these improvements produced an efficient engine which could supply rotary motion to all sorts of machinery.

As we have mentioned already, the manufacture of steam engines was closely related to the development of the engineering industry. Boulton and Watt worked closely with John Wilkinson, the great Midlands iron master, whose invention of a process for boring iron cylinders was crucial to the production of efficient steam engines. William Murdock, who began his career as an apprentice with Boulton and Watt, was responsible for many engineering advances. He was probably the originator of the 'sun and planet' motion, and in 1792 was the first to show the practicality of coal gas lighting. John Smeaton was another famous engineer who made many improvements in the design of Newcomen engines in the 1750s and 1760s.

For all its significance in early industrial Britain, we must be careful not to exaggerate the impact of Watt's engine or of steampower in general. In 1800 there were more Newcomen engines in use in the coalfields than Watt engines, while even in the tin and copper districts only a third to a quarter of engines in use were made by Boulton and Watt (many of the engines were illegal copies of Watt's designs). In textiles steam power was also well established. The first steam driven cotton factory was at Papplewick in Nottinghamshire in 1785; the first in Manchester was opened in 1792 and by 1802 there were said to be 52 steam powered cotton mills in the Manchester district. Yet these were all spinning mills. Cotton weaving remained a handicraft industry, and not until the 1830s did the quantity of cotton cloth

A view of the West Midlands 'Black Country' engraved in 1869.

woven on steam-powered looms exceed that produced by handloom weavers. Even for spinning, more yarn was produced by water-driven mules in 1800 than by steam power, although by 1815 steam had become dominant.

In other branches of textiles, such as woollens, worsteds, and linens, the advance of steam power was slower, and outside the textile factories, with a few exceptions (such as brewing), its adoption was very limited. Even in 1850, outside the textile industries, industrial technology was essentially handicraft. As late as 1870, of a total steam horse-power of 1,980,000 H.P., about 580,000 H.P. nearly a third of the total, was concentrated in textiles.

Cotton Textiles

Of all Britain's great basic industries which were the foundation of her economic growth in the late eighteenth and nineteenth centuries, cotton textiles has some claim to be considered the most significant. From around 1770 to 1840 cotton textiles were Britain's fastest-growing major industry, the fastest-growing export industry, and the first industry to be transformed by steam-powered factory production. From a position of insignificance in 1770, cotton textiles by 1805 were already Britain's most important manufacturing

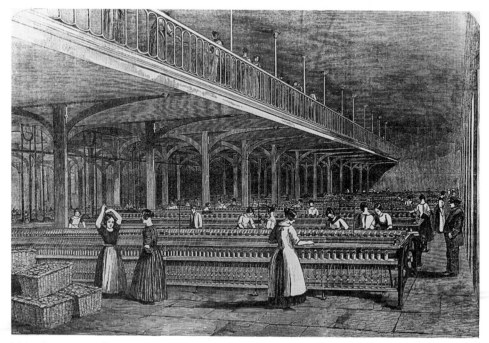

A Manchester cotton factory in 1851. Most textile workers were women and children at this period.

industry in value of output and also the largest export industry (overtaking woollen textiles in both respects); and cotton goods remained the major industry until well into the nineteenth century, continuing to be the chief export industry until 1914. In 1841, the first year for which the Census gave occupational returns, cottons employed far more than any other manufacturing sector. The census showed 378,000 working in cotton textiles (a considerable underestimate, the true figure was nearer 500,000, a large proportion of them women and girls). Coal mining, according to the same census, employed 118,000; woollen and worsteds 167,000. Thus, although small by comparison with agricultural workers (1,300,000), or domestic servants (about one million), the dominance of cotton textiles among the main industries was clear cut.

In its use of steam power (virtually complete in spinning by around 1820 and in weaving by the mid-1840s), in its early transition to factory production, and in its regional and urban concentration, cotton textiles epitomised the industrial revolution. In 1770 the industry, small as it was, had been rather scattered, though with noticeable concentration in the districts around Manchester and Glasgow. Even then, it was essentially a rural

A Manchester cotton mill in 1835.

industry, and dependence of the early factories on water power sustained the industry's dispersed character. But from the 1790s rapid concentration in growing factory towns characterised the cotton spinning industry. By 1838 some 86 per cent of all English cotton operatives were found in just two counties, Cheshire and Lancashire, nearly all of them in what was effectively a single cotton region centred on Liverpool and Manchester.

Historians have debated whether cotton textiles was **the** leading sector in the industrial revolution. Rostow suggested in the 1960s that it was soaring cotton production in the last quarter of the eighteenth century which was largely responsible for Britain's 'take-off' from a poor, traditional economy to a modern dynamic one. Scholars now place more emphasis on the relatively advanced state of the economy **before** the mid-eighteenth century, and also stress the more broadly based advance of the economy after 1780. Phyllis Deane, for example, rejects the view of any single industry playing the role of a leading sector, and points out that other industries, notably iron and coal, have claims at least as strong as cotton (she makes the significant point that cotton textiles used an imported raw material, raw cotton, so that part of the benefits of rapid growth were felt overseas). On the other hand the fast-growing cotton industry not only encouraged employment, factory building, and the installation of steam engines and textile machinery, but the very speed of change excited contemporaries and fostered a spirit of enterprise elsewhere. The cotton factories themselves often incorporated pioneering and revolutionary changes, such as new types of steam engines, iron frame buildings, steam ventilation, and coal gas lighting.

The sustained rise of the cotton textile industry is shown in Table 7.1, which gives figures for raw cotton imports. Since all raw cotton for the cotton industry had to be imported, the recorded quantities of these imports provide a good indication of the overall growth of the industry.

Table 7.1 Imports of Raw Cotton and Proportion of Cottons Exported

Year	Imports (million lbs)	% Exported
1700	1.1	-
1760	3.4	50
1780	6.6	30
1790	31	23
1800	52	62
1815	90	60
1820	141	53
1840	452	50
1860	1050	64
1900	1510	79
1912	2038	85

We can notice at once two points from Table 7.1. First is the very high rate of growth achieved between 1780 and 1860, followed by a period of rather slower growth. In the 52 years between 1860 and 1912 imports of raw cotton did not quite double; in the previous 45 years they had increased nearly twelve-fold. Especially dramatic were the increases in the very early years: a more than twenty-fold increase in the 40 years after 1780. No other sector grew so fast, either in terms of output or of productivity.

The second point from Table 7.1 is the generally high ratio of output exported, reaching a proportion of 85 per cent just before the First World War. There were, though, two periods when the export share actually fell: from 1760 to around 1790, and from 1815 until the 1840s.

This latter point suggests that it was home, rather than foreign, demand which was primarily responsible for the initial burst of rapid growth from the 1770s. During the war period, from 1793-1815, foreign trade played a leading role, followed by a long period from 1815 to 1860 when both home and foreign demand advanced more or less in step, with home demand edging ahead before 1840, export demand thereafter. From the 1860s the share of exports in total demand then went ahead rapidly, suggesting that it was now definitely overseas markets which were responsible for the expansion of the cotton textile industry.

What launched the period of rapid cotton manufacturing after about 1770? A convenient way of approaching this question is to turn the problem around, and ask why development before 1770 was limited. A principal reason for slow growth seems to have been the lack of suitable yarn for weavers. The difficulty was two-fold. There was no readily available method of making cotton yarn strong enough to be used as a warp (the length-wise thread) in woven cloth. So the early cotton industry was forced to produce mainly hybrid cloths, with cotton wefts (cross-wise threads) and linen warps. The chief products were known as fustians. There were a few all-cotton products, like handkerchiefs and heavy cotton velvets, but it was impossible for British cotton workers, with the existing technology, to match the fine cotton calicoes imported from India.

Secondly, early in the eighteenth century cotton weaving became much more efficient relative to cotton spinning. Even before the invention by John Kay in 1733 of his famous flying shuttle it was claimed that one weaver could handle the yarn produced by six spinners. The flying shuttle, originally developed for woollen weaving but widely adopted by cotton weavers after 1760, increased the disequilibrium. Kay's machine doubled the weaver's speed and enabled him to weave a much wider cloth.

Many inventive men tried to bridge the gap between spinners and weavers, which existed both for cotton and woollens, by mechanised inventions. A roller spinning machine, patented in 1738 by John Wyatt and Lewis Paul, was not a commercial success. A breakthrough at last came around 1767 with the invention of the spinning jenny by James Hargreaves, a Blackburn weaver. The jenny allowed the spinner to spin several threads at a time, at first eight, by 1770 (when the jenny was patented) 16, by 1784, 80, and later over 100. The machines were widely adopted and an estimated 20,000 were in use in 1788.

The jenny was a simple hand-operated machine made mostly of wood. The small models fitted well into the domestic family economy, for weaving was normally men's work, spinning was done by women, and minor tasks could be performed by the children. By the 1780s larger jennys were housed in factory-type buildings, but they remained part of the putting-out process, with merchant clothiers providing spinners with yarn for hand-spinning on the machines. Moreover the jenny did not solve the problem of producing a strong cotton warp, so that woven cloth still had to be of the mixed fustian type.

Of much greater significance was the water-frame, patented by Richard Arkwright (1732-92) in 1769. This was a water-powered spinning machine which would at last produce a thread strong enough for a cotton warp. A wide range of all-cotton cloth would now be woven, and the textile industry could now produce a **new product,** a cheap, light fabric which found a ready market at home and abroad. The fact that a strong cotton warp could now be produced was more significant than its cost, for yarn spun on jennys was actually cheaper. Thus the two machines complemented each other, the jenny spinning yarn for mixed fabrics and cotton weft, the water-frame making yarn for cotton warps.

The speeding up of spinning produced yet another bottleneck, the need to mechanise the carding process (in which the cotton fibres were prepared for spinning). The decisive development here, a rotary carding machine, was patented in 1775, also by Richard Arkwright. This machine, perhaps more than any other, allowed the production of cotton yarn on a mass scale. Another very significant development came in 1785 with the invention by Samuel Crompton of his spinning machine called a 'mule'. This combined the advantage both of the jenny (many threads spun at once) and the water-frame (a soft, fine thread which could be used as a warp as well as a weft). The mule was originally hand-operated and made of wood, but after 1792 they were made of iron and power driven. Later, in 1825, the 'self-acting mule' patented by Richard Roberts, greatly improved the efficiency of the machine.

The spread of power-driven mules after 1792 made cotton-spinning a wholly factory-dominated business. Costs fell dramatically, with resulting increasing markets. A piece of cloth which cost 40 shillings in 1780 cost around 13 shillings in 1812 and only 5 shillings in 1860.

The spinning jenny was essentially a cottage machine, but the water-frame needed a water wheel and hence required substantial fixed capital investment. Maximum economy could be achieved when a water-wheel powered several frames and carding machines, and this encouraged the development of large factories and the appearance of a new type of entrepreneur, the factory owner, who directly employed and controlled his workforce.

Richard Arkwright has an honoured place in the history of the industrial revolution. In addition to patenting the water-frame and carding machine he erected the first water-powered spinning factory (at Cromford, near Derby) in 1771 in partnership with Jedediah Strutt, and was Britain's largest cotton spinner until his death. He built factories at Belper and Derby, helped Samuel Oldknow build his famous large mill at Marple, in Cheshire, and built a factory with David Dale at New Lanark in Scotland. Until 1785 Arkwright had an exclusive patent right to his water-frame invention, and prior to this date the machines could only be made either by Arkwright himself or under licence from him. This is one reason why power-operated factories made slow progress before the 1780s. Sir Richard Arkwright (he was knighted in 1786) was not a great inventor; it is now accepted that his inventions were largely 'borrowed' from others. But he was a shrewd and far-sighted businessman, willing to invest capital in new technology and not afraid to contemplate wholly new forms of industrial organisation. At his death he left a colossal fortune of half a million pounds.

As we have already discussed, the adoption of steampower to drive textile machinery, which made rapid headway from the 1790s, set the seal on the emergence of cotton textiles as Britain's leading manufacturing industry. Between 1790 and 1815 output grew dramatically, based predominantly on rising export demand for yarn. These years saw a growing concentration of the industry in Lancashire, centred on Manchester and the surrounding districts. In 1800 there were 42 steam engines working in the Lancashire mills, while in the East Midlands there were only 15 in Nottingham and one in Derbyshire. Another growth area was in Scotland; there were 39 mills there in 1796, mostly in the Glasgow region, and some 120 by 1812. It was in New Lanark that Robert Owen, famous later for his pioneer work for trade unionism, introduced his utopian experiments in industrial organisation. In partnership with David Dale, Owen created a model society, in which he attempted to cater for all the needs, social and religious, as well as material, of his workforce.

Manchester and Glasgow had several advantages for the location of cotton factories: cheap coal, abundant labour, good communications both with internal markets and overseas, and a suitable damp climate (though this factor is often exaggerated). Both places were well situated to import raw cotton cheaply, for they were natural ports of entry for ships from the New World. Before 1790 the West Indies had been the major supplier of raw cotton, but the invention of the cotton gin in 1793 quickly enabled the USA to dominate the cotton trade. Between 1791 and 1821 the cotton crop of the American southern states, much of it exported to Britain, increased from 2 million lbs to 182 million lbs. In 1786-90 more than 70 per cent of Britain's cotton had come from the West Indies; by 1810 more than 50 per cent was coming from the USA, and by 1846-50 the proportion had risen to more than 80 per cent.

The mechanisation and growth of cotton spinning put pressure on the weaving section of the industry, thus reversing the position of the mid-eighteenth century. The obvious solution was to apply mechanical power

—water or steam — to cotton weaving as had occurred in spinning, but for several reasons this proved difficult. As early as 1784 the Rev. Edmund Cartwright invented a practical power-driven loom, but it was a long time before it came into widespread use. Partly this was due to problems with the machine itself, which needed several years of improvements; partly it was due to the reluctance of male weavers to abandon handlooms for the discipline of the factory. As a result, power-weaving spread only slowly, as Table 7.2 confirms:

Table 7.2 Power-looms and Handloom Weavers in Britain's Cotton Industry

	Power-looms	Handloom weavers
1795	—	75,000
1813	2,400	212,000
1820	14,150	240,000
1829	55,500	225,000
1833	100,000	213,000
1835	109,000	188,000
1845	225,000	60,000
1850	250,000	43,000
1861	400,000	7,000

The figures in Table 7.2 give only an approximate guide. Some scholars date the absolute decline in the number of handloom weavers from the 1820s, others from the mid-1830s. What is certain is that in the decade 1835-1845 power weaving made very rapid progress: the number of the power looms doubled and the number of handloom weavers fell by two-thirds. The painful struggle of the handloom weavers against the advance of the factory is one of the sadder chapters in Britain's economic history. The desperate situation of the weavers in this period contrasts starkly with that before 1820 when demand for their services increased rapidly, wages rose, and handloom weavers were among the most prosperous of Britain's industrial workforce.

Although the growth of the cotton textile industry was greatest before about 1840, and although by this date cottons had already passed their peak both in their contribution to Britain's national income and their share of exports (because the economy was becoming more diversified) the industry continued to expand until the First World War. To repeat, in 1914 cotton textiles remained easily Britain's most valuable export. Moreover, we should not let slower growth rates blind us to the substantial absolute increases which were being achieved. The amount of productive capacity added to the cotton textile industry in the decade of the 1850s alone was greater than the total productive capacity of the industry in 1840. More capacity was added to the industry in the years 1900-1913 than had existed in total in 1850. In concrete terms, this meant huge demands for textile machinery, steam engines, factory buildings, factory labour, raw cotton, and all the varied trades and services involved.

As discussed already, the initial upsurge in the cotton textile industry before the 1790s was based on home demand rather than exports. But from 1790 until 1914 exports remained a crucial element in rising demand, especially between 1793 to 1815 and between 1860 and 1914. In the war years before 1815 the most rapidly growing export markets were in the United States and Latin America, stimulated by British merchants' search for new markets as war conditions in Europe diverted trade from its traditional channels. From the 1830s there was a substantial growth of exports to India and other markets, and by 1840 India had replaced the United States as the largest single importer of British cotton goods. By 1850 India accounted for one quarter of the sales of British cotton goods.

These changes in overseas markets were prompted partly by American protection after 1815 and partly by the spread of the industrial revolution to Europe and the United States. Increasingly, developing countries in Northern Europe and America could satisfy their own home demands, so that Britain's exporters could turn increasingly to poorer, as yet non-industrialised regions. In turn there was a deterioration in the quality of cotton goods produced to cater for the markets of poorer countries.

The 1860s marked in some ways a watershed for the cotton industry. First came the temporary upheaval of the 'cotton famine' during the American Civil War (1861-1865). The collapse of cotton supplies from the American South brought soaring cotton prices and a search for new supply sources, such as India and Egypt. Many cotton firms went bankrupt, and there was mass unemployment among textile markets (who nevertheless were solid in their support of the anti-slavery Northern cause).

More permanent was the growing difficulty of exporting to Europe and the United States. From 1864 America became increasingly protectionist, and from the late 1870s most European countries also erected high protective tariff barriers. At the same time, industrialisation in both continents progressed rapidly, while in Britain itself home demand for cotton goods was rising only slowly. As a result, the trends seen already, with a growing proportion of output being sold to the markets of the underdeveloped world, became even more marked. In 1914 about 40 per cent of all exports went to India alone, and probably over three-quarters were being sold to the 'underdeveloped' world. In 1850 the proportions had been reversed, with about three-quarters going to the developed regions of Europe and North America.

Woollen Textiles

The development of woollen textiles presents some interesting contrasts and comparisons with cotton textiles. For centuries, of course, woollen cloth had been overwhelmingly Britain's main manufactured product and easily the most important export. This predominance lasted until the end of the eighteenth century, with cotton textiles making rapid inroads into woollens' lead after 1780. The pace of growth of woollen textiles output, though upwards, was much slower than that of cottons, with the result that after about 1805 cottons replaced woollens as the most important industry (by value of product) and the leading export industry.

Throughout the nineteenth century woollen textiles continued to grow, but at a slower pace than cottons, and with less marked fluctuations. The average growth of the volume of output of woollens throughout the nineteenth century was about 2 per cent a year, that of cottons was 3 per cent. Nonetheless, woollens remained a major industry. Until 1850 it was second as an export sector only to cotton goods, after which it yielded second place to iron and steel manufacturers. From 1900 woollens yielded third place to coal. But it was always one of the main basic industries, a large employer of factory workers, and a leading export sector. In 1850 woollens employed over 250,000 people throughout its various branches (about half the figure for cottons), and contributed 14 per cent of the total value of Britain's exports.

The relatively slow growth of woollen textiles can be explained principally by three factors. First, because the industry was already well established in the eighteenth century, the opportunities for dramatic expansion were less. Moreover old-established industries tend to breed a certain conservatism, and it was not accidental that in the eighteenth century the most dynamic region of development was the newest centre of the industry, the West Riding of Yorkshire. This region produced about 20 per cent of total national output in 1700, and this had grown to 60 per cent by 1800. Much of the output from the West Riding was of types of cloth called 'new draperies' and worsteds: light, cheap fabrics which were not fulled in fulling mills (fulling produced a blanket-type material). By contrast the older centres of production in East Anglia and the West Country did not grow so rapidly. The traditional heavy broadcloths produced in Suffolk and the West Country were in decline during the eighteenth century, while the Norwich industry, which concentrated on output exported overseas after 1870. This stands in contrast to the earlier period, for it is clear that the growth of the industry between the 1830s and the 1860s was dominated by growing export demand which absorbed an increasing share of total output. After 1870 it was the home market which became more important, and the share of woollens in total exports declined.

The second reason for slow growth lies in the nature of the market. The bulk of woollen cloth output, unlike cottons after 1800, was always produced for the home market. The home market could not have the possibilities for rapid expansion (but also more violent fluctuations), which new export markets could bring. Moreover, being a relatively warm cloth, the markets for woollens were mostly in temperate regions, in Northern Europe and the United States. These countries developed their own mechanised manufacturing sectors during the nineteenth century, and from the 1870s especially, the growth of protective tariffs in Europe and America hit the woollen industry hard. Table 7.3 gives an indication of the proportion of woollen textiles exported and the contribution of the industry to total exports.

Table 7.3 The Woollen Textile Industry, 1805-1910

Year	Value of output (£m)	Wool consumed (m.lbs.)	Share Exported (%)	Share of Total Exports (%)
1805	22	105	35	40
1830	30	170	19	13
1850	36	235	25	14
1870	59	400	43	13
1890	60	600	29	10
1910	75	770	28	9

From this table it is clear that, taking wool consumption as an indication of total output, the production of woollen textiles expanded continuously during the nineteenth century. The rate of growth of wool consumed by the industry was rather quicker between 1830 and 1870 than between 1870 and 1910, but more striking was the stagnation in the **value** of output in the last quarter of the nineteenth century. This stagnation was due partly to falling prices, but it was exacerbated by protective tariffs erected in some of the major export markets, and, as the table shows, there was a sharp slump in the proportion of worsteds and new draperies, was also in decline after 1750. The West Riding of Yorkshire had many advantages over the older centres: relative freedom from guild restrictions which stifled innovation in the old corporate towns, access to cheap supplies of raw materials, and abundant labour in the rural villages and small towns of south Yorkshire. Once mechanical power, water and steam, were applied to the industry the advantages of the West Riding, with its fast flowing streams and proximity to the coal districts, became confirmed.

The third reason for slow growth was because of the tardy rate at which technological change was introduced into the industry. Here we must make a fundamental distinction between the two principal branches of the industry, worsteds and woollens. Worsteds were much the more dynamic of the two. Mechanised power-driven worsted spinning mills became common in the 1820s and by the mid-1830s most worsted yarn was being spun in steam-powered mills. Power looms, too, spread rapidly after about 1840. The number of power looms in the West Riding of Yorkshire (which was the centre of the worsted industry) grew from only 1,800 in 1836 to 19,000 in 1845 and to 35,000 in 1856. By this latter date most worsted weaving was done in factories, and only a handful of handloom weavers remained. Many of the factories, in towns like Leeds and Bradford, were large integrated concerns, with spinning and weaving combined in the same factory.

Worsted manufacture came to be concentrated almost entirely in the West Riding of Yorkshire. Although the first mechanised factories made their appearance in the 1790s, the advent of general mechanisation was ten or twenty years later than in cotton textiles. Nevertheless, the worsted thread and the processes involved in worsted manufacture were similar to cottons, and so the pattern of mechanisation could follow cottons and benefit from advances made in that sector.

By contrast, traditional woollen manufacture remained backward, more dispersed, and grew more slowly than worsteds. The reason was partly due to slow growth of demand for these products, partly due to conservatism and resistance to innovation in the established centres of production, and partly because of technical problems in adapting production to mechanisation. This latter problem has been particularly emphasised by Landes, and the problems were not fully overcome for spinning until the mid-1820s and for weaving until the 1850s.

It is misleading to speak of woollen 'factories' before about 1825. The earlier mills were only partly mechanised and the buildings were used to bring together large numbers of hand operatives. Water-power was used from the 1790s for some processes, notably carding and slubbing, but not until the mid-1820s was spinning mechanised. Thus even Benjamin Gott's famous 'factory' at Bean Ing, near Leeds, established in 1792, was largely unmechanised. As late as 1839 only 36 per cent of woollen spinning machines were driven by steam-power (half the proportion in worsted mills) and in 1850 woollen weaving was almost entirely a hand operation. The contrast in the progress of power weaving between the three main textile branches, cottons and woollen and worsteds, which had been achieved by the mid-nineteenth century, is shown in Table 7.4.

Table 7.4 Power Looms in Textiles in 1850

Cotton Textiles	250,000
Worsteds	33,000
Woollens	9,400

Only after 1850 did power-weaving make serious inroads into the woollen industry, and handloom weavers survived in parts of Yorkshire into the 1880s and even longer in some remoter districts of Wales and Scotland.

The Coal Industry

Coal mining was a key industry in Britain's industrial development. It was of significance in its own right, becoming after 1860 the main source of industrial employment, and employing over one million people by 1913. Large sums were invested in collieries, and mining villages developed as highly localised, close-knit communities. Coal became one of Britain's principal exports, accounting for some 10 per cent of the total by 1913. But much more important was the contribution of coal in facilitating the expansion of other industries. It became the prime fuel for smelting pig iron in the 1780s, and from this time onwards the expansion of the iron industry, and later the steel industry, was based upon cheap supplies of coal fuel. Coal was also used in steam engines, and so made its influence felt throughout the length and breadth of industrial Britain, in the textile industries, for metal working, pumping water from mines, for railway locomotives, steamshipping, and innumerable other sectors. Even by 1800 there were already some 1,200 steam engines in use. Coal was also fundamental to many industries and processes which are sometimes neglected by economic historians. One example was the gas industry. Gas lighting developed during the Napoleonic War period and spread rapidly after 1820. Gas was produced almost entirely from coal, heated in retorts, and by 1860 nearly every small town had its own gas company or municipal supply. Other examples are the development of the artificial dyestuffs and pharmaceutical industries. The former grew after about 1850, and latter from the 1890s. Both were based on processing coal tar, itself a product of gasworks or coke ovens. Coal tar derivatives also became the basis of the plastics industry, although this was only in its infancy before 1914.

The very ubiquity of coal in industrial Britain makes its role difficult to assess. We should certainly be careful not to exaggerate the direct impact of coal on the economy. The total value of its output never amounted to more than one or two per cent of national income before 1850, although it reached six per cent by 1900. There are other reasons too for being cautious about the role of coal mining. Coal output never experienced the phenomenal growth rates of, say, the cotton textile industry, growing steadily rather than spectacularly in the eighteenth and nineteenth centuries (although there was a period of rapid growth between about 1835-60 when output rose more than four-fold). Also, coal is a primary product, not a manufacturing industry. Coal underwent virtually no processing, other than sorting and grading, before being sold at the pit-head. Hence its **value-added** was negligible, unlike, say, the textile industry or even more the chemical industry. Of its nature a mining product cannot make the contributions in terms of economic linkages and development of skills which manufacturing industries can make. This is why we associate primary production with underdeveloped poor countries, and manufacturing (secondary) production with developed economies. Another reason for caution about the role of coal is that from around 1880 productivity (output per man) started to decline, although total output was growing substantially.

Certainly, though, coal, being fundamental both to the expansion of the iron industry and to the development of steam technology, lay at the very heart of the industrial revolution. Coal was also both directly and indirectly responsible for some of the major developments in transport. Coal fired the railway locomotives, while the first canals and the first railways were constructed to facilitate the movements of coal. Wooden rails had been used to move coal wagons at collieries in the seventeenth century; from the later eighteenth century these were increasingly made of iron, and by 1825 (that is, before the opening of the Stockton to Darlington line using steam locomotion) there were already perhaps 400 miles of iron railways in use. And of the 165 canal projects sanctioned by parliament between 1758 and 1801, no fewer than 90 were primarily intended for the movement of coal.

In examining the growth of the coal industry in the eighteenth and nineteenth centuries a number of key points should be remembered. First, coal mining remained throughout the period a labour intensive industry. Even in 1914, when mechanical cutting of coal at the coal-face had made considerable progress in the United States, the great bulk of Britain's coal was cut by hand. Secondly, coal was subject to the law of diminishing returns. Sooner or later coal from existing pits could be won only by deeper working or by working inferior seams. This meant rising costs and falling output per man.

Of course, the opening of new rich coalfields could check this trend, as could improved technical efficiency. This helped expand output per man in the coal industry before the 1870s, but eventually falling productivity was inevitable if output was to continue to grow. These factors together, labour intensity and declining labour productivity, account for the enormous expansion of employment on the coalfields as demand for coal expanded during the nineteenth century. Thirdly, we must recognise the importance of transport costs for the coal industry. Coal's bulk made land transport before the railway age prohibitively expensive; hence the importance of water transport. Throughout the eighteenth century and until about 1830 the main market for coal continued to be London's domestic market. Virtually all this supply was 'seacoal' sent coastwise from the Northumberland and Durham mines. Even on the eve of the Second World War it continued to be cheaper to import coal to London's dockland by this route rather than bring it by rail from the Midlands' coalfields.

The fourth general point is a social one. Mining communities were of their nature highly localised, often in isolated areas, and socially self-contained. Mining communities were typically wholly dependent on the one occupation, and son tended to follow father into the pit so that it was common for several generations of one family to work together. Work was arduous and dangerous, and this further cemented a sense of community spirit and loyalty which developed among workers in mining areas. Although relatively well paid, miners were usually strongly affected by the trade cycle, with unemployment and downward pressure on wages occurring in depression times. Not surprisingly, therefore, we often find miners in the forefront of working-class movements, such as the ten-hour agitation and the development of trade union organisation.

Against this background we may now survey the main developments in coal mining. Table 7.5 shows how coal output mounted during the period 1700-1913.

Table 7.5 Growth of Coal Output, 1700-1913 (million tons)

1700	2.5	1850	50
1750	5	1870	110
1800	11	1890	182
1825	22	1900	225
1840	34	1913	287

Until 1854 no national figures for the coal industry were collected by the government, so that earlier statistics are the estimates of economic historians.

No one disputes the broad trends they show: a slow steady growth in the eighteenth century, and significantly faster growth in the nineteenth century. The peak production reached in 1913 was never subsequently surpassed, and in that year the labour force employed also reached its maximum. However, Deane and Cole's suggestion that coal output grew fastest between 1830 and 1865 (a more than four-fold increase), is disputed by some who argue for steadier growth. But Deane and Cole's figures (some of which are included in Table 7.5) are plausible, because it was in the mid-nineteenth century that the iron industry was expanding rapidly, the railway network was established, and coal prices were falling in consequence.

On the demand side the expansion of the coal industry is not difficult to explain. The continuing demand from urban households and rising industrial outlets ensured that if coal was available cheaply enough it would find a ready market. There were many purposes for which only coal could be used (for example in steam locomotives and in the coal-gas industry). For other purposes coal could be used as a **substitute** for other fuels (for wood fires in domestic grates, for charcoal in iron furnaces, and so on). During the late eighteenth century cheaper coal became more widely available and this stimulated its use at a time when timber costs were rising. The war period from 1793 to 1815 was especially significant because the interruption of imported timber and the rising war demands for timber radically altered the relative costs of coal and wood fuel.

In the eighteenth century coal had been largely a domestic fuel. In the nineteenth century it became an industrial fuel, with an increasing share going to export markets. Growing dependence on industrial and export demand naturally made the mining industry increasingly vulnerable to economic fluctuations as the nineteenth century progressed. Table 7.6 shows how between 1800 and 1913 industrial and export markets increased from only one-third to nearly nine-tenths, with exports alone accounting for a third of output by the end of the period. Exports grew from about 3 million tons (valued at £1 million) to nearly 100 million tons (valued at over £53 million) between 1850 and 1913. By this latter date coal comprised about 10 per cent of the total value of exports, contributing about the same as iron and steel goods and nearly half the total of cottons.

Table 7.6 shows clearly how industrial, and especially iron, consumption came to dominate demand. The period 1830-45, when railway construction was expanding rapidly, saw coal prices in London fall by one-third (much faster than the fall in the general price level). The expanding demand for coal was evidently fully matched by expanding supplies, but how was this expansion of supply achieved?

In 1700 the coal industry was a collection of mostly small scattered pits, few employing more than 30 or 40 miners, and most of the coal dug from shallow workings. The exception was in the North East, where the mines of Northumberland and Durham, easily the most important mining area in

Table 7.6 Sources of Coal Demand, 1800-1913 (% of total)

	1800	1840	1890	1913
Domestic	66	31	17	13
Iron Industry	10	25	16	11
Railways	-	1	13	6
Exports	2	5	16	33
Other (including general manufacturing and gas)	22	38	38	37
Total	100	100	100	100

Britain, were much more developed and highly organised. Newcastle was already a major coal port, sending to London about 250,000 tons a year (and 1½ million tons by 1780). Outside the North East coal was mined principally in the Midlands, South Yorkshire, South Lancashire, the Forest of Dean, and the Scottish Lowlands.

The major constraints on the expansion of coal mining were expensive transport (as stressed already), and, as mines became deeper, drainage and problems of safety and ventilation. By the nineteenth century various forms of mechanisation were available to improve mining efficiency. Despite the labour intensity of coal production, labour supply does not seem to have acted as a major constraint on the expansion of the industry. This may partly be explained by the early use of women and child labour for many jobs other than the actual cutting. Partly also, the coal industry was able to attract immigrant workers from Ireland and Scotland, while from around the 1870s the fact that growing coal employment coincided with a sharp decline in the numbers of agricultural workers and Cornish tin and copper miners was also significant. The total numbers employed in Britain's collieries rose considerably, from around 200,000 in 1841 to half a million by 1880, and to 1,107,000 in 1913.

Coal absorbed a great deal of capital investment, but lack of capital does not seem to have constrained the growth of the coal mining industry. This was because, of course, Britain was a wealthy country and coal was generally a very profitable enterprise. But two further points are significant. First, the vast majority of coal mines were small concerns involving relatively little capital and employing only a small number of miners. In 1850 it was estimated that there were some 3,000 mines with an aggregate capital of £30 million. Thus the average capital per mine was around £30,000, though the biggest mines, especially in the North East, absorbed many times this sum. At this period the North East was producing one-quarter of Britain's total output. In 1913 the average employment per colliery was only 340 men, while in some regions, like North Wales, the average was around 100. Secondly, some of the largest mine owners were wealthy landowners, whose estates happened to contain coal seams. The Duke of Bridgewater had the resources not only to develop his Worsley coalfields but to construct the famous Bridgewater canal to carry his coal. Other prominent landlord colliery owners included the Lowthers in Cumberland, the Dudleys in Staffordshire, the Fitzwilliams in South Wales, and the Londonderrys in the North East. Well into the nineteenth century the coal industry in most areas was dominated by the large landowning families. This was especially true of Scotland, less true of the North East where a number of wealthy merchant and banking families were colliery owners.

During the course of the nineteenth century, as collieries tended to grow in size and involve more capital, a growing number of enterprises were organised as joint stock companies. This was especially true after the limited liability Acts of 1855-62. Even so, the companies were normally controlled by a small group of people, often from the same family, and there remained a close connection between coalmining and some of the great landowning families until 1914.

The major technical problem in the eighteenth century was undoubtedly drainage. Mines tended to become flooded at deeper levels and some means of pumping the water out became necessary. The problem was overcome only slowly, by means of improved pumping engines which enabled mines to be sunk to deeper levels (the problem affected all mines, of course, tin, copper and lead as well as coal). As we have seen, Newcomen's engine spread rapidly in the coalfields during the eighteenth century. From 1775 Watt's improved pumping engine became available, and this was widely adopted after 1800, once Watt's patent had expired and the engines consequently became cheaper and more were produced. As a result, mines could be sunk deeper. Early in the eighteenth century the maximum depth reached by mines in the North East was around 400 feet. By 1793 coal was being reached from a depth of 726 feet in Whitehaven, and in 1835 a few pits were sunk beyond 1,000 feet. More important was the general deepening of pits to reach lower seams, with consequent improved productivity (or at any rate maintaining productivity, which would otherwise have fallen sharply). By the end of the nineteenth century a pit at Ashdown Moss, near Manchester, reached 2,888 feet.

Deeper mines brought attendant problems of ventilation and safety. In the eighteenth century it was common for colliery owners to employ boys to operate trap doors and fans in order to get rid of the dangerous gases which built up underground. Furnaces were also erected to circulate air. But not until the 1860s were steam-driven fans installed in coalmines, by which time other aspects of safety were also being improved under the stimulus of an Act of Parliament passed in 1850 which provided for the appointment of safety inspectors.

The danger of underground explosions was considerably lessened by the invention of the Davy safety lamp in 1815 by Sir Humphrey Davy. Davy's design was improved upon during the course of the nineteenth century, but appalling disasters from explosions or from poisonous gases continued to mar the history of the industry. In the twelve years from 1845 to 1867 there were 12,590 fatalities in Britain's collieries. A single explosion in 1844 took the lives of 95 men and boys at Haswell Colliery in the North East, while 204 were gassed to death at Hartley Colliery in Durham in 1862.

Accidents from broken winching gear, used to lift both miners and coal, were also frequent. An important improvement was the development of wire rope, first made in 1834 and widely used in pits during the 1840s. Increasingly at this time collieries used steam engines for winding gear, and the use of wire rope was especially significant as mines became deeper.

The growth of such mechanisation and the opening of new pits which could be economically exploited as transport improved, ensured that productivity in the industry rose for much of the nineteenth century despite diminishing returns from industrial pits as the richest seams were exhausted. Productivity reached its peak in the early 1880s, but then declined steadily (see Table 7.7).

Table 7.7 Output per Miner (tons per year)

1850	264
1870	373
1890	358
1913	260

Finally, Table 7.8 shows how although the North East retained its leading position among coal districts almost until the outbreak of the First World War, other coalfields grew more rapidly during the second half of the

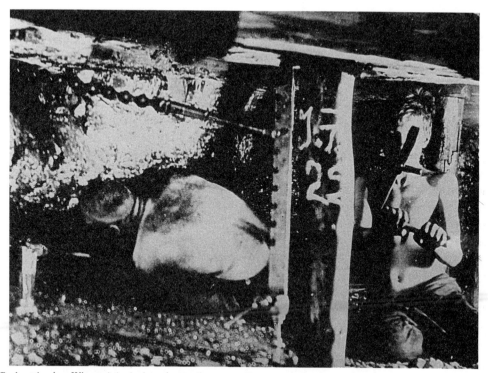

Coal cutting in a Wigan pit in the late nineteenth century. Here a boy is using a rack-drill. Temperatures in the pit could reach 80°F. Britain lagged far behind the USA in the introduction of mechanised coal cutting.

nineteenth century. In this period important new coalfields were opened up, notably in South Yorkshire, around Doncaster, and in South Wales.

Despite the key role played by the coal industry in the nineteenth century, and its continued growth and profitability prior to 1914, there were several weaknesses already apparent before the First World War. Most significant was the steady decline in productivity, so that output could only be expanded by

Table 7.8 Coal Output by Regions, 1854-1913 (million tons)

	1854	1884	1913
North East	15.4	36.1	56.4
Yorkshire	7.3	19.2	43.7
Midlands	3.9	16.1	38.8
S. Wales	8.5	24.8	56.8
Scotland	7.4	20.4	42.5
Others	22.2	44.2	49.2
Total	64.7	160.8	287.4

employing more and more labour. By 1913 the coal industry was employing about one in ten of all the male workforce, an extraordinary situation for a country which prided itself on being the 'workshop of the world' and the pioneer manufacturing nation. Although, as we have seen, diminishing yields are inevitable in an industry such as mining, the coalfields nonetheless made very slow progress with mechanisation. In 1913 only 8 per cent of Britain's coal was cut by machine, by contrast with more than 75 per cent in the U.S.A. (where output per miner was double that of Britain). It appears that there were sound geological reasons for the limited progress of mechanisation and the low productivity of British pits. Many of the seams in Britain's mines were difficult to work by machine, and in any case some of the coalfields had been worked for more than a century. Nevertheless, it is indisputable that more progress might have been made in mechanisation, and that many coal owners were short-sighted and unwilling to invest in new technology. Here was another weakness: the large numbers of small, inefficient pits. In 1913 there were still 1589 separate enterprises running 3289 collieries.

Coal was also vulnerable on account of factors lying outside the control of the industry itself. Already before 1914 rival fuels were developing rapidly: petrol combustion engines, diesel-fired ships, and electricity (which, although using coal for generation, produced power more efficiently). Processes which economised on the use of coal were being developed, while the growing export trade left the British industry vulnerable to overseas competition and tariff protection.

These various weaknesses became clear only after the First World War, but already beforehand it is clear that the prosperity of British coalmining was built on shaky foundations.

Iron and Steel

At the opening of the eighteenth century iron production was small, scattered, and stagnant. The annual output of pig iron, which may have reached as much as 35,000 tons in the 1620s and 1630s, was no more than about 20,000 tons in 1700 and still under 30,000 tons in 1750. At this stage, England's metal working industries, which were already growing rapidly in Birmingham and the surrounding districts, relied on foreign supplies for a large proportion — perhaps half — of the iron they used.

From about 1750 iron output accelerated. By the early 1780s several large ironworks had been established and output of pig iron had reached some 70,000 tons. Yet half the nation's iron was still imported and iron production could not yet be counted a major industry. From the 1780s, though, the

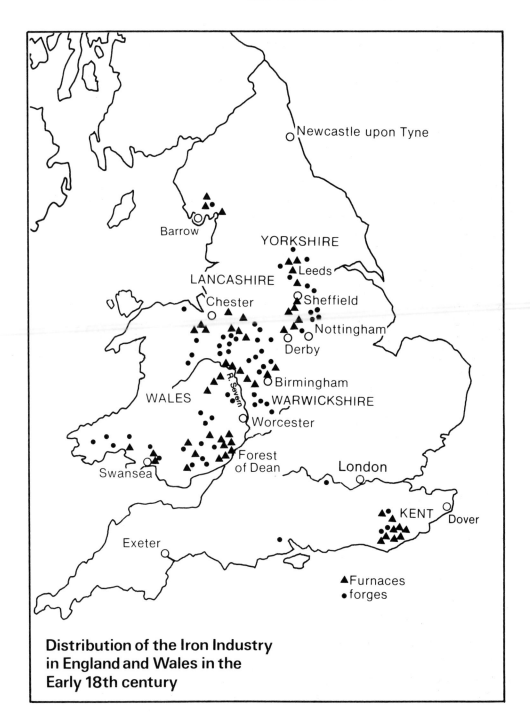

Newcastle upon Tyne

Barrow

YORKSHIRE

Leeds

LANCASHIRE

Chester

Sheffield

Nottingham

Derby

R. Severn

Birmingham

WALES

WARWICKSHIRE

Worcester

Forest
of Dean

London

Swansea

KENT

Dover

Exeter

▲ Furnaces
● forges

**Distribution of the Iron Industry
in England and Wales in the
Early 18th century**

picture changed. By 1806 pig iron production had reached 250,000 tons, Britain was a net exporter of iron, and the industry was contributing more to the national income (around 7 per cent) than even cotton textiles. Iron had become one of Britain's great basic industries. The role of the industry in Britain's industrial revolution was crucial and, as Phyllis Deane has pointed out, has as many claims as, if not more than, cotton textiles to be considered a 'leading sector'. The significance of the iron industry lies in a number of factors: in its rate of growth and contribution to the national income, both high, as we have seen; in its use of a home resource, iron ore, in contrast to cotton textiles; in its supply of cheap good quality iron (and later steel) to a wide range of other industries, like railways and shipbuilding, general engineering and machine production, gas and water pipes and many others; and in its emergence, by the 1840s, as a major export sector, helping to diversify Britain's economy away from overwhelming dependence on textiles and adding an important capital goods sector to exports. The growth of pig iron production is shown in Table 7.9 (prior to 1854 the figures are estimates only, but they give a reliable picture of the overall trends).

Table 7.9 Pig Iron Production in Great Britain, 1720-1913

Years	Output (000 Tons)
1720	25
1788	68
1805	250
1823	455
1840	1396
1847	2000
1854	3070
1864	4786
1874	5991
1884	7812
1894	7427
1904	8694
1913	10260

By 1840 Britain was producing more than 1 million tons annually and in the following twenty years output trebled, and then doubled again in the next twenty to reach 7.7 million tons in 1880. Thereafter production was stagnant, falling in the 1880s and making some modest recovery after 1895. Exports followed a similar pattern, growing strongly until the 1870s and then stagnating. In 1870 about 70 per cent of all iron and steel production was exported (it had been about one-fifth in 1830 and one-third in 1855); but by

1913 only 44 per cent of output was exported and Britain was then importing as much as 30 per cent of her consumption of wrought iron and steel, compared with 8 per cent in 1870. The steel industry, relatively unimportant in 1860 before the adoption of the Bessemer process, then grew quickly in the 1860s and 1870s. In 1870 Britain produced more steel than the United States and Germany combined. However, from the 1880s Britain's steel output, though increasing, grew far more slowly than her rivals. By this time too there were signs that Britain's productivity and technical advance were sluggish compared with her principal competitors. In the 1880s the United States overtook Britain in steel and pig iron production; by the mid-1890s Germany was producing more steel, and in 1905 more pig iron, than Britain. In 1870 Britain had produced about half the world's output both of iron and steel. By 1913 Britain produced about one-eighth and one-tenth respectively.

This sketch of developments suggests some of the questions which historians have asked about the iron and steel industry. Why did iron output grow so rapidly after the 1780s, and what sustained its development in the mid-Victorian period? And why did both the iron and steel industries stagnate towards the end of the century?

Prior to 1760 virtually all Britain's iron was smelted in charcoal blast furnaces. This produced a metal which, for a few purposes, could be cast directly into cast iron products. But the quality of such iron was unsuitable for most iron goods, being brittle and fragile. For the great bulk of ironwork, like household implements, metal tools, ploughshares, horseshoes, gun barrels, and above all nails (nails used perhaps one-third of total iron output in the early eighteenth century) a different form of iron, bar (or wrought) iron had to be used. Bar iron was produced in forges where the smelted iron from the furnaces (pig iron) was subjected to a series of re-heatings and hammerings by hammers driven by water-power. This produced a form of iron which could then, after rolling and slitting in mills, be used by the nailers and smiths. Steel, much tougher and more durable, and used for high-quality cutlery, sharp-edged tools, clock-springs, and the like, was made by further refining bar iron in a furnace or, after 1740, by Benjamin Huntsman's crucible process. The crucible process produced steel in clay crucibles in molten form which was of extremely high quality, but it was also extremely expensive. Not until after 1860, when mass-produced cheap steel became possible, did steel output become quantitatively significant.

The stagnation of the iron industry before the 1760s was principally a failure of domestic supply. Throughout the period England continued to import large quantities of bar iron from Sweden and Russia. Indeed, before the revolutionary innovations of the 1780s the proportion of imported iron used by British manufacturers (around half) was increasing.

The iron industry faced four main problems in raising output. First, as long as iron production was dependent on charcoal fuel, iron manufacture was bound to be scattered and expensive. Iron ore is bulky and hence costly to transport, and British ores contained so much waste (the metallic content of ore averaged about 50 per cent) that furnaces and forges had necessarily to be sited near sources of iron. But they also had to be sited near supplies of timber for charcoal, since charcoal is extremely fragile and virtually impossible to transport over long distances. Suitable timber supplies were scarce, for forest land had to compete with the needs of the cultivator; and as timber resources were used up in one area and charcoal costs became prohibitively expensive, iron production tended to move to other areas.

Thus the iron industry was scattered and mobile. At the opening of the eighteenth century the principal areas of production were in the West Midlands (especially Shropshire and Staffordshire), the Forest of Dean in Gloucestershire, South Wales, South Yorkshire and Derbyshire, North Lancashire, and in the North East near Newcastle. Still of some, though declining, significance were the old weald area of Kent, Surrey and Sussex.

Not only was the location of industry determined by supplies of ore and charcoal, but also by the needs of water-power for the blast, the forge hammers, and the rolling and slitting mills. Rarely were ore and charcoal supplies available near large rivers, so that water-wheels had to rely on small streams whose flow was uncertain and irregular (often drying up in summer months).

A third constraint on development was the cost of transporting the iron itself, once produced in the forges and mills. It was estimated that in the early eighteenth century a twenty-mile journey by road cost the same as the sea journey from Sweden to London.

A final problem was the varied quality of British iron ore, so that bar iron imported from Sweden or Russia was frequently of superior quality.

The development of Britain's iron industry is largely to be explained by successive solutions to these constraints on supply, so that by the 1790s the industry was fully capable of meeting the huge growth of demand which occurred during the wars of 1793-1815. Similarly when a further and even more spectacular upsurge of demand occurred with the boom in railway construction during the 1830s and 1840s, Britain's industry was not only able to supply home requirements but to develop a large and expanding export trade as well. Moreover all this iron (and steel, which developed rapidly after 1860) was produced from Britain's own iron resources. Not until the 1880s was foreign ore imported on a significant scale.

The principal technological change in iron manufacturing was the substitution of coal (in the form of coke) for charcoal fuel. Thus a cheap and abundant resource replaced a costly and declining one, and this enabled Britain's manufacturers to produce cheap iron of high quality and to locate near sources of coal rather than in remote woodland areas.

The use of coal fuel occurred in two stages. First, before the 1780s came the adoption of coke in blast furnaces. Attempts had been made to smelt iron ore with coal in the seventeenth century but the first commercially successful venture was achieved at Coalbrookdale in 1709 by Abraham Darby. Although this is rightly regarded as a landmark in industrial history, the spread of coke-smelting was very slow before 1760. In that year there were only about 14 coke furnaces in blast in England and Wales and not a single one in Scotland. The reason for the slow spread was not so much because the Darby family kept their process a well-guarded secret, but because it took several decades for rising timber prices and falling coal prices to make coke-smelting a generally economic proposition. Darby's success was due partly to a particularly suitable type of coking-coal he was able to use and partly due to his production of a very limited range of specialist products for which his cast iron was specially suitable.

From the 1760s, stimulated by demand for iron for cannon during the Seven Years War the number of charcoal furnaces went into decline and total pig iron production began to climb after a long period of stagnation. By 1790 there were about 24 charcoal furnaces and 86 coke furnaces, whereas in 1760 the numbers had been about 61 and 14 respectively.

Although coke furnaces spread from the 1760s coke-smelted pig iron often had still to be transformed into bar iron in the traditional charcoal-using forges. It was possible to use coal in the forges, but this introduced impurities into the bar iron, making it brittle and unsuitable for many purposes. For steel and for high-quality iron manufactures it was essential to use bar iron from charcoal forges, whether domestic or imported. The process of heating and reheating pig iron in the forges to make bar iron was slow, expensive, and wasteful of whatever fuel was used.

Before the 1780s ironmasters made some headway in speeding up the manufacture of bar iron, but the breakthrough came in the early 1780s when Henry Cort took out patents for his puddling and rolling process in 1783 and 1784. In Cort's furnaces the impurities in the pig iron were removed while it was still molten, and the cooled iron could then be rolled into bars. This method gave enormous advantages over traditional methods. Coal was used throughout, and the iron industry was released from dependence on charcoal. The manufacture of bar iron from pig was accelerated from several weeks to a couple of days, with consequent savings in labour, fuel and capital. The various processes of heating, puddling (melting and stirring), hammering and rolling were now combined into a single operation. And the resulting bar iron was of high quality and much cheaper than imports from overseas.

The use of coal naturally meant that the iron industry gravitated to the coalfields. From the 1760s concentration took place in South Wales, Shropshire and the West Midlands, South Yorkshire, and the Scottish Lowlands. Places without coal, like the Forest of Dean, declined rapidly. By geological chance, moreover, Britain's major sources of iron occurred near coalfields, often within the same mines. By 1806, therefore, 87 per cent of Britain's total output was located on the coalfields, and of this total Shropshire, Staffordshire and South Wales accounted for about 70 per cent.

Developments outside the iron industry also encouraged iron production, reminding us how industrial changes are often interrelated. The improvement of transport facilities, especially river navigation and the extension of the canal network, help the movement of bulky goods like coal and iron. And the availability of James Watt's steam engine in 1775 also made an immediate impact, being used for the furnace blast and for the other purposes for which water-wheels had been used hitherto. The application of steam-power to iron manufacture hastened the re-location of ironworks to the coalfields and permitted the construction of larger and more productive blast furnaces. In 1788 the average annual production of a blast furnace was 750 tons; by 1805 this had roughly doubled to 1491 tons; and by 1839 it was 3566 tons.

Alongside these technical developments went a change in industrial structure, with the emergence of several large capital-intensive enterprises. Some enterprises not only owned several iron mines and ironworks, but invested in coal mines and other related areas. Such firms included the Darby family and John Wilkinson, both based in the Midlands, the Carron Company in Scotland, and Richard Crawshay's works in South Wales. These large firms were often pioneers of new technology; John Wilkinson, for example, was the first to use the Watt steam engine in iron production.

The expansion of the iron industry until the arrival of cheap steelmaking in the 1860s rested upon the coal-using technology of the eighteenth century. Continual improvements in design and efficiency, and an overall increase in the size of furnaces, ensured that productivity rose steadily and costs fell. There were two more significant technical developments. One was the invention in 1828 of the hot air blast by the Scottish ironmaster and engineer James Neilson. Neilson discovered that a blast of hot air in a furnace gave great savings in fuel and higher output; overall smelting costs were reduced by this method by one-third. The hot blast proved particularly useful in Scotland where it enabled hitherto almost unusable Clydesdale ore to be smelted. The price of Scottish pig iron fell rapidly, and Scotland became one of the country's leading producing regions, output growing from only 38,000 tons in 1827 to nearly 1 million in 1860. The second invention came in 1840, when James Nasmyth invented the steam-hammer, permitting the production of great iron bars needed for the railways and steamships.

The figures already given in Table 7.9 show the impressive growth performance of the iron industry. What was specially impressive was the elasticity of output permitted by the new techniques of production. From the 1830s especially, output rose to meet the demands of the railway industry, of export markets (much of it for railway equipment), and, from the 1850s, increasingly for shipbuilding. From the 1860s and 1870s railways and ships used the new cheap steel. There were innumerable other calls on the output of the industry, for pipes for gas and water, for the engineering and metal trades, and for armaments.

During the 1830s and 1840s railways were the single most important source of demand for iron, although demand fluctuated considerably. In the peak year of 1847 nearly 6,500 miles of line were under construction and in that year railways absorbed over a quarter of iron output, with rising prices and high profits for iron producers. By the 1850s the main trunk railway lines had been built, and the pace of growth slackened. Now the more powerful stimulus came from shipbuilding and foreign demand.

The age of cheap steel came in the 1850s and 1860s. For many purposes steel (an alloy of iron and carbon), because of its toughness, was much more suitable than wrought iron, but its use was limited by high costs of production which, before 1850, was still based on Huntsman's crucible process developed in 1740. The transformation came as a result of three innovations. In 1856 Henry Bessemer (1813-98) publicised his new method of making steel. His converter achieved high enough temperatures to remove impurities and enabled steel to be produced directly from molten pig iron. Bessemer steel was originally too brittle to be of much use, but Robert Mushet discovered a method of adding manganese to the molten pig iron to overcome this.

The second invention was the open-hearth process developed by William Siemens in 1866 (and later improved in France by Martin). This process removed impurities in pig iron by directing a flame to the molten pig, and had distinct advantages over the Bessemer process being easier to regulate and also able to use scrap. Consequently open-hearth steel grew as a proportion of total steel output, from 12 per cent in 1875 to 22 per cent in the early 1880s and 80 per cent in 1914.

The Atlas steel works, Sheffield, 1869.

Neither the Bessemer converter nor, originally, the open-hearth process, was suitable for making steel from iron ore which contained phosphorous. Most British ore was phosphoric so that from the 1870s growing supplies of non-phosphoric ore were imported from Spain and, later, Sweden. A process for making steel from phosphoric ore was developed in 1878 by Sidney Gilchrist Thomas, a post-office clerk, and his cousin, Percy Gilchrist, a chemist. They discovered that by lining the furnace with a basic (non-acid) substance a good quality steel could be produced. The Gilchrist Thomas, or basic, process was slow to be adopted in Britain. As late as 1900 only 16 per cent of British steel was basic although thereafter open-hearth furnaces increasingly made basic steel.

As Table 7.10 shows, Britain's iron and steel output failed to match the rates achieved by the United States and Germany, and, as we have seen already, Britain was well behind both these countries in 1913.

Table 7.10 Iron and Steel Output, (million tons)

Year	Great Britain		Germany		United States		World	
	Pig Iron	Steel	Pig Iron	Steel	Pig Iron	Steel	Pig Iron	Steel
1870	6.0	0.2	1.2	0.1	1.7	0.04	11.8	0.5
1890	7.9	3.6	4.0	2.1	9.2	4.3	26.7	12.3
1913	10.3	7.7	16.5	17.3	31.0	31.3	77.9	75.1

Crucible steel making in a Sheffield workshop, around 1900.

How can we explain the slow growth and loss of world leadership? Until recently the most common explanation has been that of entrepreneurial failure. The iron and steel industry has long been a target for historians like Aldcroft who have suggested that there was a general decline of entrepreneurial ability in Britain at this time. Britain's entrepreneurs, it is claimed, were slow to adopt innovations, like the Gilchrist Thomas process, and as a result the productivity of industries in the United States and Germany rose above levels achieved in Britain. British firms were generally smaller, higher cost, and technically more backward than their principal rivals.

The supposed poor entrepreneurship has been put down to three factors. First, complacency. It is claimed that Britain's early overwhelming world leadership built up by 1870 allowed easy domination of home and foreign markets, high profits, and consequent loss of competitive drive among Britain's manufacturers. Secondly, British management and workers were inadequately trained and educated in comparison with their rivals, especially in the field of technical education. Thirdly, entrepreneurship was weak because there were too many small firms; this not only spread managerial talent thinly, but reduced the incentive to innovate and introduce new technology.

The idea that poor entrepreneurship was to blame for the slow growth of iron and steel in the last quarter of the nineteenth century has not found favour among recent historians. McCloskey suggests that Britain's iron and steel industry was not backward relative to her rivals; the different rates of technological progress can be explained by the different types of iron and steel produced, and by the size and rate of growth of the markets facing producers. Investment decisions made by British firms were rational and were designed to maximise profits in a competitive market. There was no 'blame' and no 'failure'.

The nature of markets is significant. The overall growth of market demand facing British producers between 1880 and 1914 was much slower than in the United States or Germany. This was partly because Britain's own home market was mature: the railway network was largely complete and other sources of demand were not growing sufficiently quickly. Abroad, markets for Britain's products were being closed by protective tariffs and by foreign competition. It was only to be expected that countries like the United States and Germany, with their huge natural resources of coal and iron, rapidly expanding railway networks, and large protected domestic markets, would outpace Britain.

In short, there were reasons stemming from the demand side which account for the slow rate of growth and technical innovations in Britain's iron and steel industry at the end of the nineteenth century. Britain suffered from her early start, and from the proliferation of many small concerns, for none of which was it rational to undertake a programme of massive investment in view of the limited demand for their products.

Appendix: The Darbys and Coalbrookdale

Coalbrookdale is on the Shropshire-Staffordshire border on the River Severn. An ironworks was established there in 1709 by Abraham Darby, a Bristol ironmaster. Darby died in 1717, but under his successors, all members of the Darby family, the enterprise became one of the largest ironworks in Britain.

The enterprise has a special place in British industrial history on account of four 'firsts'. The two most significant were (1) Abraham Darby (1687-1717) was the first to smelt iron ore using coke, rather than charcoal, as a fuel. This he did in 1709, using the specially favourable local coal to make his coke. (2)

Coalbrookdale constructed the world's first cast iron bridge in 1779, with a span of 100 feet. This was the famous Iron Bridge over the Severn, which still stands today. Other innovations were (3) the first cast iron rails which were laid down at the works in 1767. These replaced the wooden wagon ways first laid down in 1748 to facilitate traffic between the various coal mines and iron furnaces belonging to the works. (4) the Coalbrookdale company produced the first successful locomotive to run on rails. This was a steam locomotive built for the engineer Trevithick, and the trial took place at Coalbrookdale in 1802.

The significance of coke-smelting was profound. Hitherto iron ore could only be smelted with charcoal, which meant that iron production was dependent on dwindling and increasingly expensive timber resources. Coke smelting thus liberated the iron industry, for pig iron could be produced with cheap and abundant coal. The cast iron products made from this pig iron were of excellent quality, as Coalbrookdale's own output demonstrated. However, despite Coalbrookdale's evident success, coke smelting made only very slow progress before 1760. Until the 1750s Coalbrookdale was the only ironworks in the country smelting with coke, and the impact of Darbys breakthrough came only in the second half of the eighteenth century. This slow progress of the innovation was the result of four main factors. First, the growth of demand for iron was sluggish until after 1760. Secondly, the Darbys were reluctant to pass on to competitors some of the secrets of their processes (especially a technique of making thin castings for cylinders). Thirdly, we should emphasise that at this stage wrought iron was still dependent on charcoal smelting; it was not until the 1780s that Henry Cort's important breakthrough (puddling and rolling) allowed wrought iron to be made with coke. Fourthly, not until after 1760 did coal prices fall far enough, and timber prices rise high enough, to encourage the general adoption of coke smelting.

The significance of the Iron Bridge was both direct and indirect. Directly, it was a pathbreaking feat which inspired the construction of other bridges and structural projects. The bridge demonstrated, too, ways in which cast iron might be used, showing the strength and durability of the material. Indirectly, Coalbrookdale and the Iron Bridge became places of pilgrimage for engineers, foreign travellers, and others interested in the marvels of modern technology. Feats such as the Iron Bridge captured the public imagination (the bridge's designer, Abraham Darby, grandson of the founder, received the Gold Medal awarded by the Society of Arts), and spread a spirit of progress and innovation which was so helpful to industrial change.

We should note a number of other points of significance about the company and its founders. The works turned out a stream of high quality engineering products, including cast iron cylinders for Newcomen atmospheric steam engines. Steam engines were widely used in mines for pumping out water by the 1720s, and by 1758 the Coalbrookdale company had cast more than 100 steam cylinders and built many complete steam engines. The skills of firms such as Coalbrookdale formed a crucial link between the drawing boards of the inventors and the practical realisation and improvement of their creations.

It is interesting that the Darbys were devout Quakers and they maintained close contact with other Quaker iron-masters in the West Midlands. Quakers were notable for personal thrift, hard work, honesty, and support among fellow members of the Society of Friends. Communities such as this (and there were others) were important, for they provided a vehicle for spreading scientific information, mutual support in times of bad trade, and opportunities for borrowing among members of the group for capital investment.

Abraham's father, John, was a devout Quaker, a Birmingham nailer and locksmith. It was natural, therefore, for Abraham to be apprenticed to a local Quaker maltmill-maker, and this is where he gained his initial experience of iron casting. Later, he established a brass works in Bristol with other Quaker partners, and his experiments there with iron castings led him to his new venture at Coalbrookdale in 1709.

The Coalbrookdale company typifies in many ways the path of development taken by successful industrial enterprises in the eighteenth century. It remained a close-knit family firm, built up from small beginnings. As profits accumulated these, together with borrowing from friends, provided the capital for further development.

Coalbrookdale, and firms like it, became centres of innovation and experimentation. They bred generations of skilled workers whose skills underpinned the transition of Britain to an industrial country. Coalbrookdale influenced techniques of iron making and mechanical and civil engineering and played a distinct role in Britain's industrial revolution.

Chapter 8
Railways and the Mid-Victorian Economy

The railways were one of the great achievements of nineteenth century Britain. Between 1830 and 1850 a skeleton network of major trunk routes had been built in Britain, and by 1850 Britain was already a substantial exporter of railway equipment. In the second half of the nineteenth century railway construction spread throughout the world, often using British equipment, capital, and expertise. Together with the spread of ocean-going steam shipping, railways were one of the most powerful forces which opened up the world economy in the second half of the nineteenth century, enabling the exploitation of agricultural and mineral resources in the western states of the USA, Australia, Argentina, South Africa, and many others. Simple-sounding questions such as 'what was the impact of the railways?' can never fully be answered simply, because the changes they brought were so enormous and widespread. Even in Britain, where the railways arrived at a time when the economy was already industrialising, where the main centres of industry were already established, and where economic growth was progressing rapidly, the railways' impact was profound and affected nearly every aspect of social and economic life.

The first railway, from Stockton to Darlington, in 1825 was the product of two earlier developments. One was the laying down of rail wagon-ways which, as we have seen, were increasingly made of cast iron in the late eighteenth century. There were more than 400 miles of such rails in 1825, most of them serving coal mines. Coal wagons were pulled mainly by horses, but by 1800 stationary steam engines were used at some collieries using winding gear to haul the wagons. It was natural, therefore, for engineers to try to adapt the steam engine to a moveable engine which would run on the tracks.

The second development, therefore, was the moveable steam engine, a locomotive, to run on rails. A great many engineers tried to solve the problems involved, which necessitated not only an improved type of steam

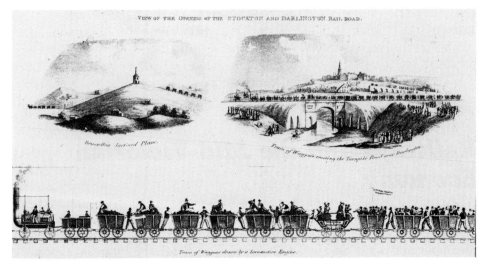

The Stockton to Darlington Railway, opened in 1825, ushered in the railway age.

engine, but producing rails strong enough to support the weight of the locomotive. As early as 1804 Richard Trevithick had built a high pressure steam locomotive to run on rails (he had earlier built a steam locomotive to run on roads), and from then until the 1820s other engineers, including George Stephenson, experimented with different designs. The high pressure engine and the use of wrought iron rails solved the major problems, and in 1825 George Stephenson's *Locomotion* was used successfully on the new Stockton to Darlington coal line, the first railway in the world built specifically to use a steam locomotive.

Yet only in retrospect can 1825 be seen as the start of the railway age. In many ways the Stockton and Darlington Railway looked backwards rather than forwards. Thus the steam locomotive shared the track with horse-drawn wagons and the winding gear of stationary engines. The Railway took tolls from competing users, just as the turnpikes and the canals did. The gauge adapted for the width of track was 4 foot 8½ inches, the traditional gauge of wagon-ways in the north-east coalfields in order that coal wagons from the collieries could be used on the new line. Later, this 'standard gauge' was adopted not only in Britain but in many parts of the world.

Of greater significance was the opening of the Liverpool and Manchester Railway in 1830. This was the first major railway to rely solely on steam locomotion. The triumph of steam had been secured the previous year, in 1829, when the promotors of the railway organised the famous trial at Rainhill, over a particularly difficult section of nearly-completed track. At the trials George Stephenson's *Rocket* locomotive was the decisive victor.

Unlike the Stockton and Darlington Railway, the Liverpool and Manchester broke completely with the earlier forms of transport and established an administrative organisation which set the pattern for all later railway companies. The company owned and operated the rolling stock, maintained its own permanent staff, and ran the entire undertaking itself without subcontracting to other carriers. In terms of scale and investment the new railway was a significant departure. Moreover from the first the railway emphasised passenger traffic. Contrary to expectations, passenger receipts provided more than half the total, and this was the experience of other early railways. This unsuspected source of demand was in effect created by the railways: people now travelled by rail where previously they would have stayed at home. The Liverpool and Manchester Railway was immensely profitable, averaging around 10 per cent return on its capital, and encouraging others to start similar projects. The result was the expansion of Britain's railway network which can be seen in Table 8.1.

Table 8.1 The Development of Railways in Great Britain

Year	Track open (miles)	Capital Invested (£ million)	Total Revenue (£ million)	% passenger revenue
1825	27			
1830	98			
1842	1,938		4.8	65
1850	6,084	235	12.7	52
1860	9,069	327	24.4	46
1870	13,562	503	42.9	43
1880	15,563	695	62.8	41
1890	17,281	860	76.8	43
1900	18,680	1136	101.0	43
1912	20,038	1290	124.0	42

From Table 8.1 we can see that the most rapid phase of railway construction was over by 1850, although there were substantial additions thereafter. By 1870 roughly two-thirds of the total track mileage was laid down, and subsequently the pace of construction was much slower. In fact, by 1870 nearly all the main trunk routes had been completed. Later additions were mostly for double-tracking, branch lines, and the suburban network (especially around London).

What the Table does not show is how uneven construction was before 1870. Most of the railway companies were formed, and a great deal of the construction carried out, in three bursts of activity. The first, following the initial success of the Liverpool and Manchester Railway, occurred in 1835-7; the second, the 'railway mania', in 1845-7; and the third in the mid-1860s. Why did railway promotion come in bursts? The main reason was that railways involved huge sums of initial capital investment before they could start earning revenue. The total capital invested in canals by 1830 was only about £20 million: the Liverpool and Manchester Railway alone cost nearly £1 million and, as Table I shows, enormous amounts were tied up by 1850. All this capital was raised privately, and, especially in the first half of the nineteenth century, private investment tended to take place in speculative waves. Indeed, one reason for the five year time-lag between the Stockton line and the next major project was the collapse of an investment boom in 1825 and subsequent loss of business confidence.

Because of the huge sums of investment required, all railway companies were promoted with Acts of Parliament, authorising the raising of capital by shares and debentures (fixed interest shares) and granting limited liability to shareholders. During the railway booms large numbers of Acts were promoted in parliament, especially in the mid-1840s. In the single year of 1846, for example, no less than 219 Acts were passed, authorising the expenditure of £133 million of capital (about one-quarter of total national income), and covering 4538 miles of new line.

Despite the unplanned and uneven nature of development the growth of the railway network had a certain logic. Like the turnpikes in the eighteenth century, the first lines to be constructed were those serving the routes likely to prove the most profitable. By 1838 the trunk route between Lancashire and Liverpool, via Birmingham, had been completed by two companies, and within a couple of years this line had been linked by other companies to Derby, Leicester, Nottingham, Leeds, and York. Cross-country routes linked important towns, like Manchester and Leeds in 1840, while trunk lines from London pushed in other directions (reaching Bristol in 1841 and Dover in 1844 for example).

Most of the lines projected before 1845 were logical in terms of existing traffic and reasonable expectations of future development. The mania of 1845-7 was different, with a great many unrealistic projects, many of them competing with each other. At one time five rival companies proposed to link London with Brighton by different routes, and of the 9000 miles sanctioned by parliament (over 600 other projects never got as far as an Act) only about 5000 miles had been built by 1858.

These waves of activity had several consequences. Since so many projects were started at the same time this tended to push up construction costs. Railway demand forced higher iron prices, for example, and encouraged landowners to demand high compensation payments for land. Already in 1844 the average cost of each mile of track in Britain was £33,000. Undoubtedly the burst of activity led to a great deal of waste and extravagance, while high prices of iron and other materials had an adverse effect on the other industries which used them.

The great numbers of different companies, with different methods of charging and sometimes in direct competition, brought numerous disadvantages. Most of the companies adopted the standard gauge for their track, but the Great Western Railway, from London to Bristol, laid down the broad 7 foot gauge at the insistence of their brilliant engineer Isambard Kingdom Brunel. This meant that no through traffic could go beyond Gloucester, where expensive and lengthy unloading and re-loading had to be undertaken. Eventually, in the 1890s, the Great Western Railway was obliged to adopt the standard gauge, which then became general throughout the country.

The main ways in which the drawbacks of large numbers of companies (there were 104 in 1844) were met were by the setting up of the Clearing House and by the process of amalgamation. The Clearing House was established by 9 companies in London in 1842 to facilitate such matters as through booking and to standardise charges. By 1850 it incorporated nearly every major railway company in Britain. By this time a number of important amalgamations had already taken place, and a few giant railway companies were starting to emerge. In 1844 the unscrupulous George Hudson, the 'railway king', formed the Midland Railway out of a number of companies operating in Yorkshire and the Midlands. The Midland soon acquired other companies, and at the height of his power in 1846 Hudson controlled about half Britain's track. Another important enterprise was the London and North-Western, which brought the whole of the London to Lancashire line under one management. This company had a capital of over £17 million, employed over 10,000 people, and was easily the country's largest joint-stock enterprise. As a result of amalgamation, by 1871 the 28 largest companies controlled some 80 per cent of the total track mileage.

The spate of amalgamations in the 1840s and various agreements among rival companies to limit competition threatened to establish powerful monopolies. The railways were rather like canals or water-companies in that they were 'natural monopolies': one company could provide such an important service that it might well make enormous profits and charge high prices, but, because of the high fixed capital investment involved, two or more rival companies could soon result in cut-throat competition and bankruptcy. In order to prevent railway companies taking advantage of their

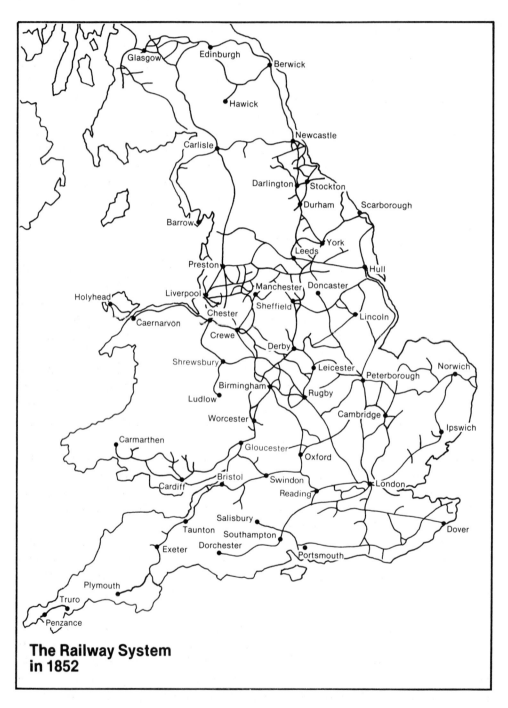

The Railway System in 1852

monopoly power parliament brought in various measures of control and regulation from an early date. The Acts granted by parliament imposed controls on charges and dividends, and in 1840 a special Railway Department at the Board of Trade was set up. In 1844 companies were obliged under Gladstone's Regulation of Railways Act to run special third-class 'parliamentary trains' for working-class passengers, charging no more than 1d (one old penny) a mile (with children under 12 half fare) and running every day of the week. This Act also gave parliament the authority to take over the railway companies after 21 years (an extension of the principle already incorporated in gas and water acts, which normally permitted local authorities to purchase the undertakings after 21 years).

The Effects of the Railways

Until the 1830s most long-distance, bulky, freight had been transported by water, either by coast or by Britain's 4000 miles of navigable waterways (two-thirds of which were canals). Valuable and perishable goods, or bulk goods over short distances, had gone by horse-drawn wagon, and passengers by coach, on the roads — mostly on the 22,000 miles of turnpiked roads.

The great significance of the railways was that they could provide a quicker, more efficient, and cheaper service for the transport both of freight and passengers. Passenger coach services disappeared almost at once, as soon as railways served their routes. Canals tended to remain competitive longer, but in 1852 total railway freight exceeded that carried by canals and after the 1850s the quantities carried by canals became insignificant.

It has been estimated that by 1850 the railways had undercut the former charges of stage coaches by perhaps one-fifth and the canals by one-third to one-half. But in addition the railways proved attractive because of the speedy and efficient service they could maintain, not subject to weather and other inconveniences which affected roads and waterways.

When economic historians discuss the impact of the railways they generally distinguish between **economic** and **social** consequences. Economic consequences may be further divided into those arising from providing transport services, and those from the construction and maintaining of the railway network.

As mentioned already, the railways provided cheap and efficient transport for goods and passengers. Transport costs are, of course, an important element in costs of production and distribution, and anything which lessens them can result in wider markets, economies of scale, and more specialisation. The impact of the railway, while felt throughout the economy, naturally varied

1. The Terminus at Bridgetown.—2. Arrival of the First Train at Carrington's Point.

British investment helped the spread of railway and other modern technology throughout the world. Here we see the British-built and financed railway in Barbados in 1882.

between different regions and goods carried. The railways seem to have made a particular impact in three areas; in the transport of **inland** coal and iron ore (thus the coal of South Yorkshire and the iron ore of Northamptonshire benefited particularly); in the transport of agricultural goods, both bulky grain and perishable products like fresh fruit and milk (the railways are generally credited with encouraging agriculture's prosperity in the 'high farming' period of the 1850s and 1860s); and thirdly in the movement of passengers. As we saw earlier, passenger traffic was very largely a 'new' creation, and, as Table 8.1 shows, passenger receipts remained a high proportion of total revenue, always more than 40 per cent, down to the First World War.

The construction of the railways was an immense undertaking, absorbing a great deal of labour and materials, especially in the peak periods of activity. As far as materials are concerned, the chief backward-linkage from railway construction came from iron, though railways also used considerable supplies of timber, glass, bricks, and, indirectly, coal. In a peak construction year like 1848 the railways consumed as much as 40 per cent of all the iron consumed in Britain (or 30 per cent of the total production), but the averages were much less than this and tended to fall after the 1850s. Thus between 1844-51 about 18 per cent of iron output went into the railways, and about 8 per cent between 1852-69. Although these were substantial amounts, and after 1870 a great deal of steel was used for rails, the figures suggest that we should not exaggerate the impact of railways on the economy. Except for very short periods railways were never a dominant source of demand.

The capital requirements of the railways was another source of influence. As we saw earlier, capital was mostly raised by issuing shares and fixed-interest debentures, and the railways were important agents for popularising investment among the general public. The coming of general limited liability between 1855-62 came in the wake of widespread acceptance by the public of investment in railway companies as a secure outlet for savings. The railways therefore helped tap new sources of savings for productive investment, and local stock exchanges in Liverpool and Manchester were established largely to deal in local railway shares.

Railways construction also involved an enormous labour force, especially in the peak periods of construction. Most of the labour was unskilled, much of it from local rural areas, though gangs of railway 'navvies' also came from Scotland and Ireland, forming a semi-permanent workforce which went from one construction site to another. At a peak construction period like May 1847 as many as 256,509 men were employed. Their wage bill that year probably exceeded £16 million (over 3 per cent of national income, a substantial figure). Yet in 1852 only 36,000 navvies were employed and the average between 1831-70 was around 60,000.

Of more lasting significance was the permanent employment brought by railway companies, which grew throughout the period, as Table 8.2 shows:

Table 8.2 Permanent Employment by Railway Companies

1850	56,000
1856	100,000
1875	250,000
1890	350,000
1910	600,000

The railways made enormous demands on engineering, both mechanical and civil, and also on other professions like law, accountancy and surveying, which were all encouraged by railway development. Some of the greatest names in engineering, like George Stephenson, his son Robert, and Isambard Kingdom Brunel, became consultants for a number of railway companies and initiated many pioneering innovations. There were also groups of prominent railway constructors, who formed large construction companies. One such individual was Thomas Brassey who undertook a great deal of construction overseas once the main period of railway building in Britain was at an end.

The social effects of railways were as diverse as their economic effects.

Lowestoft Beach, c. 1900. Cheap railway excursions brought prosperity to many seaside resorts. The use of 'bathing machines' allowed the users to enter the water with the minimum exposure to public view.

Clearly the railways encouraged mobility, and opened up the opportunities for travel among the working-classes, not just the middle and upper classes. In 1842 third-class railway journeys made up only about one-third of the total number of journeys made; by 1849 they were more than one half, and they continued to become relatively more important thereafter. During the 1840s some companies introduced cheap excursion trains for day trips, and this helped to popularise seaside resorts like Blackpool and Margate. When the railways reached Torquay in 1848 so important did the event seem to the local authorities that they granted a public holiday. The railways, too, created 'railway towns' like Swindon and Crewe, which developed as centres of railway engineering. Crewe's population in 1841 was a mere 203; by 1846 it was 2000, and by 1871 more than 18,000. Swindon's population was under 2000 in 1831; by 1901 it was above 40,000.

The railways also aided the growth of suburbs, especially around London. London's first underground railway started in 1863, while from about 1880 the expansion of the suburban railway network, served by fast and frequent trains, fostered the growth of a commuter class.

The railways generally improved communications, and so contributed to

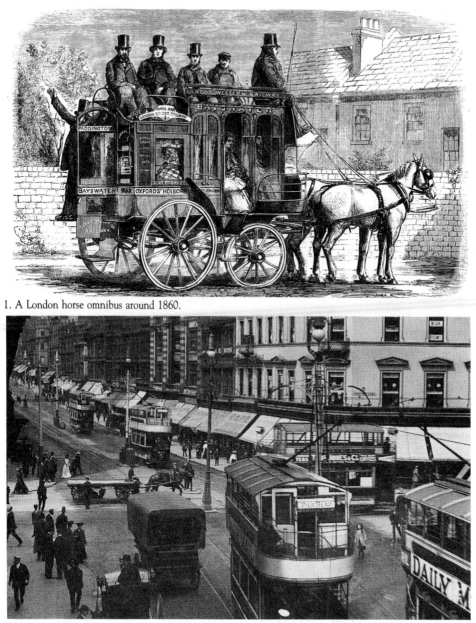

1. A London horse omnibus around 1860.

2. Trams in Liverpool in 1908.

Horse omnibuses developed rapidly on London's streets after 1830. By the 1850s there were more than 1000 in the capital. The first horse tramway was opened in Birkenhead in 1860 and by the 1880s had transformed working-class travel in London and the larger cities. From the 1890s tramways, often municipally owned, were increasingly electrified (usually with overhead wires).

the social unification of the country. Railways permitted the mass circulation of national newspapers, and allowed the growth of a fast and efficient mail service. The telegraph, started in 1843, was a direct consequence of railway development. It has been suggested, too, that the railways, of necessity having to stick to rigid timetables, made people more time-conscious, and encouraged the standardisation of time throughout the country (hitherto there had been minor regional variations).

In short, therefore, the social and economic consequences of the railways were pervasive and substantial. But how substantial? Inevitably, despite the difficulties of answering such a question, historians have tried to assess the overall impact of railways on Britain's economy. Recent historians have put forward two quite different views. Hawke, in trying to measure just how wealthy Britain would have been without the railways has concluded that the total loss would have been in the region of 10 per cent. Not, perhaps, a strikingly large figure to those who picture the railways as all-important. Hobsbawm, though, views the problem differently. He sees the railways as providing an essential boost to an economy which was showing signs of flagging in the 1830s. Railways ended the over-dependence on textiles and allowed Britain's economy to move to a new, diversified, path of growth. Coal, iron, and later steel, joined textiles as the basis of Britain's economic strength.

The views both of Hawke and Hobsbawm have their critics. Certainly few would agree with Hobsbawm that railways were **the** key force permitting further economic growth from the 1830s (the economy was more diversified than Hobsbawm allows, and foreign trade was raising demand for British exports in this period). And Gourvish has recently criticised Hawke for under-estimating the role of the railways. Thus it seems safe to conclude that the railways were significant, if not overwhelmingly so, in encouraging Britain's economic growth. But perhaps more fundamentally, they influenced in some way or other the lives of virtually every man, woman, and child in the country.

Appendix: The Work of Isambard Kingdom Brunel

Isambard Kingdom Brunel (1806-1859) was one of the great civil engineers of the nineteenth century. For economic historians his contributions lie in two directions. First, for his role in the history of technology, and secondly as representative of a new breed of civil engineer in industrial Britain.

Brunel's importance as an engineer stems partly from his own genius and the many innovations he made. But his work is of particular significance

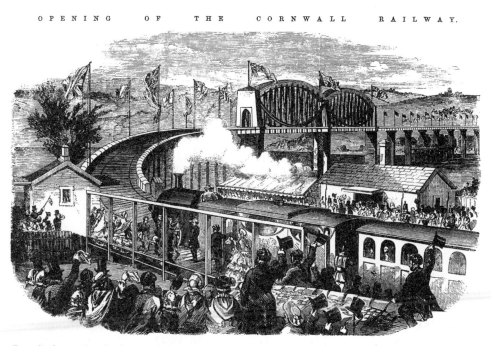

Brunel's famous Royal Albert Bridge at Saltash, opened in 1859.

because the two main areas, railways and steam-shipping, were among the main forces shaping the nineteenth century world.

Brunel's work as a railway engineer began with his appointment in 1833 as engineer to the projected London to Bristol Railway, the future Great Western Railway. It was as engineer to the G.W.R. that Brunel established his reputation, joining George Stephenson and Joseph Locke as the triumvirate of great railway engineers who met and overcame the challenge of designing the world's first railway network. The G.W.R. was widely recognised as the finest line in Britain, noted for its well-constructed and elegant bridges, tunnels, viaducts and stations.

Three areas of Brunel's railway work deserve particular mention. First were the many advances he made in the construction of bridges and tunnels. Most significant was the famous Royal Albert Bridge over the Tamar at Saltash. This was the last and greatest of Brunel's many bridges, built between 1853 and 1859, although Brunel had begun his designs in 1847. The bridge spanned 2,200 ft. and carried trains of the Cornwall Railway Company westward from Plymouth on a single track. Together with Robert Stephenson's bridge over the Menai Straits, opened in 1850, Brunel's bridge, in many ways a more complex undertaking, was one of the major feats of nineteenth century engineering. These bridges solved one of the chief early problems of railway civil engineering: how to build long bridges of sufficient strength. Cast-iron was too brittle, and Brunel and Stephenson showed how wrought iron could be used. The Menai and Saltash bridges were the first of many constructed of wrought iron before the age of steel.

Secondly, Brunel was notable for his use of engineering theory in his railway designs. Brunel was a trained engineer, learning much from his famous father, Sir Marc, who had employed his son on his Thames tunnel project (the world's first underwater tunnel) when only 18 years old. Brunel contributed many theoretical advances to the science of engineering, and his engineering expertise contrasted with the practical but untrained Locke and Stephenson. It was part of Brunel's contribution to look at each problem anew, through the eyes of an engineer. Hence his decision in 1835 to adopt a broad 7 foot gauge for the London to Bristol Railway instead of the standard 4 foot $8\frac{1}{2}$ inches. In engineering terms Brunel was right, for his gauge gave a faster, safer, and steadier journey. But it was also more expensive, for it required more land for the wider tracks and much capital had already been sunk in standard gauge lines. Brunel lost the 'battle of the gauges' in 1846 when Parliament refused to sanction any new broad gauge lines, though the G.W.R. continued to use its broad gauge until 1892.

Thirdly, Brunel made many advances in the use of materials. He made use of wrought iron in his bridges (and also ships), but also used timber widely. Many of Brunel's tunnels, bridges and viaducts used timber in a new and imaginative way, one writer suggesting that 'Brunel was the greatest timber engineer this country has ever known'.

In addition to his role in railway development Brunel designed three great steamships, each the largest ever built at the time of their launch, and each making considerable advances in steamship design and construction.

Brunel's first ship, the *Great Western,* was launched in 1838 for the Atlantic crossing to New York. The significance of this ship was that prior to Brunel no-one had thought the Atlantic could be crossed entirely by steam-power, for it was believed that no ship could carry sufficient coal for the engines. Atlantic crossings using steam had been made since 1818, but the engines were used as a supplement to sail. Brunel realised that the carrying capacity of a vessel increased more than proportionally to its need for power; thus the Atlantic could be crossed by a sufficiently large vessel using only steam power. In the event Brunel's grand design brought several rivals and the *Great Western* was not the first to make the crossing under its own steam. But the sailing of Brunel's ship in 1838 in only 15 days and 5 hours, with 200 tons of coal still left, proved Brunel triumphantly right. With this voyage the

Launch of Brunel's *Great Britain*, July 1843.

age of regular trans-Atlantic ocean crossings began.

Brunel's second ship, the *Great Britain,* launched in 1843 was another landmark. The combination of large size, an iron hull, and the use of the new screw-propeller engines, made the vessel of great importance in the history of shipbuilding design. The *Great Britain* was nearly four times the size of any iron ship yet constructed, and it remained in service until 1886. Like the *Great Western,* the *Great Britain* was used for the Atlantic run. Brunel's third ship, the *Great Eastern,* was built for a non-stop voyage to Australia. This great ship was started in 1854 and launched in 1858; it was of truly heroic size, much larger than any existing ship and a prototype of all future ocean liners. It was 692 feet in length (more than double the *Great Britain*) and the hull was over 6000 tons of iron. This ship was plagued with problems, in construction, in launching (it was so big that it took several months before it could be moved from its Thames dock into the water), and in operation. The *Great Eastern* was a financial disaster for its owners, for a depression in the Australian trade and, in 1869, the opening of the Suez Canal, undermined the purpose for which the ship had been built.

The true significance of Brunel's ships lay in their concept of economies of scale and in the multitudes of technical problems which Brunel encountered and overcame in producing such large vessels. The *Great Eastern* was not his only financial failure. Many of his projects were extravagant and financially unsound, though bearing the hallmark of engineering genius. Brunel's broad gauge is one example; another was his abortive 'atmospheric railway' in South Devon in the 1840s. Brunel has been accused of paying too much attention to grandiose engineering schemes and not enough to the interests of shareholders. Yet it is noteworthy that Brunel was able to find financial backers for his projects, and the economic historian must emphasise the many technological 'spin-offs' which came even from those projects which proved financial failures.

Brunel also stands as an important representative of a new profession of civil engineers which arose in the railway age. Men like Brunel owed much to their road and canal-building predecessors, but they encountered many new problems on an altogether larger scale. They helped improve the status of the engineering profession (both Brunel and his father were members of the Royal Society) and they brought it to a state where various specialisms, structural engineering, surveying, and so on, could develop.

Chapter 9
The State and Social Reform

Factory Reform

The reform of working conditions in factories has attracted the attention of historians for a number of reasons. First, reforms were achieved by parliamentary legislation. This therefore raises the question of the role of government in social problems, and hence of inroads into laissez-faire (the principle of non-interference by the state). Secondly, historians have been interested in who promoted the reforms, and whether agitation took place inside or outside parliament. Thirdly, the factory reform movement exposed the tremendous evils of the conditions under which labourers (often women and children) had to work. These conditions have been used to shed light on the social consequences of the industrialisation and the more general questions of changing living standards during the industrial revolution.

The progress of factory reform exhibits a number of features. Until the second half of the nineteenth century the reforms carried out were confined to textiles (mostly cottons and woollens, and thus not all textiles) and mines (mainly the coal mines, not all mining). Not until the 1860s were the workshops, where conditions were often worst, brought into line with factories. Conditions in the notoriously unhealthy 'sweated' trades, such as the clothing industries of the East End of London, remained unaffected by any legislation until the end of the century. One question we must ask, therefore, is why reforms made headway first in the textile factories and, from 1842, in mines.

Another feature of the reforms was that they were passed to protect women and child labourers, the conditions for adult male workers remaining outside their scope (although some of the legislation did affect the working conditions of adult men, too, as we shall see). Again, we must ask why parliament was willing to protect certain groups of workers, but not others. We should note also that not until 1833 was a really effective reform passed, and even this was limited in scope; and, as we have mentioned, not until the 1860s were

Table 9.1 Progress of Factory Legislation, 1802 — 1908

Date	Act	Main Provisions	Industries Affected	Impact
1802	Health and Morals of Apprentices	1. Employers to provide some education for working children 2. Working day for children limited to 12 hours 3. Night work for children abolished 4. Factories to be whitewashed annually	Cotton and woollen factories	Negligible
1819	Factory Act	1. Work prohibited for children under 9 2. Working day for children 9-16 limited to 12 hours	Cotton factories only	Negligible

(1825 and 1831 : 1819 Act improved by raising age for children workers from 16 to 18, and abolishing nightwork for those under 21, but legislation still not effective.)

Date	Act	Main Provisions	Industries Affected	Impact
1833	Factory Act (Lord Ashley's Act)	1. Work for children under 9 prohibited (except in silk factories) 2. Children under 13 to work only 9 hours a day (48 hours a week) 3. Children 13-18 to work only 12 hours a day (69 hours a week) 4. Nightwork for under 18's prohibited (except in lace manufacture) 5. 2 hours schooling a day for factory children 6. 4 full-time factory inspectors appointed	Textile factories (including silk and linen factories as well as cottons and woollens)	Effective because inspectors provided. But much evasion by employers
1842	Mines and Collieries Act	1. Underground employment for females and for boys under 10 prohibited 2. Winding gear to be operated by those over 15	Mines	Limited, with much evasion

Date	Act	Main Provisions	Industries Affected	Impact
1844	Factory Act	1. Children under 8 not to work 2. Working day for children 8-13, limited to 6½ hours, children to attend school at least 3 hours a day 3. Dangerous machinery to be fenced 4. Hours for females limited to 12 hours a day, and no nightworking	Textile factories	Limited, with much evasion
1847	Factory Act (Ten Hours Act)	Working day for children, 13-18, and women limited to 10½ hours (58 hour week)	Textile factories	Limited before 1850 because children could be used, in 'relays', thus keeping the working hours of adult men long
1850	Factory Act	1. Work for those covered in the 1847 act to be between 6 a.m. and 6 p.m. (Saturday 2 p.m.) 2. 1½ hours a day to be allowed for meals	Textile factories	This Act and the 1853 Act prevented 'relays' and so established a standard working day for adult men as well
1853	Employment of Children in Factories Act	Provisions of 1850 Act extended to children, 8-13	Textile factories	
1860	Coal Mines Regulation Act	Earlier safety regulations (of 1850 and 1855) strengthened		Considerable improvement to earlier legislation

Date	Act	Main Provisions	Industries Affected	Impact
1867	Factory Extension Act	1. Earlier Factory protection extended to non-textile trades 2. Children under 8 not to work 3. Children 8-13 to receive at least 10 hours schooling a week	Non-textile trades and industries (some already protected, like pottery industries in 1864)	Greatly widened scope of protective legislation
1867	Agricultural Gangs Act	1. Children under 8 not to work 2. Women and children not to work with men in field gangs	Agriculture	First extension of protection to agriculture
1872	Mines Regulation Act	1. Boys under 12 not to be employed full-time 2. Boys 10-13 to attend school one half-day a week	Coal mines	First significant decline in employment of young children in mines
1878	Consolidating Act	Over 100 separate items of legislation consolidated in one act	All industries	
1908	Coal Mines Act (Eight Hours Act)	Working hours for all miners limited to 8 hours a day	Coal mines	Legislation directly on working hours for adult men for the first time

workshops included in legislation. Thus another question which must be asked is why progress was so slow and so narrowly confined.

The major landmarks in factory and other industrial legislation are shown in Table 9.1, and it is against this background that the progress of reform may be examined.

The earliest legislation came in 1802, and was designed to rectify abuses in the recruitment of child labour to the new factories. These factories, it should be remembered, were often situated in remote country areas in order to take advantage of fast-flowing streams to drive water-wheels. Where population was sparse, and labour recruitment difficult, some of the northern factories

A view of the New Lanark Mill around 1820 where Robert Owen introduced his utopian experiments, including a school and model housing for his workers.

took in pauper children as 'apprentices' from parish authorities in the big cities, London, Birmingham, Manchester and elsewhere. The system provided the factory owners with cheap labour, and it relieved the parish authorities of burdens on the poor rates. But the dreadful conditions in some of these factories prompted Sir Robert Peel, himself a humane cotton manufacturer (and father of the famous prime minister) to persuade parliament to pass an Act in 1802. But the measure achieved little. It applied only to parish pauper children, so that employers could simply recruit their child labour elsewhere. Once the general adoption of steam-powered machinery enabled factories to locate in populous urban areas the need for pauper children was lessened anyway. Moreover, no independent inspectors were appointed. Local JPs were put in charge of operating the Act, but they were often either themselves factory owners or they represented the interests of factory owners.

The next Factory Act was not passed until 1819, and resulted from the joint work of Sir Robert Peel and Robert Owen. Owen, who had already set up a model factory at New Lanark, demanded in 1815 that factory work should be forbidden for children under 10, and that work for under 18s should be limited to $10\frac{1}{2}$ hours labour, with $1\frac{1}{2}$ hours for meals and 30 minutes for education.

As a result of pressure from Peel and Owen Parliamentary Committees heard evidence between 1816 and 1819. The Bill's supporters produced evidence of long hours, harsh working conditions, and sometimes brutal treatment suffered by factory children. Manufacturers countered with arguments that factory children were healthier than those in other occupations; that the income they received kept their families from starving; that the morals of the children were good and that the children enjoyed their work; and that the alternative was to throw the children on the streets to beg or starve, or into the parish workhouses.

The vigorous opposition from the manufacturers caused the original proposals by Peel and Owen to be watered down considerably, and the final Act of 1819 was both weak and ineffective. From this time Robert Owen became disillusioned with parliamentary action as a useful way of promoting better working conditions.

The long delay in passing any strong or effective measures was the result of many factors, one of which was doubtless simple ignorance by rich landowners and professional classes of the true conditions under which factory operatives laboured. Even when parliament's measures were ineffective, the gradual accumulation of evidence assembled by parliamentary committees of enquiry was a major factor in promoting further change. Parliament was also reluctant to interfere with the free play of market forces, such interference being held to go against the principles of laissez-faire. Following Adam Smith, the dominant economic philosophy was that any state action to restrain trade, to impose monopolies, or to interfere with free bargaining between employers and employees, was wrong.

This is the reason why parliament was first persuaded to help child labourers, and later women. Factory reformers, even when their ultimate object was to improve conditions for all workers, realised that parliament would never agree to legislate on behalf of ordinary adult male workers, who were deemed perfectly capable on looking after themselves. They were quite right; not until 1908 did parliament take such a step. The reformers thus concentrated their efforts on exposing the abuses of child labour, arguing that young children were as yet incapable of protecting themselves and needed the protection of parliament. At the back of much of the agitation for reform, though, and of the opposition to it, was the realisation that regulation of child and female labour could affect the work of adults too. This was because in many processes the work of women and children was essential: if limits on their working day ever became effective, this would in practice limit the working day of adult men too.

The attempt by reformers to distinguish between child (and female) labour on the one hand, and ordinary male adult labour on the other, helps to explain a number of features of the factory reform movement. The movement was very much a moral crusade, in which leading humanitarian reformers like Lord Ashley (later Lord Shaftesbury), Richard Oastler, and Michael Sadler tried to shock the nation's conscience by exposing the plight of helpless children. The moral aspect of reform was clear from the many prominent churchmen who supported the cause, from the calls for the provision of education for factory children (which usually meant religious education), and by constant references to immorality and drunkenness in factories.

The distinction made by reformers between children and adults also helps to explain why for so long legislation was confined to the textile factories. It was in the factories that the exploitation of child and female labour occurred on the largest scale, was most novel, and most visible. With the advent of simple machinery a great deal of factory work could be done by women and children. Indeed, for some tasks children were preferred by employers, for not only were they cheaper and more docile, but they were often more nimble and dextrous than adults. In all the early nineteenth century textile factories women and children formed a very high proportion of the labour force, representing perhaps three-quarters of all operatives in the spinning mills.

The emphasis placed by reformers on protecting child workers in factories also explains why the reform movements were essentially middle or even upper-class campaigns, led from above, as it were, rather than from below. Many of the leading reformers were Anglican Tories, aghast at the horrors of the new factory system and its apparent threat to traditional family ties and religious values. Campaigns against factory abuses were often joined with campaigns against slavery, against the employment of boy chimney sweeps, against drunkenness, and other social movements. Adult male workers were often bitterly opposed to the factory legislation. For example they resented Lord Ashley's 1833 Bill because it meant that their children would earn less from shorter hours, and so reduce the family incomes, while less child labour would lead employers to demand more hours from their adult work force (this happened after the Mines Act of 1842 too).

The first real successes for the factory reformers came in the 1830s when the Factory Movement began a powerful humanitarian crusade against factory conditions. From 1830, as Hunt has put it 'pressure was more co-ordinated, more institutionalized, and on an altogether greater scale'. The leadership, largely Tory and Anglican, intitiated something of an 'establishment backlash' against the manufacturing classes, often Whig Dissenters. The reformers concentrated upon reforming the conditions under which children worked, but their ultimate objective was to improve factory conditions for all workers.

The true founder of the Factory Movement was Richard Oastler (1789-1861) whose experience of Leeds woollen factories convinced him of the need for reform. He won widespread support in the north of England, where he became known as the 'Factory King'. He campaigned through public meetings (he was a powerful orator) and through a mass of pamphlets and newspaper articles drawing attention to the evils of child labour. His most effective thrust was to liken child labour to slavery, and he compared the conditions suffered by factory children unfavourably with those of adult slaves in the colonies. This stung humanitarian consciences at a time when the anti-slavery movement was reaching a peak (slavery in Britain's colonies was abolished in 1833).

Oastler's campaign started in 1830. His rallying cry was for a ten hour day for factory children, and during the next two years he organised a network of Ten Hour Committees (or Short Time Committees) in the textile districts. In parliament the ten hour cause was taken up by Michael Thomas Sadler (1780-1835) who, like Oastler, was an Anglican Tory and similarly out of sympathy with the harsh new industrial code presented by the political economists. Sadler proposed a Bill in 1831 which called for the prohibition of factory work for children under 9 and a ten hour maximum working day for those aged between 9 and 18. So radical a proposal had little chance of success. Parliament procrastinated by appointing a Committee (with Sadler as Chairman) to investigate the problem, but before the Committee could complete its work parliament was dissolved and Sadler lost his seat in the first election to the reformed House of Commons. But the work of Sadler's Committee was of great significance, for it startled the nation with its revelations (often exaggerated and distorted) about the conditions of child labour. A further Commission was set up in 1833, in which Chadwick this time played a leading role, and which largely confirmed the abuses to which Sadler had drawn attention.

The result was the passage of the famous 1833 Factory Act, the first effective measure, which was drafted by Chadwick and promoted in parliament by Lord Ashley. The Act fell far short of the hopes of the reformers, though it did exclude children under 9 from the mills and introduce a twelve-hour day for those aged between 13 and 18. The Act also attempted to provide some schooling for children, though this provision proved impossible to enforce. Most important, though, was the appointment of full-time independent factory inspectors. Although few in number, the reports of the inspectors gradually provided better evidence of the actual conditions of factory work and so prepared the way for later reforms. Lack of effective enforcement had undermined the earlier Acts, and at least the new inspectorate provided some mechanism for making the legislation effective. But little could be done to prevent employers (and children) giving false information about their ages, for not until 1837 did it become compulsory to register births, deaths, and marriages.

With the passage of the 1833 Act legislation for factory reform slackened for a few years. The Chartist and anti-Poor Law movements helped divert the attention of reformers for a time, but from the early 1840s the question of labour conditions again came to the fore. Lord Ashley in 1840 called for an enquiry into the working of the 1833 Act, and the results were two shocking reports, the first, in 1842, revealing conditions in the mines, and the second in 1843, dealing with other industries. The report on mines used illustrations for the first time as part of a parliamentary enquiry, and the vivid pictures of young children toiling alone underground in the dark produced a sensation. Parliament therefore hurried to pass Lord Ashley's Mines Act in 1842, which forbade the employment of women and girls underground and set a minimum age of 10 for boys.

Lord Ashley (from 1851 the 7th Earl of Shaftesbury) dominated the ten hour movement until 1850, and devoted his life to social reform. A Tory and an Anglican, he campaigned tirelessly on a wide range of social issues, factory reform, housing, climbing boys, the reform of lunacy laws, and moral and religious welfare. He was responsible for the 1844 Factory Act, which made the significant advance of extending protection to women employed in factories as well as children and young persons. For the first time also, employers has to fence dangerous machinery, which had caused a great many horrifying accidents. Nevertheless, this Act actually lowered the age at which a child might work in a factory, from 9 to 8 years.

A further landmark was achieved in 1847 with the passage of the so-called Ten Hour Act. In fact the Act fixed working hours for women and children at $10\frac{1}{2}$ hours, and the reduction to ten hours was not finally achieved until 1874. The 1847 Act was promoted by John Fielden (1784-1849), an industrialist who had taken over leadership of the Factory Movement in the House of Commons (Ashley having temporarily resigned his seat). The significance of Fielden's Act was two-fold. First, the ten hour day was at last achieved (if we ignore the additional half-hour); and secondly, if the provisions of the Act were carried out effectively the hours of adult male workers would be controlled too. As we have discussed already, the Act was strengthened in 1850 and 1853 to prevent child labour being used in relays, so that by this

Illustrations like these in the Report of the Mines' Commission in 1842, shocked the public by their depiction of the exploitation of child labour.

time a ten hour (and a half) day had been won for nearly all textile factory workers.

The achievements of the factory reform movement should be put in perspective. In 1850, the legislation affected only textile factories and mines, and these employed only a minority of all women and child workers. Indeed, these occupations accounted for only one-quarter of all children under 15 in employment. Agriculture (for boys) and domestic service (for girls) were the principal occupations and they remained untouched by legislation. Moreover, conditions outside the textile mills and mines were often as bad, or worse, than these inside. Especially bad were conditions in the Staffordshire pottery industries where young children of six or seven worked long hours in dangerous and unhealthy conditions, and where no fewer than 17 per cent of the workforce were under 11 years old.

Progress from 1860 was piecemeal, steadily widening the barriers of application beyond the textile mills and mines, gradually confirming and strengthening the provisions already enacted, and enlarging and improving the factory inspectorate. In 1860 and 1861 protection was extended to black and dye works and lace factories. In 1864, following a report by the Children's Employment Commission which revealed appalling conditions in brickworks, metal trades, match factories, and the potteries, an Act extended protection to these and other industries. This Act for the first time made provisions for adequate ventilation. In 1867 came further Acts which covered most handicraft workshops and any industrial establishment employing more than fifty workers. The major consolidating Factory Act of 1878 marked the end of a period of more than three-quarters of a century of agitation and reform. Much had been achieved, although, of course, not all of the improvements in working conditions were brought about as a result of legislation. The activities of trade unions, enlightened employers, and general social awareness all played their part. The growth of parliamentary intervention in the economy was of great significance. It marked a triumph for the utilitarians, humanitarians, and others who opposed the non-interventionist creed of the political economists. Representative of these latter was Nassau Senior, Professor of Political Economy at Oxford, who led the intellectual fight against factory reform in the 1840s. Senior opposed factory legislation on many grounds: on principle, since it went against the laissez-faire doctrines; on theoretical grounds (he argued, incredibly, that since all factory profits came in the last hour of a twelve hour day, a reduction of working hours would wipe out all profits and lead to bankruptcy); and even on the grounds that factory work was so effortless for children that it could hardly be called work. He wrote of 'the extraordinary lightness of labour, if labour it can be called'.

Social Change and Social Improvement

During the eighteenth and early nineteenth centuries the government's involvement in domestic social affairs was largely confined to the problems of

Death of two climbing boys in a chimney flue (from an engraving in 1824).

law and order (hence with the Poor Law) and with the eradication of particular social evils often brought to the public attention by humanitarian reformers. Examples of the latter were prison reform, where some progress was made after 1808 largely through the efforts of Sir Samuel Romilly and later of Sir James Mackintosh; and the abolition of the slave trade in 1807, inspired by the work of William Wilberforce.

The growth of industrial society slowly changed attitudes towards state involvement. A major force of change, as we have seen, was urbanisation. By 1850 the doctrine of laissez-faire was in retreat in various ways, and state involvement embraced public health and factory reform, with the Poor Law reformed and centrally administered. The state had also imposed controls on the railways and had taken the first tentative steps towards involvement in education in the 1830s. The area of local authority expenditure had also risen, largely as a result of urbanisation. The local authorities administered the Poor Law and public health improvements; by 1850 some ran their own gas and water undertakings and more came to do so in the following decades. By the 1860s a 'civic improvement' movement was underway, with towns like Birmingham taking the lead in slum clearance, better medical and sanitary conditions, and improved water supplies.

From around 1870 the area of state activity widened even more, both in

Some Board schools introduced swimming lessons in public pools at the beginning of the twentieth century, as here in Bradford in 1907. The poor physical condition of many of these boys is very evident.

traditional areas and in new directions. Two periods of particular activity were the late 1860s and early 1870s, and again between 1906 and 1913.

Why did state involvement in social matters increase? To some extent, of course, the earlier pressures stemming from industrialisation and urbanisation continued. Individuals continued to make their mark on particular causes. One such was Charles Kingsley, whose *The Water Babies,* published in 1863, exposed the wretched lives of young climbing boys employed by chimney sweeps; his work led to more effective parliamentary action than Shaftesbury had been able to achieve in the 1830s and 1840s. But we can see some more general pressures for change. One was a shift in public attitudes, reflected by a new political philosophy. The laissez-faire ideal of Adam Smith and his followers gave way to a more positive view of the state. Both socialism and such 'collectivist' doctrines as those propounded by T. H. Green played their part, but there was also practical realisation that growing wealth had self-evidently not brought benefits to all, the huge pockets of poverty which

In 1907 school medical examinations became compulsory. The top picture shows children being weighed and measured in Bradford in 1907, while the bottom picture shows children being examined for head lice (a common ailment).

continued to exist troubled the Victorian conscience, and the famous social investigations made by Booth and Rowntree at the turn of the century heightened awareness.

In many respects the late nineteenth century was a time when society was prepared to look at itself anew, encouraged by significant changes which were taking place and by the growth of mass communications. The rapid expansion of Britain's empire after 1880 was accompanied by a belief in Britain's civilising mission to the world; but revelations about Britain's own destitute tribes in the squalor of its urban slums brought obvious questions and comparisons. The Boer War (1899-1901) also brought its shocks. A direct result of the appalling physical state of the young army recruits, many of whom were unfit for military service, was the provision of school meals (1906) and school medical inspections (1907).

Political changes were significant, too. Large numbers of working-class men acquired the vote in the Reform Acts of 1867 and 1884 (the latter Act extended the franchise to nearly 60 per cent of all males). This brought pressure on the existing parties to 'buy' working-class votes through social legislation and to check the growth of a separate labour movement; it also brought the need to bring education to 'our future masters'. It was not accidental, therefore, that the years 1868-75 saw many important social reforms, including both educational and trades union reform.

A final force of change was foreign influence and example. Britain's superiority, which had seemed so permanent and unshakable at the time of the Great Exhibition in 1851, seemed less evident by 1880. The 'great depression' of these years brought a spirit of questioning and unease. Technical education seemed better in Germany and the United States, for example, and the idea grew that Britain should learn from other countries. There were also foreign examples of social welfare legislation; Germany introduced a national insurance scheme in 1885 and New Zealand pioneered old age pensions in 1898.

The result of all these pressures was the growth of state involvement in social concerns. One way of showing the growth of state influence is to look

Table 9.2 State Expenditure (including local authorities) (at constant 1900 prices)

Year	1792	1831	1870	1880	1910
Total (£ million)	17	48	74	103	264
Per capita	1.2	2.0	2.4	3.0	5.9

at the growth of total government expenditure (only a part of which was for social welfare, of course), and this is done in Table 9.2.

Most of the increases, as Table 9.2 shows, took place after 1870. A great deal of the social welfare expenditure came from local authorities, and it is an indication of the widening area of their involvement that whereas in 1820 Poor Law expenditure accounted for about 80 per cent of local authority spending, by 1890 the proportion was down to 12 per cent.

A number of the areas of state involvement, such as public health and the Poor Law, have been dealt with already and will not be discussed here. Instead we will look at two particular areas which illustrate the general points made above, the development of state education and the Liberal social reforms of 1906-13.

Education

The state's first tentative steps into the field of education came in 1833. School provisions, largely ineffective, were attached to the Factory Act of that year, and a small grant of £20,000 was made to the two principal religious bodies which had set up a national network of schools from the early part of the nineteenth century. These bodies, the National Society (Anglican) and the British and Foreign Society (Nonconformist), provided only limited education for working-class children, as did the other forms of schooling existing at the time, such as the Sunday Schools (started in 1780 in Gloucester by Robert Raikes) and the Dame Schools, so called because they were often run by women earning a few pennies from the children who attended them. Nevertheless, modern research suggests that earlier historians have been too dissmissive of these early forms of working-class education, and too impressed by state-provided education after 1870. These early schools, especially the 'self-help' Dame Schools, for all their drawbacks, did reach a high proportion of poor children, and there is evidence that literacy rates among males and females were improving **before** 1870.

Middle and upper class children were catered for by the fee-paying private and public schools, by the endowed grammar schools (a very few of which still offered scholarships for poor boys) and the universities.

Following the grant of 1833, the amount was increased in 1838, and Dr. James Kay-Shuttleworth became the first Secretary of a special committee to supervise the expenditure. Kay-Shuttleworth introduced a number of important reforms, both in teaching methods (he introduced a system of 'pupil-teachers' in the 1840s), teacher-training, and a schools inspectorate. By 1860 the state grant had risen to more than £500,000. From about this time

A village 'dame school' around 1840.

the state became increasingly concerned with the provision of education generally, reflecting the widespread view that Britain was falling behind the standards reached in other countries. Little concrete was achieved, but important enquiries into the private and grammar schools, the public schools, and the universities produced a great deal of evidence of inadequate teaching methods and outmoded curricula, and helped instil a spirit of self-questioning and self-improvement among these institutions.

Forster's Education Act of 1870 is generally regarded as a landmark in education history. So it was in the sense that for the first time a national scale of elementary education was envisaged. The Act set up local School Boards which were to establish elementary schools, financed out of local rates, where no adequate religious schools existed. But the limitations of the Act must be stressed. No national system of education was established; the Act aimed to 'fill in' existing gaps and so made no attempt to improve the standard of existing education. There was as yet no compulsory school attendance, and schooling was not made free, though the Boards could waive fees. In 1876 attendance was made compulsory up to the age of 10, then up to the age of 12 in 1899, and to 14 in 1918. Not until 1891 was education made free.

A second major landmark, in many respects more fundamental than Forster's Act, was the Balfour Education Act of 1902. The Act was largely the work of the great civil servant Sir Robert Morant, who, along with Edwin Chadwick and Dr. John Simon, was one of a small group of powerful and influential civil servants who made a significant mark on social reform.

Morant was among those who were greatly concerned by Germany's technical leadership, and his interest was therefore focused on secondary education. In 1902 less than one in ten of Britain's 14 year olds was in full-time education.

The 1902 Act had a two-fold significance. First, it brought schools directly under elected local authorities, abolishing the School Boards, and replacing them with local authority education committees. The committees were placed under the overall supervision of the Board of Education (in effect a government ministry) which had been set up in 1899. Secondly, the Act brought the state for the first time into the sphere of secondary education, empowering local authorities to build and maintain secondary schools.

The combined effects of legislation passed between 1870 and 1902 was to set up a national network of local authority schools in which every child in the country was entitled to free elementary education. With the provision of 'scholarship' and 'free places' after 1902, an increasing number of the ablest working-class children could have free secondary education too.

Social Reform, 1906-13

The years between 1906 and the outbreak of the First World War marked an enormous step forward in social legislation. The significance of the measures was two-fold. First, they marked a substantial increase in overall state involvement in social and economic life. The twentieth century trends towards higher government expenditure, higher taxes, and an enhanced governmental role in the economy were all to be seen in this pre-1914 period. Secondly, a number of the Acts broke new ground and established new principles in social welfare legislation. The changes were in quality as well as quantity, and have been held to mark a distinct move in the direction of the modern welfare state.

Table 9.3 lists the main pieces of social legislation passed by the Liberals, inspired especially by Lloyd George and Winston Churchill.

The table gives some idea of the range of issues tackled. Notable is the concern for workers, for the unemployed, for the very old, and for the very young. It is worth stressing the new departures involved in some of this legislation. Unlike the Poor Law, the pension and insurance schemes were funded not by local authorities and rates, but by the national budget out of national taxation. The Eight Hour Act for coal-miners was the first to regulate conditions for ordinary adult workers; nineteenth century legislation had been concerned solely with women and children. The Trade Boards Act was the first to introduce minimum wage legislation.

Historians have naturally tried to explain these new departures and to

Table 9.3 Social Reform, 1906-11

Year	Act	Aim
1906	Education Act	Provided cheap school meals
1906	Trades Disputes Act	Unions not liable for losses caused by strikes
1907	Education Act	Provided medical inspection in schools
1908	Coal Mines Act	Fixed maximum 8 hour day for miners
1908	Children Act ('Children's Charter')	Protected children in various ways. Juvenile courts established and prison for under 14 year olds abolished. Under 18 year olds not to enter public houses
1908	Old Age Pensions Act	Introduced old age pensions for the first time
1909	Labour Exchanges Act	Established labour exchanges
1909	Trade Boards Act	Fixed minimum wages in some 'sweated' trades
1909	Housing and Town Planning Act	Amended law on working-class housing and allowed for town planning schemes
1911	National Insurance Act	Provided insurance against sickness and unemployment
1911	Shops Act	Weekly half-holiday for shop assistants

account for the upsurge of activity. Many of the explanations have been referred to already in general terms, and here we will examine some of the causes which received special attention.

The Boer War was, as we have seen, directly responsible for the attempts to improve the physical condition of schoolchildren. There was also a more general awareness of the need to protect children, especially in the light of some of the revelations contained in Booth's survey of London. This survey was also partly responsible for action on the sweated trades which had been a matter of public agitation since the 1880s. The Trade Boards Act covered four trades, tailoring, box-making, lace-making, and chain-making, employing 200,000 workers, 140,000 of whom were women and girls. Later, in 1913, six more trades were covered.

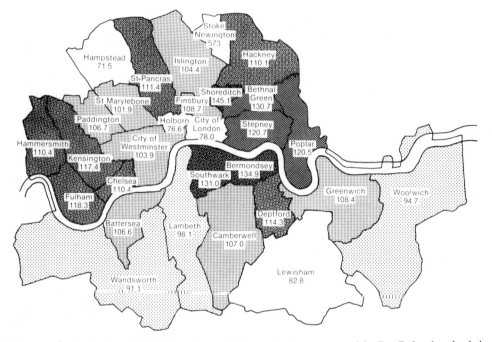

Infant mortality in London, 1907-10. Note the very high rates in the poor areas of the East End and in the dark areas south of the Thames.

The significance of Booth's London survey, and also that made by Rowntree of the city of York, in arousing public concern and directing attention to particular issues, was so great that we must examine them in a little more detail.

Charles Booth's *Life and Labour of the People of London,* begun in 1886 and completed seventeen years later in 1903, has been called 'the greatest social enquiry ever undertaken in England'. In 17 volumes Booth amassed a wealth of detailed evidence about the living conditions of the working classes. He showed that no less than one-third of London's population were living on or below the poverty line (which he set at about 20 shillings a week). Most of them lived in overcrowded and squalid conditions, and Booth proved that the death rates varied almost exactly with the levels of poverty. At the bottom of the social pile were the 10 per cent of the population, around 300,000 individuals, who were unable to scrape together even the bare minimum for a reasonable physical existence. Many of these were too old to work, though another important cause was periodic unemployment.

The methods of investigation used by Booth were as significant as his evidence. He relied entirely on hard statistical facts, and he let these facts

Marylebone workhouse in 1900. Poverty among the elderly became a major cause of concern at this period.

speak for themselves. He offered no solutions and few explanations. Such a rational, scientific approach was well calculated to make the maximum impact on an age ready to be impressed by scientific methods and empirical research.

Alongside Booth's mammoth enquiry must be placed the work of Benjamin Seebohm Rowntree of York. Rowntree's survey, undertaken in 1899 and published in 1901 as *Poverty: A study of Town Life,* was inspired by Booth's work and used similar methods and obtained similar results. The difference, of course, was that York was not London. What might have been dismissed as the inevitable consequence of a vast metropolis could hardly be ignored for a small country town. Disturbingly, Rowntree found that even in York no less than 28 per cent of the population, nearly as many as in London, lived below the standard Rowntree reckoned necessary for bare physical health. As in London, poverty and high death rates went hand in hand, mortality among the poorest being twice that of the better-off. Rowntree also demonstrated the relation between poverty and physique: at the age of 13 boys from the poorest homes were on average 11 lbs lighter and 3.5 inches shorter than boys from better-off houses, even among the working-classes.

These surveys made a deep impression on public opinion, and were certainly factors in the development of social legislation. Their emphasis on the problems of old age and unemployment in particular was reflected in much of the subsequent legislation. But it must be emphasised that the surveys merely added weight to a cause already finding increasing support. Their findings produced detail but uncovered little that was actually new. Moreover the writing of other contemporaries, like Beveridge and the Webbs, were at least as influential in shaping opinion among Liberal MPs. As we have noted already, there were numerous factors combining to make the time suitable for change, factors such as the growth of the Labour Party and the development of trade unions. Moreover ten countries already had pension schemes when Lloyd George introduced them in Britain, and Lloyd George himself went to Germany in August 1908 especially to investigate the social services provided there.

The actual details of the various Acts are less important than their causes or what they later developed into. Many, indeed, were very modest in effect. For example the Old Age Pension Act did not apply universally, providing a maximum of 5 shillings a week for individuals and 7 shillings and six pence for a married couple, only if their incomes were below £21 a year. Those earning more than £31.10 shillings received no pension at all. The National Insurance Act was a bolder measure, but even here the original act confined unemployment insurance to only a limited number of trades (including building, shipbuilding, and engineering). The health insurance provisions went further, becoming compulsory for all manual workers and voluntary for those earning less than £160 a year. The self-employed and non-employed were excluded. workers contributed 4d a week towards the insurance fund, employers 3d a week and the state 2d.

Historians have naturally viewed the Liberal social reforms as progressive, many seeing in them the foundation of the welfare state (though others see the origins much earlier, in Victorian public health and factory legislation). Some socialist historians, though, see the reforms as the response of the authorities to a revolutionary situation, the minimum possible response to stave off a widespread upheaval. Some use the term 'social control' to indicate a policy of providing a safety-valve for working class discontent, yet maintaining authority and control firmly in the hands of the existing, governing classes. As we have seen, though, the causes of the reforms were not simple; some of the reforms had their origins far back into the nineteenth century, some to events in other countries. Of the immediate causes the Boer

War was probably at least as important as the threat of industrial unrest in sharpening parliamentary interest in favour of social reform.

Chapter 10
Working-class Movements: Chartism and Trade Unions

The Chartists

Among working-class movements in the first half of the nineteenth century the most significant was the Chartist movement. This was a movement which advocated democratic parliamentary reform, though underlying the surface political demands was the aim to bring far-reaching social change. Chartism spread rapidly in the years 1838 and 1839, and became a powerful force in the depressed years of 1839-42. Thereafter it declined, making a brief reappearance in 1848.

What was the significance of Chartism? It was both national in scale, involving most major English cities and taking root also in Wales, Scotland and Ireland. It was also essentially working-class in leadership, distinguishing it, therefore, from the Anti-Corn Law League or the factory reform movements of the same period. Also the language of some of the more militant of Chartism's colourful leaders was often violent in tone, and there were a number of outbreaks of violence. This has led some historians to liken Chartism to a revolutionary socialist movement, akin to various continental movements which came to a head in the 'year of revolutions' in 1848. Historians often draw a contrast, too, between the failure of Chartism and the success of the Anti-Corn Law League (the Corn Laws were repealed in 1846). Chartism was characterised by working-class, disunited leadership, with diverse and often unrealistic aims, and by agitation outside parliament. The Anti-Corn Law League was firmly middle-class led and supported, with limited and coherent aims, and with powerful parliamentary support from Peel and Cobden.

Chartism grew out of a number of reformist movements which gathered strength in the 1830s. The soil for such improvements was fertile. The 1832

Parliamentary Reform Act had bitterly disappointed working-class leaders and this severed the uneasy alliance which had existed between the working classes and middle-class radicals. The new parliament did not represent the mass of the population at all, but extended the franchise only to owners of property. Employers now had political representation, but not the employed. Both the Factory Act of 1833 and the New Poor Law of 1834 were resented (the former reduced the hours and earnings of workers' children without altering the conditions of adult workers). Moreover various groups of workers, such as the handloom weavers and some agricultural labourers, were suffering from unequal competition with new machines. And the fluctuations of the trade cycle were cutting deeper. In 1837 a trade downturn began which between 1839 and 1842 turned into one of the worst depressions of the century with mass unemployment in the textile districts. It was in 1837 that the authorities began to extend the New Poor Law to the industrial North, forcing paupers into the workhouse 'bastilles' just at a time when unemployment, and hence those needing relief, was mounting rapidly.

The aims of the Chartists were diverse. In fact they covered such a wide area of the country, with so many differing conditions and problems, that it was impossible to have a single set of goals. The common core was adherence to the 'People's Charter', which had been drawn up by Francis Place in 1838. Place put forward six demands: annually elected parliaments; every man to have the vote (and possibly women, though Chartists were vague about this); voting by secret ballot; the right of anyone to stand for parliament, not just property owners; all electoral areas to be equal; Members of Parliament to be paid.

None of these proposals was new in the 1830s, and all had been put forward by reformers even in the eighteenth century. But the novelty in the 1830s lay in the underlying aim of improving working-class conditions through political action. Thus Chartism marked a stage in the development of a working-class consciousness, working for social reform through political power.

The Chartist leaders were split into two broad camps as to the best ways of achieving their aims. One, most strongly represented in the northern industrial districts, advocated violence and physical force. The other more moderate wing wanted constitutional methods, education, and moral persuasion. The main moderate leader was William Lovett who, together with Francis Place, had founded the London Working Men's Association in 1836. Other groups pressing for political reform before the emergence of Chartism included the Birmingham Political Union, under the leadership of the banker Thomas Attwood, who advocated printing paper money to get out of trade depressions. Much more significant was the Northern Union, led by the Irishman Feargus O'Connor (1794-1855). O'Connor was a brilliant and impassioned speaker whose views and language represented the more extreme and violent reformers. In 1837 he founded the *Northern Star* in Leeds, a radical newspaper which soon had a circulation of 50,000 and became the principal Chartist newspaper.

The Chartist movement was at its most powerful in the first few years. A large People's Convention was held in London in 1839 at which Lovett was elected Secretary and plans were made to draw up a vast petition in support of the six demands. The petition, which received over $2\frac{1}{4}$ million signatures, was rejected by the House of Commons in July of that year. The government, alarmed by the level of agitation, sent troops to the northern counties.

Nothing like a general revolt occurred, although there were sporadic violent incidents in Birmingham, London, and South Wales. The worst disturbance was at Newport when a group of miners tried to release a Chartist leader from prison. The authorities opened fire on the miners, killing ten and wounding fifty.

The failure of the Newport uprising brought to an end a period of violent agitation and for a time the movement collapsed. It was rekindled in 1840 with the foundation of the National Chartist Association in Manchester, which claimed to represent some 400 separate Chartist Societies all over the country. Another petition was drawn up, this one with $3\frac{1}{4}$ million signatures, and again, in 1842, parliament rejected it.

As in 1839, the authorities acted against the Chartist agitation of 1842 with considerable repressive force. The leaders were arrested, many of them receiving long prison sentences and others being transported. For a movement so short of able leaders the government's reaction was a crushing blow. From 1842 also two further events pushed Chartism into the background. One was the general improvement of economic conditions and the onset of a period of high employment and rising living standards. The other was the growth of the Anti-Corn Law League, which deflected support from the defeated and discredited Chartists. In 1848, a year of trade depression and revolution in Europe, there was a brief revival. Once again the Chartists collected a huge petition, this one claiming over 5 million signatures. The movement's leaders, Feargus O'Connor and Ernest Jones, planned to take the petition in a mass procession from Kennington Common to Westminster. In the event the demonstration was a fiasco, and marked the final eclipse of the Chartist movement. First, only about one-tenth of the expected number of demonstrators actually turned up (the leaders had predicted half a million). Secondly, the authorities forbade the march, and troops and special constables were stationed at key points on the planned route. Rather than challenge the authorities O'Connor and Jones abandoned their original plan and took the petition unescorted to parliament. Thirdly, the petition was found to contain less than half the number of signatures claimed, and a great many of the names were forgeries and inventions. Chartism became a laughing stock and never recovered.

The failure of Chartism was due to several causes. From the start, divided and often inept leadership weakened the movement. Leaders were divided both on ultimate goals and on the methods of achieving them. Critical was the lack of middle-class support, which deprived Chartism of funds, leadership, and 'respectability', so important in nineteenth century Britain. Resolute and often brutal reaction by the authorities also weakened the movement. Moreover Chartism tended to thrive in times of economic depression and fade in trade revivals (thus confirming that at root Chartism was a 'knife and fork', or social movement, rather than a purely political one).

It must be stressed that Chartism was never a single coherent movement. To describe Chartism as 'socialist', or 'working-class', is to oversimplify. Under the umbrella of the six demands Chartism included a whole mass of fragmented social reform movements, some of them distinctly regional. Also, like most working-class movements of the period, Chartism was essentially conservative and reactionary. Most reformers looked backwards, to a supposedly ideal world of regulated relationships between masters and men, where machines did not threaten jobs, and where the trade cycle did not mean periodic bouts of poverty. The real radicals were the employers, creating a new industrial society. Only slowly, after 1850, did working-class movements, led by the new labour aristocracy, adjust to the changing conditions of industrial Britain.

Working-class Movements: Trade Unions

The growth of industrialisation during the nineteenth century brought with it the gradual formation of a distinct working-class and the development of a number of working-class movements. Some of these movements had political aims, like the Chartists and the various groupings from which they sprang, although underlying the political demands of the Chartists were the goals of social improvements for the working-class. Other movements had limited objectives, often connected with the ideals of 'self-help' and 'self-improvement'. Such were the Friendly Societies, which encouraged their members to save when times were good in order to have money available during periods of unemployment, or to meet exceptional expenses like funerals. The Mechanics Institutes aimed to provide skills for workers and so enable them to improve their wages and prospects. The Co-operative Movements began in Lancashire in 1844 when some weavers — the 'Rochdale Pioneers' — banded together to obtain cheaper food. From this modest and limited start the movement grew into a major retailing and wholesaling business, and branched even further into politics and education. Of all working-class movements, though, the most significant was trade unionism. The significance of trade unions lay in the numbers of workers involved, the methods used to obtain their ends, and their contribution to working-class politics; they became the major force behind the growth of a working-class political party, eventually known as the Labour Party.

The growth of the trade union movement took place against the background of four major forces. One was industrialisation. This produced a growing number of workers, increasingly concentrated in industrial cities, and the appearance of a distinct working-class consciousness as the different interests of employers and employees became more sharply defined. An important distinction occurred between the better-off workers, often those with craft skills or some particular expertise, and the mass of the unskilled workers. It was the former who were at first more successful in establishing permanent organisations. Industrialisation also brought improved communications, through railways, the telegraph and postal services; these in turn facilitated the growth of national organisations and the dissemination of information.

A second force, also a product of industrialisation, was the trade cycle. Generally speaking, combinations of workers were most likely to succeed in increasing wages or reducing working hours when demand for labour was strong. In times of unemployment the bargaining position of workers was weaker, and in depressions the ability of employers to afford concessions was also reduced. The growth of the trade union movement was therefore affected by the ups and downs of the trade cycle: unions tended to be strong in boom periods and weak when conditions were depressed.

The trade cycle was important for another reason. The nineteenth century saw for the first time alternate bouts of industrial prosperity with rising wages and high employment, and depressions with lower wages and unemployment. This experience sharpened the clash of interests between the employers and the employed, fostered the growth of a working-class consciousness, and encouraged groups of workers to grasp what concessions they could in good times and to resist lower wages in bad.

The third force operating on union development was the legal environment, as established by various Acts of Parliament and interpreted by the courts. Table 10.1 summarises some of the more significant landmarks in trade union legal history.

Only gradually during the nineteenth century did trade unions gain a secure legal footing, and at times the tide of legal protection ebbed and flowed. Between 1799 and 1824 parliament forbade the very existence of unions, or combinations as they were called. Thereafter union activities, such as strikes

Table 10.1 Trade Unions, Political and Legal Landmarks

Year	Act	Aim
1799	Combination Act	These two acts forbade
1800	Combination Act	'Combinations' of workers.
1824	Combination Act repeal	
1825	Trade Union Act	Permitted unions to exist, but strictly limited action.
1871	Trade Union Act	Reversed Hornby v Close decision of 1867 and gave protection to union funds.
1871	Criminal Law Amendment Act	Forbade picketing and other union activities, including strikes.
1875	Conspiracy and Protection	Legalised peaceful picketing and legalised strike action.
1906	Trades Disputes Act	Reversed Taff Vale Judgement, 1901, and protected unions from liability for civil wrongs (e.g. consequences of strikes on profits).
1913	Trade Union Act	Reversed Osborne Judgement, 1909, and permitted unions to pay a political levy to the Labour Party.

or picketing, and the security of their funds was very much in doubt until Disraeli's fundamental Act of 1875. Even subsequently, an adverse court decision in 1901 threatened to deprive unions of the strike weapon until the passage of a further Act of Parliament in 1906.

Fourthly, from the 1880s especially, various forms of socialist thought became a significant force in the trade union movement. Just how influential the forms of 'revolutionary socialism' and syndicalism which thrived on the European continent were in Britain is a matter much debated among historians; but certainly from the late 1880s the British trade union movement became increasingly involved in politics. Union members started to stand for parliament, and the movement actively supported the formation of the Labour Party.

Table 10.1 shows a progressive though uneven development of the acceptance of the trade unions by the authorities as the nineteenth century went on. Trade unions, as groups of workers organised to pursue collectively various common aims, were by no means a product just of the nineteenth century, nor did they disappear completely during the repressive period of the Combination Acts at the beginning of the century. Their origins have been traced back before the eighteenth century, and certainly in the late eighteenth century a growing number of 'trade clubs' emerged and sometimes engaged in successful strike action. These combinations of workers were mostly short-lived, formed for some specific purpose, and then disbanded. They were not, therefore, the types of permanent organisations we have come to associate with the trade union movement. Historians have tended to underestimate the achievements of these trade clubs which, although never affecting more than a small minority of the total workforce, nevertheless were frequently successful in attaining their limited objectives.

We should not exaggerate the impact of the Combination Acts in stifling union activity. These Acts were passed in 1799 and 1800 at a time of revolutionary upheaval in France and of fear of similar outbreaks in Britain. But historians now recognise that the Combination Acts were of little consequence for the development of the trade union movement. Various unions were, in fact, formed between 1800 and 1824; that they were ineffective was due not to government repression but to the severe depression after 1815 and to the problems of organising labour combinations at a time of a rapidly growing labour force and general hostility from employers.

The period from about 1829 to 1834 was notable for the rise and collapse of movements for general unions, embracing on a national scale workers in different occupations. Most spectacular was Robert Owen's Grand National Consolidated Trades Union launched in 1833, but there had already been several earlier attempts. Robert Owen (1771-1858) was a great social reformer who had made a considerable impact with his radical views expressed in *A New View of Society* in 1814. Earlier, he had established his famous experimental factory while manager of the New Lanark Mill; as a humane employer he paid good wages, provided decent housing, and did not employ children under the age of 10. He also established schools for the children of his workforce. Owen was a pioneer of early factory legislation, helping Sir Robert Peel to secure the passage of the 1819 Factory Act. He preached the advantages of co-operation rather than competition, and went to America in 1824 to put his ideas into practice; he set up a model community there called New Harmony , but the principles upon which the community was founded proved too visionary and idealistic and the experiment ended in failure.

Owen returned to England in 1829 where 'Owenite' co-operative movements had gathered strength. It was in this year that another major trade union figure John Doherty, a disciple of Owen, set up in Lancashire a cotton-spinners' union which attempted to enrol members on a nationwide scale,

1834: Unionists rally against the deportation of the Tolpuddle Martyrs.

including Scotland and Ireland. More ambitious was Doherty's National Association of United Trades for the Protection of Labour. This was launched in 1830 and was the first of the general unions to achieve any success. Neither of Doherty's unions lasted long, and in October 1833 Owen himself launched the GNCTU, a general union which soon claimed to have 800,000 members. This union, too, was short-lived, and had effectively collapsed by the summer of 1834.

Historians differ in their interpretations of this burst of activity in the years 1829-1834. Some contrast the 'mass movements' of these days with their radical and socialist ideologies both with the earlier period of inactivity and the later period of craft exclusiveness and sectional interests. Other historians, like Musson and Hunt, considerably play down the significance of the general unions. They stress the continuity of craft union activity both before and after the 1830s; many craft unions, for example, held aloof from the Owenite movements. They stress, too, the ineffectiveness and insignificance of the general unions. Despite the unions' claims, the numbers of actual paid-up members was very low (only 16,000 in the case of the

GNCTU) and they achieved very little in practice. Despite their avowedly general and national aims, the unions which joined them tended to pursue narrow sectional interests, and to withdraw when these aims were disregarded.

In a wider perspective, though, the union upsurge in the early 1830s was significant in two respects. It certainly furthered the growth of a working-class consciousness. This was given an unwitting boost by the hostility of the authorities, especially in the transportation of six Dorset agricultural labourers, the 'Tolpuddle Martyrs', who in March 1834 were sentenced to seven years' transportation for taking illegal oaths when planning to join the GNCTU. Secondly, the difficulties of organising general unions were vividly brought home to the union leaders. Divergent and often conflicting aims and interests between different groups, battles for leadership among the various component unions, problems of communication and planning concerted action, as well as constant hostility from the employers (most of whom refused to employ GNCTU members, for example) all instilled a spirit of realism and caution which was to characterise the union movement in the third quarter of the nineteenth century.

Union activity did not disappear between 1834 and 1850, though it undoubtedly became relatively dormant. Apart from the shock of the 1834 defeats, one reason was that other reform movements, such as Chartism, the Anti-Corn Law League, the Ten Hour Movement, and the Anti-Poor Law agitation deflected attention. These years also saw the growth of 'self help' movements among the working classes and, from 1844, the growth of the Co-operative movement. From around 1850, though, the trade union movement took another step forward, though on lines very different from that of the earlier phase. Most significant was a growing split within the working class between the craft-dominated 'labour aristocracy' and the unskilled working classes. It was the former which dominated the trade union movement before 1889, while from that date unskilled manual workers became increasingly involved in union activity.

The great social historians Beatrice and Sidney Webb gave the term 'New Model' trade unions for the craft organisations which appeared after 1850. Their prototype was the Amalgalmated Society of Engineers, founded in 1851. In contrast to the mass unions of the 1830s, here was a union of skilled men, in a single trade, with a high subscription (one shilling a week), and whose aims included those of friendly societies, such as providing sickness and unemployment benefits. The ASE was essentially a moderate union, avoiding strike action if possible, accepting the existing organisation of capitalist society between employer and employed, and obtaining the best deals it could

Membership card of the Amalgamated Society of Engineers, the first of the 'new model unions' founded in 1851.

for its members by cautious negotiations. Unions similar to the ASE grew up among other skilled crafts in the 1850s and 1860s, for example the boilermakers, carpenters, and bricklayers. Many of these unions set up headquarters in London with paid full-time officials. Here a small group of such men, labelled the 'Junta' by the Webbs, who included Robert Applegarth of the Carpenters and William Allen of the Engineers, exerted a considerable influence on general trade union policy. Partly as a result of the activities of such men the union movement gained in status and respectability, and was probably a contributory factor to the extension of the franchise to the working classes in 1867.

Nevertheless, the significance and the newness of the New Model Unions should not be exaggerated. They certainly did not embrace all the union movement. Some of the large unions, including unions among miners and textile workers, recruited far more widely than terms like 'craft skills' and 'exclusiveness' would lead us to believe, and they did not accept Junta leadership. Neither did the New Model leadership win approval from many small unions of the skilled and semi-skilled. There were also several instances of unions among unskilled workers, especially in the boom of the early 1870s. They included dockers, gas workers, and even agricultural workers (among whom Joseph Arch organised the short-lived National Agricultural Labour Union in 1872). Furthermore the new moderation of the New Model unions has been exaggerated. Fewer strikes was not necessarily a consequence of moderation but was more probably the discovery of more effective ways of bargaining (and always with the strike weapon in the background). Moreover the right to strike was by no means legally established and unions supporting strikes faced losing their funds by breaches of contract under Master and Servant legislation.

The late 1860s marked a critical time for the trade union movement. In 1867 came the appointment of a Royal Commission to enquire into trade union matters. The Commission was set up in the wake of increasing pressure by the unions to reform their legal status, especially after the adverse Hornby v Close judgement in 1867 by which it appeared that trade unions could not protect their funds if an official absconded with them. At the same time there was public anxiety about unions, especially after the 'Sheffield Outrages' of 1866 when the house of a non-union worker was blown up.

The Commission's Report in 1869 was broadly sympathetic to unions, and a series of legal changes meant that by 1875 the status of unions was clearly recognised, as was their right to strike action and peaceful picketing.

In another respect too the movement had taken an important step forward. This was the establishment in 1869 of the Trade Union Congress, a product

Table 10.2 Trade Union Membership, 1834 - 1913

Year	Number of members
1834	800,000
1842	100,000
1850	250,000
1873	1,100,000
1879	500,000
1888	750,000
1892	1,600,000
1900	2,000,000
1910	2,500,000
1913	4,100,000

of earlier regional trades councils and at first a rival to the Junta for leadership among unions. By 1871, though, the TUC (within which the Junta continued to exercise great influence) had emerged as the leading spokesman for the union movement.

Before 1892 there are no really reliable figures for the membership of trade unions and for the early years the estimates given in Table 10.2 are only a rough guide.

Table 10.2 brings out three key points. First, the enormous fluctuations before the 1880s and the much steadier growth thereafter. Secondly, the generally higher plateau, even in times of acute depression (like 1879) which had been reached by the 1880s. In the depression of 1842, for example, union membership slumped to only 100,000. Thirdly, we may note two periods of exceptional growth, 1888-92, when membership roughly doubled, and 1910-13, when it rose by two-thirds. All in all membership rose from about 5 per cent of the workforce in 1888 to just under 25 per cent by 1913.

The rapid growth after 1888 is associated with the rise of so-called 'new unionism', the spread of unions among the working classes on a large scale for the first time. What was new was not simply the growth of organised unskilled labour, but a growing use of the strike weapon and other less moderate forms of collective bargaining, and a new radicalism within the trade union movement. There was growing industrial unrest, and a particularly large number of strikes and disturbances in the years 1910-14. It was also in the period from the 1880s that the TUC became more politically active and the Labour Party emerged.

As with so many labels attached to movements by historians we must take care with 'new unionism'. There were, indeed, new unions, most prominently in large towns among gas workers, dockers, and seamen. Their 'newness' lay in several directions, occurring among workers not previously organised, imposing few entry qualifications (unlike exclusive craft unions), and

Banner of the National Union of Gas Workers, one of the 'New Unions' of the 1880s. Note the inclusion of 'General Labourers' in this union.

frequently being led by socialists from the middle classes or labour aristocracy. Typical of new unionism (through exceptional in size and success) was the Dock, Wharf, Riverside, and General Labourers Union, set up in 1889 with the socialist Tom Mann its first president. The term 'general labourer' indicates this union's open entry policy; membership reached 50,000 by 1891, though falling thereafter. Yet more than half the increase in union membership shown in Table 10.2 after 1888 came in 'old' previously established unions, many of them craft-based. After their initial success the membership of new unions declined; in 1891 they contained perhaps one in four of all unionists, but by 1896 only one in ten. Not until 1910-14 did the new unions make further rapid relative gains. Also, as Lovell has pointed out, the socialist sympathies of many new union leaders does not mean that socialist principles were responsible for the growth of the union movement. The more mundane goals of higher wages and better working conditions were always to the fore.

Why did new unionism advance after 1888? One factor was certainly the upward turn of the trade cycle, which increased the bargaining power of labour. Another factor was a series of symbolic strike victories which won a great deal of public sympathy and support. First came a successful strike by girl workers at Bryant and May's London match factory in 1888. The following year came two victories of greater significance: a gas workers strike in East London led by Will Thorne and the great 5 week strike at the London Docks led by John Burns, Tom Mann, and Ben Tillett. The cause of the 'dockers' tanner' was taken up far from the crowded slums of London's docklands: Cardinal Manning gave his support, and £30,000 arrived from sympathisers in Australia.

Nevertheless, the burst of new unionism was not sustained, and numbers fell back in the depressed years of the 1890s. Not until 1910 was there a renewed upsurge of union growth, when all unions, new, craft, and also various white-collar unions and railway unions gathered strength. Between the mid-1890s and 1910 the policies of the new unions were also more cautious, avoiding strikes and confrontation where possible. More moderate policies were doubtless strengthened by the adverse Taff Vale Judgement, not repealed until 1906. This case resulted from a strike on the Taff Vale Railway in South Wales, and a subsequent claim for damages by the company against the union was upheld, the courts awarding £23,000. Thus even successful strike action might result in financial ruin for the unions. By this time the TUC was becoming increasingly involved in politics. In 1900 a special conference was called by the TUC, at which representatives from various socialist political bodies were represented including the Fabians, the

Liverpool Unionists' rally during the transport strike of 1911. There was a wave of industrial unrest in Britain at this time.

Independent Labour Party, and the Social Democratic Federation, as well as trade unionists. The conference established a Labour Representation Committee, known from the outset as the Labour Party, a name formally adopted in 1906. Two candidates were elected to parliament in 1900, 29 in 1906, and 42 in 1910. The new Labour Party depended heavily for its finances on a levy being raised from among trade union members, for in those days MPs received no pay (until 1911) and ordinary working-class candidates could obviously not finance the costs of elections or sitting in parliament. The legality of a political levy was challenged by the Osborne Judgement in 1909, but the Trade Union Act of 1913 permitted the levy unless the individual member 'contracted out' of the payment.

As mentioned already, the years 1910-14 saw not only a considerable upsurge in union membership, but also a growth of industrial unrest, with strikes, lock-outs, and a number of violent incidents. How do we account for these outbreaks and disturbances? In particular, should we see the strikes as part of a general socialist revolutionary trend, stemmed only by the outbreak of war in 1914 as some historians maintain?

Unrest was certainly widespread. There were major strikes in 1910 in the

Clyde and Tyne shipyards, in the railways in the North East, and in several coalfields. In 1911 the dockers and merchant seamen struck, and in Liverpool there was general rioting and two men were shot dead by troops. 1912 was even worse in terms of days lost by strikes (over 40 million days were lost). There was a national coal strike, a London dock strike, and many others. In 1913 three major unions formed a 'Triple Alliance' which seemed a threatening move held by some to herald a general strike and a major clash between labour and the authorities. The unions involved were the National Union of Railwaymen, the Transport Workers' Federation, and the Miners' Federation. But before any general confrontation could take place the Great War broke out in August 1914, and in the mood of patriotism and reconciliation which followed, the wave of industrial unrest subsided.

Recent historians (with the exception of some socialist historians) have largely dismissed the role of socialist influence as a cause of the wave of industrial unrest. Lovell rejects the view that the Triple Alliance was formed as a prelude to a general strike, and he and others prefer to emphasise two other factors. First was the undoubted check to real wages which took place after the 1890s which, coupled with mounting resentment at the evident inequalities in society, spilled over into growing working-class demands for better conditions. Second was the influence of the trade cycle. 1908 was a year of depression, and the attempts by employers to cut wages in a number of trades led to resistance and strikes. But from 1910-13 came a period of prosperity, rising prices and falling unemployment (unemployment among unionists was only 2 per cent in 1913). Under these circumstances it was natural for unions to seek to use their growing bargaining strength and for non-members to join unions.

Trade Unions in Perspective

In discussing union developments students should be careful to place the movement in perspective. In particular, four factors are of prime importance. First, unions during the nineteenth century never embraced more than a small proportion of the total workforce, even in peak years. As Hunt rightly says 'until the end of the century, in fact, the great majority of British workers had no part in trade union history'. Workers outside the movement included domestic servants, sweated trades, those in retailing, and, except for brief periods, agricultural workers. Secondly, some historians have been too ready to attach labels, like 'New Model Unions' and 'New Unionism' to the movement. We must continue to use these terms for convenience, but recent studies have emphasised that it is impossible to compress such a diverse movement into neat categories. Thirdly, early historians, like the Webbs, were over-impressed by the unions as vehicles for socialism, and tended to stress the movement as forward-looking, radical, and 'important' at times when it was not (as in the early 1830s).

Finally, we must remember that industrialisation in Britain was not the dramatic event sometimes conjured up by the term 'industrial revolution'. As we know, as late as 1850 not all even of the textile industries had been transformed by mechanised production methods, and the typical unit of industrial production was still the small workshop. It is hardly surprising therefore that industrial unions should have made progress only slowly, and that among unions craft interests should have been so often and so long to the fore.

Chapter 11
The Victorian Economy: Prosperity or Depression?

The Pattern of Economic Change, 1850-1914

There are many ways of expressing the overall performance of the economy. For some purposes we can look at total national income, or income per head, and we can adjust these series for price changes to get **real** income. If we are interested only in that part of national income generated domestically, we can look at total domestic product. Again, as we saw in our discussion of the industrial revolution, we may also look at particular sectors, such as industry or agriculture. We might also want to examine foreign trade, or productivity, or many other areas of activity.

The usual measure of a country's economic performance is its national income. Another key indicator is the growth of industrial production. Table 11.1 therefore shows the percentage annual changes for real national income and industrial production over certain periods.

Table 11.1 Economic Growth Rates (% per annum)

Years	Industrial production	Real national income	Real national income per head
1853-73	2.7	2.1	0.9
1873-99	2.2	1.9	0.8
1899-1913	2.0	1.9	0.8

It must be emphasised that the calculation of such measures as national income and industrial production is an extremely complex matter. There are problems both of definition and data, and in the nineteenth century many gaps in data exist. The figures in Table 11.1, therefore, which are taken from recent calculations by W.A. Lewis, must be considered only rough guides, and estimates given by other authorities may differ somewhat.

Before we consider Table 11.1 in any detail let us simply note that a growth rate for national income of about 2 per cent a year which occurred in the second half of the nineteenth century was not very remarkable, either by comparison with some other countries in the late nineteenth century or with many countries today (in the 1960s Japan grew at about 10 per cent annually). Something which grows at an annual rate of 2 per cent will approximately double in 35 years and multiply 3.3 fold over 60 years: something growing at 1 per cent annually will double in 70 years. To double total national income in 35 years is not, of course a negligible achievement; nor is the doubling of total real income per head in 70 years, especially at a time of fast-growing population. But such growth rates should make us cautious about using phrases such as 'revolution', 'rapid economic growth', and so on.

The periods shown in Table 11.1 have been selected because they broadly coincide with the 'long swings' into which the second half of the nineteenth century is normally divided. In particular it is common to find the years 1850-73 referred to as 'the great Victorian boom', and the period 1873-96 called 'the great depression'. Our task is to see how appropriate these labels are.

No economy progresses smoothly, of course. In the eighteenth century the main influences on year-to-year fluctuations were the state of the harvest and wars. After 1815 economists were aware of a different sort of cycle of activity, although harvests still continued to exert an influence. The nineteenth century saw a pattern of alternative booms and slumps, the trade cycle, which occurred rather regularly, on average lasting about 9 years between the peaks and troughs of each cycle. Recent historians have been less concerned with this cyclical pattern than their predecessors. Partly this is because the cycles themselves vary so much, some quite intense, as in the slumps of 1842 or 1879, others very mild; partly because the theoretical explanation of cycles do not allow economists to predict when they will occur again; partly because the cycles seem to have been unduly influenced by foreign trade, so that some domestic changes show a different sequence (much railway building, for example, while projected during booms, was actually constructed during the cyclical downturns); and also because historians have found other cyclical patterns, like a building cycle, which do not conform with the trade cycle.

Modern interest has shifted to the 'long swings' in the state of economic growth. In particular historians have focused on the apparent slowing-down of the economy in the late nineteenth century. Some have suggested a turning-point, or 'climacteric', in the 1870s, which appears to have occurred in industrial production. The timing of the change in real income, though, is not clear-cut. Real income grew quite rapidly in the 1880s, but only slowly in the 1870s, and some historians prefer to see a 'climacteric' in the 1890s, therefore. In a later section we shall look further at this question of the deceleration of the economy after 1870. Here we will look at how appropriate it is to label the period 1850-73 'prosperous', and the years 1873-96 'depressed'.

The Mid-Victorian Boom, 1850-1873

Table 11.1 shows clearly that as far as overall growth rates are concerned we should be very cautious about labelling the years 1850-73 'boom' or those of 1873-96 'depressed'. The rates of growth of national income were not markedly different between the periods, nor, as mentioned already, were they particularly impressive. Moreover there is no distinct break of trend in the 1890s.

The notion that the third-quarter of the nineteenth century was one of sustained prosperity comes from the idea that these years were generally years of rising prices, in contrast to the periods 1815-50 and again 1873-96 when prices were falling. However, as Landes and Church have shown, the period 1850-73 was not one of price inflation. Except for a brief period of price rises in the 1850s prices were generally falling or stable. Moreover the connection between prices and prosperity is not at all clear. Victorians were quite right to connect periods of rising prices with prosperity and high profits **in the short-run.** But in the **long-run** such factors as technological change, which was lowering real costs of production, were operating to bring prices down. This is what was happening throughout nearly the whole of the 19th century, and it is misleading, therefore, to associate generally falling prices over a long period with 'depression'.

If the period 1850-73 was not one of sustained growth or price rises, neither was it one where cyclical booms were especially marked. There was certainly a very strong cyclical upturn in the years 1868-72 (thus sharpening in contemporary minds the division in 1873 between good times and bad times), but there was also a very difficult period during the 'cotton-famine' of 1861-5, when Lancashire's supplies of American cotton were cut off during the Civil War. Exports were maintained at a high level, and the rate of industrial production was certainly higher than in the late nineteenth century (see Table 11.1). On the other hand, neither export growth nor industrial growth were higher than in the 1830s and 1840s, so that the notion of the period after 1850 as being one of particularly distinct prosperity is misleading.

In one respect the third quarter of the nineteenth century does seem to have been a 'golden age', and that was for the agricultural sector. The Repeal

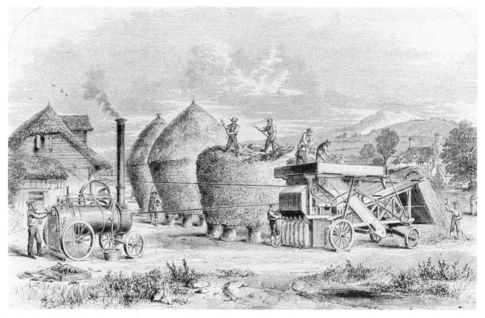

In the first half of the nineteenth century, the use of farm machinery became increasingly common on larger farms. Here a steam engine is used for threshing, around 1850.

of the Corn Laws in 1846 had not been followed by a flood of cheap grain imports, contrary to the fears of contemporary farmers. Instead, the effects of rising incomes, growing population, urbanisation and railways development brought a long period of agricultural prosperity. This was the period of 'high farming' marked by large-scale investment by arable farmers in drainage and machinery. Thompson has written of these years as a 'second agricultural revolution', noting in particular the increasing use of artificial fertilisers and machines as a way of raising agricultural productivity.

But agriculture apart (and even here there were marked regional differences, with livestock farmers generally doing better than arable producers) the labelling of the period as a 'great boom' cannot be justified. There was no great break in the broad aggregate trends of economic growth either at the beginning or end of the period, and the unifying feature once thought to occur in the period — price inflation — simply did not take place outside a brief burst in the 1850s.

The Great Depression, 1873-1896

Saul has rightly termed the 'great depression, 1873-96' a myth. As we saw in Table 11.1 there was no marked slowing of overall growth rates at this time. Indeed, if we look in more detail at narrower periods, as in Table 11.2, we can see that real income per head actually grew faster in the 1880s than in any other decade before 1914 (this would be true of the entire period 1780-1914).

As Table 11.2 shows, the low growth of real incomes in the 1890s continued after 1900, and the trends of industrial production and

Table 11.2 Economic Growth (% per year), 1850-1913

Years	Real income per head	Exports
1850-60	1.4	5.7
1860-70	2.5	3.2
1870-80	0.8	2.8
1880-90	3.5	2.9
1890-1900	1.2	0.4
1900-1913	0.4	5.4

manufacturing productivity similarly continued. Thus the period 1873-96 cannot be considered a distinct unity in a number of important respects.

The supposed unity of 1873-96 derives from three elements: falling prices, slower export growth, and a depressed agricultural sector. Certainly there was a marked fall in prices. Nearly all prices fell, especially those of certain basic agricultural products, and overall the index of wholesale prices fell by 40 per cent (though retail prices not so far). Yet it is difficult to link this fall with a 'depression'. As we have seen already, a basic cause of falling prices was technological change. The growth of steam-power, the spread of railways, the development of steam-shipping, and better communications helped by the opening of the Suez Canal in 1869 and many other factors all exerted a downward force on costs of production. But the impact can hardly be called a depression; for falling prices brought rising real incomes to wage earners, and the last quarter of the nineteenth century was a time of rapidly improving working-class living standards in Britain.

A slower growth rate of exports is also difficult to link with depression. Three points are relevant here. First, the volume of exports continued to rise throughout the period, and there was no evidence of particularly high unemployment in any of the major export sectors. Some, like coal and ship-building, grew substantially in these years, with high profits and rising employment. Secondly, the falling growth rates had set in prior to 1873, as Table 11.2 makes clear. Thirdly, even when the rate of export growth picked up markedly after 1900, other sectors of activity, like industrial production and productivity, remained stagnant.

As in the case of 'mid-Victorian prosperity' the case for a depression appears best to fit some sections of agriculture. By 1850 Britain was already a major net importer of grain, and exports continued to rise in the 1850s and 1860s. But the huge imports feared by farmers in 1846 failed to materialise, as we have seen. From around 1875, though, the situation changed. The combination of railway and steamship opened up vast temperate lands in the United States and elsewhere for commercial agriculture. In the 1870s significant supplies of American wheat entered Britain, supplanting the traditional European supplies from Russian and elsewhere. Later on Australia, Argentina, Canada, and India became important additional suppliers. From the 1880s, too, cheap supplies of refrigerated meat began to arrive from Australia, New Zealand and Argentina. These developments seriously affected many British farmers, especially those dependent on wheat production who had often invested heavily in the period of 'high farming'. Their costs were high and, since Britain clung to free trade, they could not compete with cheap supplies from overseas. Wheat prices fell rapidly, from around 54 shillings a quarter in the early 1870s to 27 shillings in the late 1890s. Other grains, like oats and barley, also fell in price, though not so dramatically, but wool prices, due to competition from Australia and New Zealand, fell even more. As a result, for the first time grain production began to fall, and the land under arable agriculture shrank. Between 1870 and 1900, about 2.5 million acres of arable land in England was switched to other uses, most of the fall, about 1.7 million acres, coming in wheat.

Yet historians now recognise that the notion of a general agricultural depression is misleading. Grain farmers, especially in the South and East of England were certainly depressed. But other farmers in other regions fared much better, for example those specialising in meat production, dairy farming, and market gardening. In other words, we cannot generalise about agriculture as a whole. Not all farmers faced overseas competition, and many of the underlying trends were favourable to agriculture. These included rising incomes, population growth and urbanisation. As incomes rise, proportionally less may be spent on very basic foodstuffs like bread or potatoes. This was one problem faced by cereal farmers. But for other agricultural products like fresh fruit or vegetables rising incomes might also bring proportionally rising demand. Milk prices, for example, did not fall at all, cheese prices fell only 15 per cent, and beef and mutton prices fell less than the fall in the average level of prices. Some farmers who bought grain as a feed for animals even benefited from the slump in cereal prices.

A balance sheet of gains and losses is difficult to draw up, but Thompson has suggested that perhaps a third of all farmers, especially in the western

Harvesting in a Berkshire village around 1906. Note the use of female labour.

counties, 'enjoyed moderate to quite unmistakable prosperity'. Another third were the depressed grain farmers of East Anglia and the Midlands. And the middle third were not markedly better or worse off in the period. Of course sufferers are always more likely to cry out than those better off, and the grain farmers, many of whom still wielded substantial political power, were a particularly articulate group. But the notion of a general 'agricultural depression' cannot be sustained.

In short, therefore, we must dismiss the conventional 'great depression' label for the last quarter of the nineteenth century. There was no obvious break in trend for many key variables either in the 1870s or 1890s. Just as we saw earlier that the 1850s and 1860s were not particularly booming, so the 1870s were not particularly depressed. Economic change was both less dramatic and more complex than conventional labels suggest.

The Economy, 1875-1913: Decline or Plateau?

On several occasions in this book we have noticed that parts of the British economy fared less well after the 1870s than before. It is now well established that by a number of important criteria the British economy slowed down after

The typewriter was introduced into many offices in the 1880s and provided new opportunities for women workers. This picture dates from 1889.

about 1873. There was no uniformity. Some indices, for example export growth, slowed down sharply; others, like real income (which rose in the 1880s), less so. But across the board there was a slow pace, in industrial growth, agricultural output, productivity, and exports. For some of the indices, such as exports, there was an upturn after 1900. But for others, including productivity and real income (per capita incomes probably did not rise at all in real terms between 1900 and 1910) there was continued stagnation. Students must be careful, of course, to distinguish between growth **rates** and **absolute** levels. In most respects the economy was growing after

Table 11.3 Growth Rate of Real Gross National Product (% p.a.)

Year	Rate of growth
1858-1873	2.8
1873-1900	2.0
1900-1910	1.2

1870, especially if we allow for price levels which fell sharply between 1873 and 1896, but the rates of growth were generally less than before.

Was there, then, a 'failure' of Britain's economy? In two respects it looks as though there was. First, as Tables 11.3 and 11.4 show, there was a failure of the economy to maintain the previous growth rates (the differences are greater than indicated in the earlier section, in part because of different time periods used, and also looking at national product rather than national income).

Table 11.4 Growth Rate of Industrial Output (% p.a.)

Year	Rate of growth
1856-1873	3.2
1873-1900	2.2
1900-1912	1.6

Secondly and very disturbing to contemporaries, was the failure of Britain to match the performance of its principal rivals, notably the United States and Germany. In the early 1880s the United States overtook Britain as the world's leading industrial power, while around 1905 Germany moved into second place. Moreover, Britain found her export markets suffering from competition from other industrialising countries, and Britain's overall share of world trade fell from about 33 per cent in 1870 to 17 per cent in 1913. Table 11.5 shows how Germany and the United States outperformed Britain in these years.

Table 11.5 Growth Rates of Britain, Germany and USA, 1870-1913 (% p.a.)

Country	Industrial Output	GDP per head	Output per man-hour
USA	4.7	2.2	2.4
Germany	4.1	1.8	2.1
United Kingdom	2.1	1.3	1.5

However, to speak of 'failure' suggests that we would have a clear standard of success, and this raises a problem. For it is by no means obvious that we can always expect economies to grow at stable or increasing rates. Indeed, there are good reasons why we might expect the British economy to slacken in the 1870s irrespective of any 'failure'. For one thing, as an economy develops, and people get richer, structural changes usually take place. Normally the service sector expands relatively quickly, and this sector tends to have lower productivity than the manufacturing sector. Also, as economies develop working hours may fall and workers may receive longer holidays. Eventually, therefore, rates of economic growth may slacken anyway. Again, the enormous boost given to the Victorian economy by the rapid spread of steam technology could not last forever. Unless new technologies come along with similar impacts (and new technologies may well suit other economies even better) there will be a tendency for growth rates to slacken.

Another reason for declining growth rates was simply the inevitable consequence of industrialisation elsewhere. This could harm Britain both by competition in export markets and by loss of markets in the industrialising countries themselves. From the 1870s there was a general rise of protectionism in Europe and the United States, and this further harmed Britain's exports.

That other countries should grow faster than Britain is not necessarily evidence of British failure. After all, in the 1890s Russia's industrial growth rate was much higher than that either of the United States or Germany, but nobody would use this as an evidence of German and American failure. The extraordinary combination of circumstances which had given Britain its early start and mid-century dominance could hardly last forever. It was inevitable that countries like America and Germany, with abundant natural resources and fast-growing populations, with high educational standards and often with favourable government policies, would catch up with Britain sooner or later. Perhaps it would be more appropriate to ask how Britain held its leading position for so long, rather than to see the erosion of Britain's lead as a failure.

Nevertheless, in several respects weaknesses seem to have appeared in Britain's economy during the last quarter of the nineteenth century. The most telling criticisms are that new industries were not developed, or were developed too slowly; and existing industries were slow to adopt new techniques which were being introduced elsewhere. In Britain, output per worker was not rising as quickly as in rival countries, and some historians have claimed that there was inadequate investment and loss of entrepreneurial vigour.

The Hypothesis of Entrepreneurial Failure

Was poor entrepreneurship responsible for declining growth rates after the 1870s? The hypothesis has proved attractive for several reasons. Some economists, notably Schumpeter, have always laid great stress on the role of dynamic entrepreneurs in initiating periods of growth. It is natural therefore, to see periods of slower growth as a result of reduced entrepreneurial dynamism. Another argument is that weaknesses in Britain's economy, lack of new products and innovations, weak marketing, and so on, were in exactly the areas where entrepreneurship is most important. Also, there was no lack of contemporary criticism of Britain's entrepreneurs. Recent historians like Aldcroft and Wiener, who lay the blame for Britain's economic weaknesses squarely on the shoulders of the entrepreneurs, have been able to quote many such comments by contemporaries. British consuls abroad frequently complained that British businessmen were complacent and unenterprising compared with their rivals. The Economist and other journals pointed to the slow rate at which British entrepreneurs took up new technological advances. Examples here included ring spinning of cotton textiles, the Solvay process in the production of soda, the use of phosphoric ones in steel production, and machine cutting of coal.

Just why Britain's entrepreneurs should have lost dynamism in the late nineteenth century, having led the world in the industrial revolution, is not obvious. Among the most common explanations are those which emphasise sociological and cultural factors. Public schools have been criticised for teaching traditional subjects like classics rather than more relevant subjects like applied science or mathematics. It has been claimed, too that public schools bred an attitude of contempt for industry and trade, directing the most able of Britain's youth towards the professions, the services, or the Empire.

In recent years, however, historians have been less critical of Victorian entrepreneurs. Studies of individual industries have generally concluded that where particular techniques were adopted only slowly in Britain there were sound economic reasons. This was true of the various examples mentioned earlier: ring-spinning, the Solvay process, machine coal cutting, and phosphoric steel.

It has also been pointed out that in areas where market conditions were favourable Britain showed no lack of dynamic entrepreneurship after 1870. In shipbuilding, for example, Britain continued to dominate world markets before 1914. In retailing, too, there were many striking examples of entrepreneurial initiative and innovation, for example, by Lever, Lipton, and Montague Burton.

More fundamentally, McCloskey has argued that it is not possible to speak of any failure of Britain's economy, and it follows, therefore, that no 'blame' can be attached to entrepreneurs. McCloskey's point is that entrepreneurs behave rationally when they try to maximise profits; if the economy is competitive the result of entrepreneurs behaving in this way will be the best possible growth rate for the economy. The economy in late nineteenth century Britain **was** competitive, argues McCloskey, and entrepreneurs **did** try to maximise profits. Hence there was no failure, and it was not possible for Britain to achieve higher growth rates than were actually reached.

Why should it be rational for entrepreneurs to use old-fashioned methods rather than adopt the latest techniques? When markets are growing only slowly it may well not pay entrepreneurs to invest in expensive new machinery, especially if other costs, like redesigned buildings, are involved. Old machinery may already have been paid for ('written off' as accountants say) and hence cost little to run. Some new technology, like blast furnaces, requires large volumes of output to make installation worthwhile. It was a feature of Britain's economy in the late nineteenth century that markets were often growing only slowly (for example export markets partly due to the effects of foreign tariffs), and that many markets were small, specialised and fragmented (for example textile firms often exported to particular overseas markets). Thus the opportunities for investing in new technology were often limited by the nature of the markets facing British entrepreneurs.

The Early Start

Many of Britain's problems which began to emerge towards the end of the nineteenth century may be put down to Britain's early start as an industrial power. Historians have suggested that the economic and industrial structure built up in the nineteenth century was no longer adequate by the end of it. Many examples of such weaknesses have been put forward: the stock of antiquated and outdated machinery; the fragmented industrial structure which came from small self-financing firms; and the locations of many industries appropriate enough when started (drawn, perhaps by the availability of canals, coalfields, or cheap labour) but increasingly unsuitable with the passage of time. Another factor was the 'inter-relatedness' of much previous investment, which meant that some improvements could not be made because they would have involved costly related investments (for example more efficient steam locomotives might pull more wagons, but this might be of little benefit without longer platforms and stations).

The 'early start' hypothesis is not without merit, and there certainly were many disadvantages of being a pioneer. But such disadvantages can have played only a small part in the slower growth rates after 1870. There were advantages as well as disadvantages in an early start — a skilled industrial labour force, a wealthy market, and so on — and we know today from the experiences of Japan and Germany, that pioneer industrial nations do not necessarily suffer from industrial retardation.

Inadequate Investment

The suggestion that Britain invested too little contains three main criticisms. First, Britain invested too little as a proportion of national income. Secondly, out of this inadequate total, too much was invested overseas rather than in home industries. Thirdly, of investment in home industries, too much was committed to the traditional staple industries, like textiles, and not enough to new industries like chemicals or electrical engineering.

Certainly a higher level of investment in industry would have raised industrial output, and compared with her main rivals Britain invested a smaller share of her national income (see Table 11.6).

Table 11.6 Domestic Investment as a proportion of Gross Domestic Product, 1850-1914

Country	Proportion (per cent)
United States	22
Germany	20
France	19
United Kingdom	9

Table 11.6 looks at investment made within the country and expresses this as a share of domestic output year by year. On average Britain's share was less than half that of the other countries shown. Partly this was because of Britain's extensive foreign investment, which in some years exceeded domestic investment. Overall about one third of all Britain's savings in the period 1870-1913 went overseas. Yet allowing for this, and looking at total investment as a proportion of Gross **National** product, we still find Britain far behind the other countries: 13 per cent in this country, over 20 per cent in the other three.

Yet we should not jump to the conclusion that slow growth rates after 1870 were the result of inadequate investment. In the first place, Britain was a wealthy country; until around 1880 British real incomes were the highest in the world so that the lower proportions of investment still produced very high absolute amounts. This was especially true by comparison with Germany, where per capita incomes remained much lower than those in Britain in 1913. Secondly although Britain invested a relatively low share of her national income, this share did not decline after 1870; it is not obvious, therefore, that the growth of the economy can have been affected by the rate of investment.

Thirdly, those who blame overseas investment should remember that such investment was not unproductive. It yielded higher returns than home investment, bringing incomes and wealth to British investors, and in many cases directly encouraged British export industries since British-financed foreign companies often bought British equipment. Fourthly, and perhaps most significantly, there is little evidence that British industries were starved of capital. Investment rates were low throughout the period 1870-1913, the Bank Rate usually standing at around 2 per cent. This implies that there was no lack of investment funds if British firms had actually wanted to borrow money. Some scholars have countered that Britain's capital markets were at fault, gearing their lending towards overseas rather than home borrowers. Yet few studies of individual firms have concluded that failure to innovate or adopt new technologies was caused by difficulties in raising capital.

Slow Export Demand, Trade Union Influence and Stagnant Productivity

After growing in volume at around 5 per cent a year between 1840 and 1870, Britain's exports grew only about 2 per cent annually for the rest of the century. Without doubt it was this slower growth which was partly responsible for the overall slow growth rates of industry and the economy. All Britain's major industries were heavily dependent directly or indirectly on export markets, and it has been shown that if export demand had not slackened total industrial growth rates would have maintained their previous levels. Most of the causes for slower export growth lay outside Britain, in demand factors. These factors included the raising of tariff barriers against British products in Europe and the United States, and the effects of industrialisation elsewhere.

Nevertheless, after about 1900 the growth rate of exports picked up once again. Between 1900 and 1913 total exports grew in volume at about 3.5 per cent each year, and exports of cotton textiles, coal, and other staples were all buoyant in this period. Yet if anything the overall performance of the British economy was even more disappointing in Edwardian Britain that it had been in late Victorian times. The rates of growth of national income and of industrial production were lower than in the period 1870-1900, which suggests that slower export volumes were not the whole story of declining growth rates.

Slower industrial growth rates in Britain occurred alongside lower rates of productivity (output per man), and alongside growing trade union strength. Some historians have therefore suggested that trade unions were to blame, by demanding higher wages and shorter hours, and by introducing various restrictive practices which resulted in overmanning.

Like so many of the arguments put forward, this one may have a grain of truth, but no more than that. Unions were strong in only a minority of industries, and in the period 1900-1913, when growth rates were lowest and productivity stagnant, real wages were also not rising and hours of work not falling. Moreover not only in Britain, but in the United States, Germany and elsewhere, output per man in industry was tending to fall after 1870 (although British levels were lower). This suggests that there may have been some general factors influencing industrial productivity in these years. One possibility is that the last quarter of the nineteenth century saw the ending of massive productivity gains which had occurred from the great innovations of the industrial revolution, steam power and the railways. The new technologies of the late nineteenth century, such as cheap steel and electric power, were insufficient to maintain the previous rates of productivity. Another possibility is that industrial dependence on natural raw materials, coal, iron, timber, tin, copper, and so on, produced an economic structure where diminishing returns would sooner or later set in. Diminishing returns could, for a time, be offset by new resources or mechanised production, but eventually output per man would fall. Only in the twentieth century has dependence on such resources been lessened by the development of artificial, man-made, materials like plastics (though these, too, of course are ultimately dependent on finite resources).

Summary

Debate over the causes of slower growth after the 1870s, and even the extent of the decline, has not been settled. Doubtless a great many factors were involved, and no single explanation can be put forward. However, if we divide explanations into supply factors and demand factors we can see that the balance of modern work is tending to emphasise demand. Under supply we would include such factors as entrepreneurial behaviour, inadequate investment, the nature of the labour force (size and skills), the various 'early start' suggestions, and trade union influences on productivity. Under demand we would include the growth rates both of export and home markets, and stress also the often scattered and specialised nature of markets which made massive high volume investment impracticable.

Appendix: The Great Exhibition, 1851

The Great Exhibition, held in 1851, was one of those events which capture

The Great Exhibition at Hyde Park, 1851.

the mood and values of a nation and symbolise an age. The significance to the historian lies in just this symbolism.

From an international perspective the Exhibition marked the zenith of Britain's industrial leadership. Britain was the 'workshop of the world', the world's only industrialised country. The huge scale of the Exhibition itself and the gathering together of the many wonders which British workmanship and ingenuity could produce demonstrated starkly both the potential of new technology and the extent of Britain's supremacy. From a domestic perspective the Exhibition marked a general rejoicing and self-congratulation at Britain's achievements, and of the acceptance and respectability of industrialism. Royal patronage was important. So was the coinciding of the Exhibition with a period of social peace at home and also of international peace. The path of industry seemed suddenly a moral one: the path towards peace, progress, and prosperity.

Put simply, the Great Exhibition marked a turning-point between the 1840s, with its social tensions, fear of famine, Corn Law agitation, and cholera epidemics; and the 1850s, a period of social stability, with free trade triumphant, a new acceptance of industrial capitalism by the working classes, and the onset of a more obvious era of prosperity.

The Great Exhibition, 1851. Interior view of the Crystal Palace.

The Exhibition by itself, of course, merely reflected these changes. If it did have a direct impact, such as helping the country to come to terms with industry, improving class relationships, or setting other countries on a similar path of industrial development, the impact can only have been minor. Probably the main direct consequence was a series of other great international exhibitions held in other capitals, which fostered peaceful competition among nations and helped the spread of technological knowledge.

What the Great Exhibition demonstrated was Britain's supremacy, the power of technology based on iron, coal, and railways, the triumph of private enterprise, and the emergence of an industrial society.

Britain's supremacy was seen partly in the enormous size of the Exhibition itself, which no other nation could have financed or constructed. It was held for five months, attracted 6 million visitors, and displayed 109,000 separate exhibits from 14,000 exhibitors from all nations. Dominating everything was the exhibition hall itself, a vast glass building erected in Hyde Park and popularly called the Crystal Palace. The Crystal Palace was in effect the major exhibit, consisting of 300,000 identical plates of glass (a dramatic illustration of standardisation and mass production) and delicate cast-iron ribbing. Covering 19 acres of the park it was one-third of a mile long and, at its highest point, 108 feet tall.

Britain's dominance was visible in many spheres. The full title, the 'Great Exhibition of the Works of Industry of all Nations' stressed the international nature of the event. But of the 14,000 exhibitors, 7,400 represented Britain and her colonies and only 6,600 the rest of the world. It was British achievements, British workmanship, British technology, and British ingenuity which attracted most attention; and British exhibitors carried off most of the prizes for excellence awarded by special international juries. To be sure, there were one or two pointers to a different picture: the successful exhibits of agricultural machinery shown by American firms, for example; and some criticisms of British design in the 'Fine Arts' sections. But overall the Exhibition revealed for all to see Britain's clear leadership in nearly every aspect of technology and machine-building.

Power-driven machinery and metal working dominated the exhibits. The exhibition of 'Works of Industry' was intended to display all industrial achievements, and there were separate categories for raw materials, machinery, manufactured goods, and fine arts. But metal products and power-driven machinery, mostly British, were the main objects of wonder and attention. The Exhibition included locomotives, models of iron bridges and iron steamships, and machines for a vast range of uses, from sugar-cane crushing to folding envelopes. Even the entrance to the Exhibition was dominated by a huge 28 ton block of coal.

In many ways, too, the Exhibition displayed the passenger potential of the railway. Railways were, of course, already well established in Britain, but were only in their infancy outside the United States, Germany and France. (There were none at all in Asia, Africa, Australasia, or Latin America.) Large numbers of visitors to the Exhibition arrived by railway, many travelling by rail for the first time. The South-Eastern Railway ran a special cross-channel ferry service for continental visitors, and most railway companies serving London put on special cheap excursion trains.

The Exhibition was a triumph for private enterprise. It was sponsored by the Royal Society and all the capital was raised privately. Not a penny of taxpayers' money was spent by the government, the entire operation being self-supporting and financed largely by a one-shilling admission fee (five shillings on special 'upper-class' days). The Exhibition ended with a profit of £186,000. Much of the construction of the Crystal Palace was carried out by the engineering firm of Sir Charles Fox, and the whole operation was completed in only seven months by 2000 workers, yet another tribute to

British skill and organisation. The design for the building was selected from open competition, the winning design being the brilliant idea of Joseph Paxton. Paxton was not a trained architect; he was a gardener who had taught himself engineering (hence the 'greenhouse' concept of the Crystal Palace). This example of self-improvement from humble origins fitted exactly with the kinds of virtues being prescribed by Samuel Smiles and others. It was an optimistic view, stressing the opportunities brought by industrial society rather than the problems and evils.

Finally, and perhaps most fundamentally, the Exhibition reflected the full emergence of an industrial society within Britain. 1851, the year of the Exhibition, was also the year when the Census showed that, for the first time, the majority of Britons lived in towns, while the agricultural population failed to rise. The year also saw the formation of the Amalgamated Society of Engineers, a step usually held to mark the acceptance by the working-class (or rather the skilled labour aristocracy) of the new capitalist society. The coincidence of these three events illustrates the emergence of the world's first industrialised nation, in terms of social adaptation as well as physical production.

In this respect three features of the Exhibition deserve particular attention. One was upper-class patronage and support, which helped give status and respectability to industry and industrialists. The Exhibition was opened by Queen Victoria on May 1 at a magnificent ceremony. The prestigious Royal Society sponsored the event and Prince Albert, Queen Victoria's husband, President of the Royal Society, was one of the leading supporters and patrons. It was Prince Albert who had pressed originally for the Exhibition to be held in Hyde Park as an international event, rather than as a smaller-scale exhibition of British achievements.

The acceptance of industrial society came not only from the top but from below. Great numbers of ordinary working-class folk flocked to Hyde Park (many coming to London on the special excursion trains) to revel in Britain's achievements. Gloomy forecasts by some of riots, murders, and even revolution which would result from such congregations of the masses were completely confounded. Five months and six million visitors later not even a flower had been wantonly picked in the Park.

The undoubted success of the Great Exhibition, finally, owed something to good fortune. At home it coincided with an upturn of the trade cycle and the inauguration of a period of social peace and prosperity. Abroad, too, there was peace after the upheavals of 1848. Gold discoveries in Australia and California were bringing movement and excitement. And May 1, was a dry, fine spring day.

Chapter 12
Foreign Trade, Investment, and Banking.

Foreign Trade and Economy, 1700-1914

The significance of foreign trade can be seen in at least three main ways. First, economists recognise that foreign trade may play a role in promoting economic growth, and historians have debated whether Britain's economic growth during the eighteenth century was led by the expansion of trade. Did trade provide an 'engine of growth'? Did it stimulate rapid industrialisation?

Secondly, whatever its overall influence on the economy, foreign trade certainly played a significant part in the prosperity of particular regions, ports, industries, and merchant groups. The story of the growth of ports like Bristol, Liverpool, and Glasgow; of industries like woollen textiles, and in the last quarter of the eighteenth century, cottons; and of great merchant companies such as the East India Company were all very much bound up with the fortunes of foreign trade.

Thirdly, foreign trade was of great strategic importance, and for this reason trade was subject to close government control and regulation in the eighteenth and early nineteenth centuries. Partly this was because the state relied heavily on duties on trade for its revenue (in the eighteenth century customs and excise duties were about 70 per cent of total government income). Partly also trade encouraged shipbuilding and the training of seamen, an important consideration for a nation dependent for its security upon naval strength. Partly, too, the balance of foreign trade largely determined whether gold and silver flowed into or out of the country. Any excess of imports over exports would have to be settled by paying bullion. There was a widespread view during the eighteenth century that precious metals were a source of national wealth, and hence of power (this view was part of the so-called mercantilist doctrine). Not surprisingly, therefore, governments took measures to stimulate exports and reduce imports.

There were other reasons, too, why overseas trade played a significant role in eighteenth century Britain. Many of Britain's growing number of colonies, for example in the West Indies and in the Indian sub-continent, were developed as an adjunct to trade. Also, long-distance foreign trade, such as the East India trade, required large sums of capital locked up for long periods. Thus several of the great trading companies were organised as joint-stock companies, with capital divided into marketable shares. Such companies, like the East India Company and the Levant Company, were among the pioneers of joint-stock company organisations, and they provided a vehicle for the effective mobilisation of capital held by merchants.

In brief, therefore, foreign trade was significant because of its role in promoting economic growth and the development of particular sectors and regions, and because the organisation and pattern of trade involved issues of state policy. Against this background we will now examine some of the main trends which took place in the development of foreign trade during the eighteenth and nineteenth centuries.

During the course of the eighteenth century Britain's overseas trade underwent a number of important changes. Chief among them was rapid overall growth. Slowly until the 1740s, more quickly until around 1770, and then very rapidly for the rest of the century, imports, exports, and re-exports all expanded. There was also a shift in geographical division. At the opening of the period, in 1700, Europe held pride of place, accounting for the bulk both of imports and exports. But by 1800 Europe's place had diminished considerably, largely at the expense of the West Indies and North America. Trade with Ireland also expanded. The geographical changes favoured Britain's western ports, like Bristol, Liverpool, Glasgow and Whitehaven, and they grew relative to London and the east coast ports where the European trade was concentrated. Also, the commodity composition of Britain's trade changed. By 1800 cotton goods had overtaken woollens as the leading export, while grain, one-fifth of total exports in 1750, was no longer a net export.

Trade grew substantially, but not smoothly. Wars and harvest conditions were among the causes of trade fluctuations, although until the outbreak of war with France in 1793 only the American War of Independence (1776-1783) brought serious disruption to Britain's commerce. Wars, indeed, often brought trade opportunities: new commercial channels were opened by conquests, rivals temporarily or permanently displaced, or new colonies acquired.

Table 12.1 shows the 'official' values of foreign trade between 1700 and 1815. The system of assigning fixed prices, or official values, to goods imported and exported was begun in 1696 (1755 for Scotland). Thus instead of recording actual, or real, values of goods imported and exported, customs officials simply took note of the quantities involved and valued them at the official rates, which might or might not be the same as the true values. Since these rates were mostly fixed in 1700 (though with new values given to new commodities from time to time) the official values diverged increasingly from actual values as time went on. From the official values it is impossible to know exactly how much exporters received or importers paid in any particular year, and, of course, we do not know the balance of trade.

Table 12.1 Overseas Trade, 1700-1815 (£ million, official values)

Year	Imports	Domestic Exports	Re-exports
1700	5.8	4.3	2.1
1750	7.8	9.5	3.2
1790	17.4	16.1	4.8
1800	28.4	22.4	18.4
1815	33.0	43.0	15.7

Official values of trade are nonetheless useful because they give a good idea of changing volumes, or quantities, of trade. As we can see from Table 12.1, quantities of imports and exports expanded at more or less the same rates during the eighteenth century, with growth much faster after 1750. During the Napoleonic War years, though, between 1800 and 1815, the volume of exports expanded much more rapidly than imports and grew at a rate faster than ever before. Re-exports (goods imported and later exported to other countries) grew only slowly before 1790, but reached exceptionally high levels during the war. We should however note the continued relative importance of re-exports, which was a half the official value of domestic exports in 1700 and still one-third in 1750.

Until the 1780s these official values are the only totals we have for imports and exports, but from this time we are fortunate to have the re-computation

Table 12.2 Real Values of Foreign Trade (£ million)

Year	Imports	Exports	Re-exports
1784-6	22.8	13.6	3.6
1794-6	37.9	24.0	8.3
1804-6	55.6	41.2	9.8
1814-16	71.8	48.0	17.7
1824-6	66.4	40.0	9.6
1834-6	70.3	46.2	10.2
1844-6	82.0	58.4	10.8
1854-6	151.6	102.5	21.0

of scholars which enables us to have a series of actual values. Table 12.2 gives a summary of these figures.

There are a number of interesting contrasts between Tables 12.1 and 12.2. Most significant is that export values rose less quickly than import values, largely because of lower export prices as new techniques of production took effect. As a result the balance of trade was actually negative, even including re-exports, throughout the period between the 1780s and 1850s.

The overall growth of British trade was accompanied by changes in geographic direction, which are shown in Table 12.3.

Table 12.3 Direction of Trade (% of total, official values)

	Imports from		Exports to	
	1700-1	1797-8	1700-1	1797-8
Europe	61.3	29.2	82.0	21.0
N. America	6.4	7.1	5.7	32.2
W. Indies	13.5	25.0	4.6	25.2
E. Indies	13.3	24.0	2.6	9.0
Ireland	4.9	13.1	3.2	9.0
Other	0.6	1.6	1.9	3.6

Table 12.3 does not show re-exports, the markets for which remained almost entirely in continental Europe. The trends shown here need little elaboration. We should note first the relative decline of Europe, especially as a market for domestic exports. The most rapidly growing markets for exports were in the Americas — the Caribbean and the United States. Imports from the West Indies and East Indies also grew rapidly relative to imports from Europe.

How do we account for these shifts? One factor of extreme importance was the growing wealth and population of the American colonies (the United States became an independent country after the War of Independence 1776-1783). Between 1750 and 1783 the number of European settlers in the American colonies more than doubled to reach two and a quarter million. Another factor was the changing commodity composition of trade. Cotton goods, which were 6 per cent of total exports in 1784-6 and 40 per cent by 1804-6, were better suited to warmer, non-European, markets.

Re-exports were also a significant component of British trade. Negligible in 1660, re-exports accounted for one-third of the total value of exports in 1700, as we have seen. Although re-exports did not retain this high share, they remained substantial. The real value of re-exports, for example, was always higher than the value of woollen textile exports after 1790. Most re-exported goods were tropical or semi-tropical products like sugar, tobacco, tea and coffee, which could not be grown in Europe. Re-exports did not, of course, contribute their full value of British exporters, since the goods already had to be bought from their overseas producers (the mark-up for re-export was generally around 15 per cent). But their significance was considerable. Britain's role as a major entrepot brought lucrative opportunities for finance, warehousing, shipping, and port facilities. Also re-exports to Europe helped pay for products such as bar iron, grain, and naval stores, which otherwise would have involved a larger drain of bullion and might have checked the trade itself.

The growth of trade which had accelerated in the latter part of the eighteenth century continued into the nineteenth century. Until around 1875 the value of exports grew very rapidly, especially during the 'long boom' between 1826 and 1873. Trade grew faster than national income, and trade thus became an increasing proportion of total income. From the 1870s there was a marked slowing down, with exports especially showing only slow growth. Despite some revival of growth rates after 1900 the overall picture between 1870 and 1913 was distinctly less satisfactory than at the mid-nineteenth century.

The structure of Britain's exports remained narrow, as it had been in the eighteenth century. Until the 1840s dependence on textiles was overwhelming. No less than 75 per cent of all Britain's exports consisted of textiles in 1830, cottons alone reaching their peak share of 51 per cent. Thereafter there was substantial diversification, although cotton goods remained the most important single export before 1913 and all textiles still accounted for one-half of exports in the 1870s and one-third in 1913.

Diversification came mainly with growing exports of various capital goods, especially those connected with railway construction which was developing rapidly overseas. From the 1840s came the 'iron phase' of export growth, followed from around 1880 by the 'steel and coal phase'. Nevertheless, the continuing narrowness of Britain's exports must be stressed. Even in 1913 around 70 per cent of all exports consisted of textiles, iron and steel products, and coal. Only to a very limited extent were 'new' industries embracing advanced technology represented among Britain's exports, industries like chemical dyestuffs, pharmaceuticals, telephones, cash registers, lifts, cameras, and electric motors. In such industries Britain lagged behind her rivals, especially the United States and Germany, and Britain became increasingly an importer of such products after the 1870s.

Before the 1870s though, the growth of British exports grew in volume at the very high rate of 5 per cent a year, and as a proportion of national income they rose from around 15 per cent in 1800 (they had been no more than 7 or 8 per cent in 1700) to 22 per cent in 1870. In these mid-Victorian years Britain far outstripped her rivals, accounting for about one-third of all world trade and some three-quarters of all trade in manufactured goods. British ships, too, came to dominate world carrying, especially with the growth of steam-shipping for long-distance routes from the 1850s and 1860s.

What accounts for this rapid growth of Britain's exports? On the supply side, trade was stimulated by falling costs of production as the benefits of the industrial revolution were felt. Lower prices meant wider and wider markets for British products. The general level of prices of British domestic commodities fell by about one half between 1815 and 1850, those of cotton goods by two-thirds. Although price levels stabilised between 1850 and 1873, there was no distinct upward trend, contrary to the view expressed in some of the older textbooks. These years, moreover, saw the spreading benefits of the railways and steamshipping, so that final costs were continuing to fall and deliveries became speedier and more reliable.

Demand for Britain's products was also buoyant. British goods were wanted both by the developing and industrialising countries of Western Europe and the United States, and the underdeveloped regions like India. The former, developing their own industries and railways, needed the capital goods they could not yet produce for themselves. The latter bought the cheap consumer goods turned out in Britain's mechanised mills and workshops. By 1850 India was already the single largest purchaser of British cotton products, taking nearly one-quarter of the total exported.

The expansion of both types of markets, developing and underdeveloped, is a key factor explaining the success of Britain's export industries, for Britain at this time had a virtual world monopoly of industrial exports since Britain had first achieved an industrial revolution. Two further factors helped the growth of trade at this time. One was general liberal trade policies which meant that goods could move relatively freely without tariff barriers. The United States moved towards free trade in the 1850s, France greatly reduced its tariffs under the Cobden-Chevalier Treaty of 1860, other European countries (including Germany and Russia) also became less protectionist, while Britain kept her colonial empire, including India, as open markets. The second factor was Britain's own free trade policy. After hesitant moves in the 1820s, this was finally achieved in the 1840s and 1850s. The main landmarks were Peel's budgets of 1842 and 1844, the Corn Law repeal in 1846, and Gladstone's final measures in 1853 and 1860. By 1860 there were only around 50 items carrying import duties, whereas in 1840 there had been more than 1100. The ability of other countries to raise their incomes by exporting to Britain, and also to earn

As a result of the Opium War, 1839-42, Britain forced China to open its doors to foreign trade; China was obliged to allow European 'factories' at Five Treaty Ports, as here at Canton.

foreign exchange (pounds sterling or gold) with which to finance their imports from Britain was a further factor boosting Britain's trade. Nevertheless, recent work suggests that trade policies were not so fundamental to the growth of world trade as was once thought.

After the 1870s the growth rate of Britain's exports slackened. The volume of exports grew at little more than 2 per cent annually, compared with the previous rate of around 5 per cent, while the value of exports, due to falling price levels, grew even more slowly.

The causes of this slowdown of exports have been among the most vigorously disputed questions in Britain's economic history. Some historians put the blame squarely on the shoulders of Britain's entrepreneurs, arguing that they were short-sighted, undynamic, and complacent. The argument that something was wrong with the British economy stems from the fact that Britain's competitors were doing so much better. Both Germany and the United States saw their exports grow at double Britain's rate in the years 1880-1913, and Britain's share of world trade slumped from about a third in 1870 to a sixth by 1913. Moreover both Germany and the United States were developing exports in new technologically advanced sectors like electrical goods and chemicals while Britain remained wedded to the traditional staple

PUNCH, OR THE LONDON CHARIVARI.—September 5, 1896.

CAUGHT NAPPING!

By the 1890s there was increasing concern about German competition, as this *Punch* cartoon of 1896 shows.

exports. Some historians argue that Britain invested too much abroad in these years, and so failed to invest enough in home industries.

Recent studies of Britain's economy have largely dismissed these supply factors, such as entrepreneurial behaviour, capital investment, and the skills of the labour force. Instead they draw attention to the slow-growing demand for Britain's products. Slow demand arose from several factors. As industrialisation spread, newly industrialised countries like the United States were able to manufacture for themselves those goods hitherto imported. Britain's basic industries, like textiles, were easy to establish elsewhere. By 1900 countries like India and Japan had sizeable cotton textile industries, while countries like Germany, France and the United States now imported very little from Lancashire. In addition to the spread of industrialisation came the growth of protectionism. Britain remained committed to free trade, but every other major economic power adopted protective tariffs. The United States raised tariffs in 1864 and increased then further in the 1880s and

1890s. Germany imposed a high tariff in 1879 and by 1890 most European countries had become protectionist.

This rise of protection had a double significance. Not only were some of the wealthiest markets for sophisticated manufactures denied to Britain's manufacturers but German and American industrialists could develop powerful industries based on protected home markets and abundant supplies of raw materials.

After the 1870s both the value and volume of Britain's exports slowed more than those of imports, with the result that the balance of trade deficit grew substantially (see Table 12.4).

Table 12.4 Britain's Foreign Trade (£ million)

Years	Imports	Exports (plus re-exports)	Balance
1824-6	66.4	50.5	− 15.9
1854-6	151.6	123.5	− 28.1
1871-5	360.2	297.7	− 62.5
1896-1900	474.3	313.7	− 160.6
1911-1913	731.2	596.9	− 134.3

How can we explain the apparent puzzle that even at the height of Britain's industrial revolution, even in the mid-years of the nineteenth century when Britain was the 'workshop of the world', the value of merchandise exports was never sufficient to cover payment of imports? Partly the answer lies in Britain's high propensity to import. Britain's growing wealth led to rising demand for many goods like tea, sugar, coffee and tobacco which could not be produced at home. Such goods had been luxuries in the mid-eighteenth century, but they had become necessities a century later. Many of Britain's growing industries, too, were dependent on imported raw materials. By 1913 Britain was dependent on overseas sources for 100 per cent of her raw cotton, more than 90 per cent of her copper, tin, and lead, 80 per cent of her raw wool, and 60 per cent of her iron ore.

A further factor was the impact of falling prices at various times which meant that export values did not keep pace with export volumes. This was especially true in the years 1820-1850, when export prices fell faster than import prices (that is, the terms of trade moved against Britain).

Britain's free trade policy kept home markets open to foreign producers. Of particular significance was the repeal of the Corn Laws in 1846. This was not of immediate importance because not until the 1870s and 1880s did the

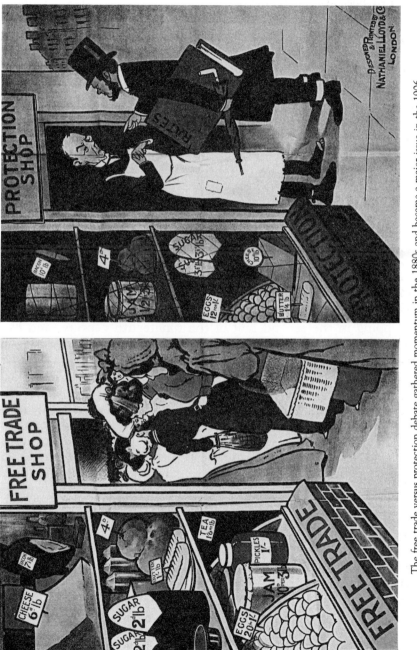

The free trade versus protection debate gathered momentum in the 1880s and became a major issue in the 1906 General Election (won by the free trade Liberals). This poster of the period shows typical free trade propaganda, concentrating on the price of basic foodstuffs.

combination of vast temperate lands in the Americas and Australia, the spread of railways, and cheap ocean going steam shipping, produce huge grain surpluses which could be exported to Europe. During the 1870s the United States replaced Russia as Britain's main source of wheat imports, and later on considerable grain imports also arrived from India, the Argentine, Australia and Canada. In 1913 Britain imported no less than 80 per cent of her wheat and 45 per cent of her meat and dairy products.

Although imports exceeded exports throughout the nineteenth century, so that the balance of merchandise trade showed a deficit, these deficits were more than covered by **invisible** earnings. Invisible exports are those exported services, like shipping, banking, insurance and other financial services, and also returns on foreign investment, which yield income for British subjects. Shipping was always one of the principal invisible exports. Most of Britain's huge trade (even in 1913 approximatley 40 per cent of all the world's trade went through British ports) was carried in British ships, and all over the world even trade between foreign countries was often carried by British ships and financed through London. In 1913 British ships carried about two-thirds of all the world's foreign trade and shipping receipts were more than £100 million a year (nearly as much as the value of cotton textile exports). Britain's dominance of world shipping increased with the development of ocean-going steam shipping in the second half of the nineteenth century, and by 1890 over half the world registered tonnage was British-owned. Until the 1870s shipping earnings were Britain's most important invisible export, but thereafter even greater earnings came from her mounting overseas investments.

Trade and Growth

Having surveyed the broad trends in Britain's overseas trade in the eighteenth and nineteenth centuries, we can now return to the important question of the role of Britain's trade in her economic growth. Was it trade expansion which led and sustained the industrial revolution?

Table 12.5 shows the overall ratio of foreign trade (exports plus imports) to national income.

Table 12.5 Trade as a Proportion of National Income

c. 1700	16
c. 1800	32
c. 1830	26
c. 1855	35
c. 1875	50
c. 1900	42

What this table shows is that trade was much more important at the end of the eighteenth century than it had been at the beginning. In the early nineteenth century (when the figures become more reliable) we can say with some confidence that domestic demand rather than foreign trade became of growing significance, but from the 1830s, and especially in the period from the 1850s to around 1875, foreign trade played the leading part in Britain's growth. The role of trade in the critical years of the late eighteenth century can be further examined with the help of Table 12.6.

Table 12.6 Production and Exports of Cotton Textiles (£ million)

	Value of production	Value of exports	%exported
1772-1774	0.9	0.3	33.3
1784-1786	5.4	0.9	16.7
1798-1800	11.1	5.1	45.9
1815-1817	30.0	17.4	58.0

This table shows clearly that the very early boost to cotton textile production before the 1790s came from domestic demand. Thereafter, however, it was foreign demand in the war period which led the growth, so that by 1815 well over half of total output was exported. The pattern shown by cotton textiles was shown also by other sectors of economy: an initial period of rapid home market development succeeded by growing overseas sales.

In summary, therefore, it appears as though foreign trade played a more significant role in Britain's economic growth after the 1780s than before, and that such trade was of greatest significance in the boom years of the mid-nineteenth century.

Trade and State Economic Policy

The eighteenth century was a period of state regulation and control over foreign trade; in the nineteenth century these controls were gradually relaxed after the 1840s government policy was characterised by free trade and laissez-faire.

By 1700 the age of the great monopolist trading companies was passing. Between 1688 and 1700 the monopoly privileges of the Merchant Adventurers in Northern Europe, the Russia Company, and the Royal Africa Company, were ended; the Eastland Company had lost its exclusive privilege in the Baltic even earlier, and the Levant Company was never able to enforce its legal monopoly of the Turkey trade against interlopers. The great exception was the East India Company, which for special reasons (notably the great risks and capital involved, and the political role of the Company in India) retained its control of British trade with India and China until the nineteenth century.

The other forms of state regulation were more enduring. These were two principal types: various duties, tariffs, and export bounties; and the Navigation Acts. As we have mentioned earlier, customs and excise duties were the major source of government revenue, and the chief motive for the imposition of duties was undoubtedly revenue collection. It was during war periods, when government needs were greatest, that duties were raised to their highest levels. Between 1690 and 1704, for example, there was a ten-fold increase in import duties. But high import duties had the effect of protecting home producers and boosting domestic output, and for this reason tariff policy, especially under Sir Robert Walpole in the 1720s, became refined into an instrument of economic policy. Duties on imported raw materials were kept low, but many finished manufactured products, like cotton goods from India, were kept out by high tariffs or prohibitions.

The Navigation Acts dated from the second half of the seventeenth century. The main Acts were passed in 1651 and 1660 and they were not finally abolished until 1849. To the Navigation Acts were added the Staple Act of 1663 and the Plantations Duties Act of 1673, which together formed the so-called Old Colonial System.

The main provisions of the various Acts were (1) all major exports from England's colonies had to be sent directly to England or another colony; they could not be sent directly to a foreign port. (2) These major exports (the so-called 'enumerated goods' which included sugar, tobacco and cotton) had to be sent in English or colonial ships. (3) If a colony wanted to buy goods from a foreign European country, these goods had first to be sent to England, in English ships. (4) Goods from beyond Europe imported into England or her colonies had to be sent in English ships. (5) English imports of non-European goods had (with some exceptions) to come from where the goods originated or were normally sent from. (6) England's imports of European goods had (with some exceptions) to arrive in English ships, or in ships of the country from where the goods originated.

These provisions seem complex, but their purpose was simple. First, they were designed to weaken the carrying trade of the Dutch and the entrepot role of Amsterdam, for the Dutch were England's main rivals in the late seventeenth and early eighteenth centuries. Secondly, they were to maximize the use of English ships and English crews, so providing the basis of naval strength.

As Dutch commercial power lessened in the first half of the eighteenth century the purpose of the Old Colonial System changed and became more and more part of colonial economic policy. The Acts were used to encourage the colonies to fulfil the role of supplier of primary products to the mother country and as purchaser of her manufactured goods. The list of enumerated commodities was extended, so that iron, copper, naval stores (timber, tar, pitch, and hemp), and hides could only be exported by colonies to England. Other measures restricted the colonies' manufacture of woollen cloth, hardware, agricultural implements, and other products in the interests of British manufacturers.

Historians have judged that the impact of the Old Colonial System on the pattern of British trade was slight. Most colonial trade would have been channelled to England anyway, and after American independence was achieved in 1783 that country became even more important as supplier to Britain of raw materials (especially cotton), and a purchaser of British manufactured goods. Doubt has also been cast on the profitability of the colonial trade (including the slave trade) to Britain anyway. Certainly individuals made huge fortunes, among them plantation owners in the West Indies, British merchants and slave traders (this appalling trade was not prohibited until 1807). But the net benefits to the British economy of the West Indian trade and even the North American trade were very limited when the full costs of the Old Colonial System are allowed for. We cannot, therefore, include 'mercantilism' as a springboard from which the eighteenth century British economy took-off.

The abandonment of control and regulation was a slow process, as we have seen. In 1776 Adam Smith, the great Scottish economist and philosopher, published his famous *Wealth of Nations.* Smith argued that economic wealth was best achieved by the 'invisible hand' of free market forces, operating without state control or intervention. He advocated 'laissez-faire', the doctrine of minimum state interference in economic matters (though for strategic reasons he supported the Navigation Acts).

Smith's theories mark a great divide between the 'mercantilist' views of the early eighteenth century and the triumph of laissez-faire in the nineteenth century. But modern historians are reluctant to see the change in quite such simple terms. They point out that 'mercantilism' was never a dominant or particularly coherent force in Britain's economic life. The extent of state intervention was always limited, and the arena of private enterprise in industry, agriculture, and commerce, always predominated. 'Laissez-faire',

The slave trade flourished throughout the eighteenth century. Many African slaves were taken to work on the plantations of the New World and the Caribbean. Here slaves are forced to work on a West Indian Sugar Plantation.

too, is not a very apt description of nineteenth century economic policy, except in the special field of free trade, and even then only fully from the 1850s. It took seventy years between the appearance of the *Wealth of Nations* and the repeal of the Corn Laws, for example. Pitt's hesitant measures in the 1780s to introduce lower tariffs on imported goods were cut short by the outbreak of war in 1793. At the close of war, in 1815, the highly protectionist Corn Law was passed, prohibiting wheat imports unless prices rose above 80 shillings a quarter. Steps to lower tariffs were not undertaken again until Huskisson brought in a sliding scale for the Corn Laws and various other modifications to existing duties in the 1820s. But a really significant dismantling of protective duties did not come until Peel's Budget of 1842, and free trade was not fully achieved until Gladstone's Budgets of 1853 and 1860. Outside of trading policy laissez-faire is best viewed as a way of thinking, which, though powerful, was never all-embracing. Even at the high watermark of economic liberalism, say in the third quarter of the nineteenth century, there were all sorts of exceptions. For example in matters of public health, factory conditions, and railways policy, the state found it necessary to intervene, and from the 1870s the sphere of such intervention grew steadily.

The Export of Capital

A striking feature of British economic history before 1914 was the large flow of capital into overseas investment. Already by 1850 a slow and fluctuating export of capital had built up a stock of investment worth around £200 million. Thereafter the pace quickened. The cumulative total was around £1000 million in 1870 and perhaps £4000 million by 1913. Between 1870 and 1913 approximately one-third of all Britain's domestic savings was channelled abroad, a quite remarkable figure and unmatched by any other country. It has been said, indeed, that in the late nineteenth century Britain ceased to be the workshop of the world and became instead the banker to the world. In some years enormous sums were invested. In 1913 alone, for example, the amount was equal to about 10 per cent of the entire national income. In other years, though, very little was exported. In 1901, during the Boer War, only about 1 per cent of national income was invested abroad, while the years following the Baring crash of 1890 (the famous merchant banking firm had made very injudicious investments in Argentina) were also years of low investment. Nevertheless, the importance of foreign investment grew progressively. Expressed as a proportion of national income, investment abroad had averaged around 2 per cent between 1811 and 1850; 3.3 per cent in the 1850s; 4 per cent in the 1860s; and 5.2 per cent between 1870 and 1913. By 1913 Britain's investments were producing an annual return of some £200 million, about double shipping earnings.

Nearly all of this investment was undertaken by private individuals, buying shares in railway companies, mines, plantations, and other enterprises operating abroad. Many of these companies were British owned, with the original capital raised in London. Others were foreign owned, but many of these, too, sought to raise capital in London. Although it is not easy to generalise about British overseas investment, covering as it did such an enormous variety of enterprises in nearly every country in the world, it is possible to highlight some of the main features. First, a great deal of the investment went into financing economic projects (rather than, for example, foreign government loans), many of which were connected with opening up new areas for commercial exploitation. Thus about 40 per cent of all foreign

British capital was invested throughout the world in railways, mines, plantations and other enterprises. Often such investment brought orders for British equipment. This illustration shows the beginning of the construction of Argentina's first railway in 1864, financed by British capital.

investment in 1913 had been placed in railway loans (some of them were foreign government loans raised specifically for building railways). Plantations and mines were other favourite outlets for investment, as were loans to improve harbour and dock facilities. Relatively little investment went into overseas manufacturing enterprises.

British investments were made throughout the world, but they were concentrated above all in the United States and in the white-settled dominions of the British Empire. The United States was the single most important outlet for investment, but between 1900 and 1913 there was a large investment boom in Canada, South Africa, and Australia. Other major areas of British investment were India (whose railways were mostly financed from Britain) and Argentina.

What was the impact of British investment? There can be no question that British capital played a leading role in developing the resources of the world before 1914. Indian tea, Argentinian wheat, Malayan tin, Siamese (Thai) teak, Northern Rhodesian (Zambian) copper, are only a few examples of hundreds where British investment and enterprise were paramount. The opening up of the world's resources was naturally of benefit to Britain as the world's leading industrial nation (until the 1890s) and the leading importer of virtually very major traded raw material.

It has been argued that Britain provided other countries with investment with which to industrialise, and so ultimately to compete with Britain. This argument would seem to have little validity. British investment in overseas manufacturing was very limited, and in any case British investment was only a small proportion of total investment in both of our major commercial rivals before 1913, Germany and the United States (British investment in Japan in 1913, where exports of cotton goods were making inroads into Britain's Asian markets, was also very low). Much more important was the positive boost such investment gave foreign countries in enabling them to purchase British goods. The link between capital exports and exports of merchandise was often a close one. For example, British-financed railway companies in India almost always bought their imports of rails and rolling stock from Britain.

Foreign interest also provided incomes for British investors. From around 1875 such incomes were more than sufficient to finance new net investment, so that foreign investment did not directly draw on domestic savings.

As well as providing incomes, and food and raw materials, foreign investment also helped close the gap in the balance of payments by providing a major source of invisible earnings. As mentioned already, returns on investment became the single most important source of invisible exports after the 1870s, and helped turn the current account balance of trade deficit into a balance of payments surplus.

Some historians have suggested that Britain exported too much capital abroad before 1914, and that it would have been better to have invested in British domestic industries instead. The argument is that had Britain invested in new industries, such as chemicals and electrical goods, instead of in foreign enterprises, Britain would have been better able to meet German and American competition and to have grown at a faster rate.

This argument is not convincing. To start with, we simply have no way of knowing whether, in the absence of foreign investment, domestic savings would have been channelled into domestic industries like chemicals and electrical goods. There is very little evidence that Britain's industries were starved of capital in the years before 1914. Indeed, interest rates were generally low, and the main reason why so much capital flowed abroad was simply that returns on overseas investment were much higher than on investments at home. Also, as we have seen, many British industries benefited directly from overseas investments, both by gaining access to cheap supplies of raw materials and by gaining valuable export markets.

The Growth of the Banking System

Money is a commodity which has very special characteristics, most significantly being instantly exchangeable for goods and services and being a store of value. This is most obviously true when money takes the form of gold and silver, for in some countries at some periods paper money has not been acceptable and has lost its value. Many commodities have some, though not all, the characteristics of money. Exchange may take place as barter, without using money or expressing values in money terms. But only in primitive societies with very limited trading has barter been the main way of exchanging goods and services. The supply of money in the form of gold and silver coins has nearly always been a state monopoly, the state making a profit by the difference between the rate at which it produces bullion and the value of the coins it mints. Long before 1700 Britain had a well-developed money economy, with gold and silver coins used for major transactions, and copper coins made from other low-value minerals, used for day-to-day trading. Long before 1700, too, various types of paper money and 'commercial paper' were in existence, especially bills of exchange which were used to finance both domestic and foreign trade.

The use of money long preceded the development of special banking institutions which dealt in money and money-like commodities, although some banking functions, like money-lending, were as old as money itself. The growth of England's banking system is best seen as the growth of groups of separate specialist institutions which only gradually, towards the end of the eighteenth century, merged into what might truly be called a 'system'. Note that we say England, not Britain. Scotland's banking developed along very different lines to those in England, and cannot unfortunately be considered here.

Banks originated in England during the seventeenth century as a result of four main factors. First, there was a growth of wealth and business opportunities. More wealth meant more savings, and one function of a bank was to provide a safe place in which savings could be deposited. The growth of business opportunities meant that more individuals wanted to borrow money for their enterprises. Particularly important was the rise of long-distance trade which tied up money for long periods, perhaps as long as two years between the beginning of a voyage and its final return with cargo, but which stood to make huge profits. Lending to overseas merchants required specialist knowledge and large resources, and some banks became active in this area. Banks were, of course, only one way in which foreign and domestic trades might be financed. The very expensive long-distance trades, like the East

India trade, were financed by the setting up of joint-stock companies, raising capital through the issue of marketable shares.

An obvious mechanism by which merchants, farmers, and others might borrow money was by giving in return an IOU to be paid at some future date. The growth of such IOUs, called **bills of exchange,** was a second main factor in the growth of specialist banks. Bills of exchange were not money, but they were like money, and the nearer they got to maturity, the nearer to money they became. By buying bills of exchange at less than their face value, at a discount, and holding them until maturity, the banks could make a profit. Specialist knowledge, sometimes about localities or particular commodities, was, of course, essential, if banks were to select trustworthy bills.

In practice not all who deposited money (gold or silver) with a bank would ever all demand their deposits back at once. Banks found that they could make profits by keeping a reserve of cash, but lending out further sums at interest to borrowers. One way of lending was to issue banknotes (the banks' own IOUs, but promising instant cash repayment to the value of the note to the bearer). Bank notes were a net addition to the money supply and their issue was an important feature of the banking system in the eighteenth and early nineteenth centuries. Banks could also lend by granting overdraft facilities and allowing cheques to be drawn against overdrafts, though this form of lending did not become widespread until the second half of the nineteenth century, by which time inland (domestic) bills of exchange were on the decline.

The fourth factor in the growth of the banking system was the need of the government to borrow money. The needs of war finance led to the formation of the Bank of England in 1694, an ingenious scheme whereby a group of wealthy merchants formed a 'joint stock' to lend £1.2 million to the government at 8 per cent interest. £$\frac{1}{2}$ million of this amount was lent in paper — Bank of England notes. Additional sums were later lent, and the Bank came to manage the National Debt for the government. At the same time the Bank acted as an ordinary bank, taking deposits and making loans, and only very slowly did it become a true 'central bank'. Nevertheless, from the outset the Bank was in a very privileged position through its acting as banker to the government, manager of the National Debt, and custodian of the national gold reserves. Moreover in 1708 the new Bank was given a privilege which was to shape English (not Scottish) banking until the nineteenth century: it was given a complete monopoly of joint-stock banking in England. All other banks had to be private partnerships of 6 individuals or less, thus ensuring that no large banks with multiple branches could exist. The Bank's position

Child's Bank, 1745.

was further strengthened as note issues by London private banks soon ceased, and these banks came to use Bank of England notes instead.

Banking before 1825

The eighteenth century brought three significant banking developments. First came the growth of a group of London private banks. These emerged after 1660, sometimes from the activities of goldsmiths. By the 1690s there were some 40 such banks, including such famous names as Hoare's, Child's and Coutts; by 1750, though fewer in number (perhaps 30), they had developed into sound and well-established institutions. Some specialised in the finance of trade and were located in the City; others, based in the West End, catered for the well-to-do gentry.

Secondly, from the 1750s, came the growth of provincial banks, the country banks. The first bank outside London had been established in 1716 in Bristol, but in 1750 there were still no more than a dozen. Thereafter their numbers grew, to perhaps 120 in 1784, 370 by 1800 and 650 in 1810. The actual numbers are not known with accuracy; both births and deaths were high, but of the general expansion of country banks, especially during the Napoleonic War period, there can be no doubt.

Country banks were much smaller enterprises than the London banks, and their activities also differed. They accepted local deposits and lent locally, but they also maintained agencies with London banks, buying and selling bills. In this way the country banks provided a mechanism for transferring surplus funds from one region to another, via London. Also, unlike the London banks, the country banks issued notes of their own, usually in small denominations of £1 or £2. This helped ease a shortage of cash which at times became acute as commerce expanded in the eighteenth century.

Third was the growth of the Bank of England, which, as we have seen, had a monopoly of joint-stock banking in England. The Bank did not, in the eighteenth century open any branches outside London. The London private banks held accounts at the Bank of England and used Bank of England notes. In fact, therefore, at this period the Bank could more properly be regarded as the Bank of London rather than as the Bank of England.

By the late eighteenth century it is possible to speak of a loose 'three-tier' banking system emerging, with the Bank of England, London private banks, and country banks all inter-linked. But the links were loose, and there was little control over the note-issues of the country banks. Increasingly the weaknesses of the system became evident, especially during the Napoleonic War period and the two financial crises of 1815 and 1825 when many country banks failed.

Banking after 1825

The story of nineteenth century banking has three threads: the growing strength of joint-stock banking at the expense of the country banks; the development of the Bank of England as a responsible central bank at the head of the banking system, with a virtual monopoly of note-issue; and the rise of other specialist banking institutions concerned largely with the finance of foreign trade, the merchant banks and the discount houses.

The causes of these developments were several. One was parliamentary legislation which encouraged the creation of joint-stock banks with multiple branches and which also sought to strengthen the position of the Bank of England. A second factor was the growth of banking experience, which in turn influenced legislation. From the various financial crises, for example the 1825 panic or the failure of the discount house of Overend Gurney in 1866, came a realisation of the necessity for strong central Bank control, of the soundness of large joint-stock banks compared with small private ones, and of the importance of such policies as Bank Rate in Bank of England control over the banking system. Moreover as the economy became more sophisticated, its demands for banking services became more specialised and changed in other ways too.

The legislation which led to the growth of joint-stock deposit banking after 1825 and which concentrated note-issue in the hands of the Bank of England may be quickly outlined. The first important measure came in 1826, in the wake of the financial panic of 1825 when as many as 80 country banks closed their doors. The aim of the 1826 Bank Act was two-fold, to encourage the formation of joint-stock banks (hitherto forbidden in England under the Act of 1708) and to restrict note issue. Accordingly, joint-stock banks were permitted as long as they were outside a 65 mile radius of London (this protection for the Bank of England was withdrawn in 1833, when joint-stock banks, though without the right to issue notes, could be established anywhere). The result was the appearance of large joint-stock banks with multiple branches. For example the London and Westminster bank was launched in 1834, and within a decade more than 100 joint-stock banks had been founded. The country banks slowly went into eclipse. Further Acts in 1858 and 1862 extended limited liability to joint-stock banks, and a number of hitherto private banks (Barclays in 1862, Lloyds in 1865, for example) became joint-stock. By 1880, by which time amalgamations among the joint-stock banks were producing larger banks with more branches, the joint-stock banks held more than one-half of the nation's total bank deposits.

Another landmark came with the Bank Charter Act of 1844, which aimed primarily to restrict the note issues both of the Bank of England and of the other issuing banks. Ever since the wartime inflation at the beginning of the nineteenth century there had been an argument between the Currency School and the Banking School as to the causes of monetary instability. The Currency School argued that excessive note issues were to blame for inflation

1866 Bank Panic: The failure of the famous discount house of Overend, Gurney and Co.

and instability, and wanted all banknotes to be backed in full by gold (except for the period 1797-1821, Bank of England notes were always convertible into gold at a fixed rate). The Banking School thought that banks should be free to regulate their note issues as they saw fit, as long as their notes were quickly convertible into gold. The panic of 1825 and further, lesser, disturbances in the 1830s had convinced parliament that excessive note issues were, in fact, to blame. The 1844 Act was thus a triumph for the Currency School. The Bank's issues of notes were to be strictly limited. Except for a fiduciary issue of £14 million, each note was to be backed pound for pound by its gold reserves. Moreover the banking and issuing departments of the Bank were to be kept separate, so that gold amassed in the issue departments as backing for notes could not be used, even in emergencies, by demands on the banking department.

The 1844 Act also tried in various ways to curtail note issues by the other issuing banks. Any bank which amalgamated automatically lost its right of note issue, no new banks of issue were to be created, and no issuing bank could exceed its current note issue. By these and other steps it was hoped to concentrate all note issue in the hands of the Bank of England, an object very

1878: The failure of the City & Glasgow Bank. This failure led to the adoption of limited liability by many banks.

nearly achieved by the 1870s (even in 1844 three-quarters of all notes were Bank of England notes), although the last private bank did not cease to issue notes until 1921.

Until around 1815 the banking system had been largely geared to domestic needs. Foreign transactions were normally financed by wealthy merchants or by continental banking houses. From around 1815 came the growth of merchant banks and discount houses, dealing specifically with the needs of foreign trade. The London-based merchant banks, most prominent of which were the Rothschilds and Barings, were a close-knit group whose financial dealings had grown often out of general merchanting and commodity trading. Their main business was 'acceptance', the accepting of foreign bills of exchange. From the 1820s they also became involved in 'issuing', mainly the issuing in London of loans raised on behalf of foreign governments. In this way merchant banks were involved both in the finance of foreign trade and in the export of British capital, and played a significant part in the growth of London as a major international financial centre during the nineteenth century. The discount houses, as mentioned already, grew up in the 1820s as dealers in bills (mainly foreign). They provided an important link between the various financial institutions, borrowing from the domestic banks normally but, in times of stringency, from the Bank of England. It was in lending to the discount market as 'lender of last resort' that the Bank was able to make its Bank Rate policy effective.

By 1914 England had a well developed, stable banking system. The Bank of England had become a true central bank, acting in times of financial disturbance to minimise upheaval and prevent the spread of panic. Below the bank, the large joint-stock banks and other specialist institutions operated smoothly, sound and respectable, and benefiting from the country's growing wealth and London's central position in the international economy.

The Role of Banks

To describe the growth of banks in terms of legislation and the development of particular institutions is to say nothing about their 'role' or 'importance'. What part did the banks play in the development of Britain's economy? There are two conflicting views. The traditional approach emphasises the soundness and success of the system, especially after the growth of joint-stock banking and the growth of responsible management exercised by the Bank of England after 1844. There were few bank failures, bank deposits swelled the nation's money supply, and the City was an important source of invisible earnings for the economy. The banks showed initiative and readiness to change, for example in the growing use of cheques and overdrafts, and in the movement by the joint-stock banks into new areas from the 1870s, such as the finance of foreign trade.

The alternative view stresses that, unlike their American and continental counterparts, British banks did not invest in long term fixed capital, and lent little to industry. They have been accused of 'starving' British industry of capital, and of being obsessed with soundness, security, and 'self-liquidating' loans (like trade bills, or advances to agriculturalists prior to harvest). Certainly the structure of the City was geared very much to international rather than national finance.

It is difficult to make an overall assessment of the role of banks. There is probably some truth in the accusation of 'conservatism' and foreign-trade bias, especially after 1870. Indeed, recent studies are beginning to uncover quite considerable banking involvement in early industrial and transport projects, prior to 1850. On the other hand Britain certainly gained immensely from her role in the world economy and the prestige of her financial institutions. There were both costs and benefits from this role, and as yet no historian has drawn up a satisfactory balance.

Conclusion
Britain's Achievement

Looking back from the perspective of the depressed 1920s, across the dreadful abyss of the 1914-18 war, many Britons were inclined to view the years before 1914 as a kind of 'golden age', a period of prosperity, stability, and tranquility. The British Empire was at its most extensive and magnificent. British leadership of the financial and commercial world was beyond dispute. Britain's political strength and influence, bolstered by the world's most powerful navy, was felt throughout the world.

From what we know now of Britain's economic performance in the decade or so before 1914 such a golden view seems inappropriate. While Britain's economy stagnated, other countries grew. In Britain there was much disquiet, especially at the obvious signs of German economic expansion, and the failure of the British to match American and German ingenuity in the development of new technologically advanced industries. Socially, too, there was much to be concerned about, as the great social surveys at the turn of the century had shown only too clearly.

Why should Britain, having led the world for so long, start to fall behind towards the end of the nineteenth century? In this book we have begun to unravel some of the answers, although there are no simple solutions.

First, we must put Britain's achievement in perspective. The industrial revolution did not appear suddenly out of the blue in the late eighteenth century. Already by 1700 England was, by contemporary standards, a prosperous country, with many areas of industrial specialisation and a well-developed commercial system. Keys to understanding the early eighteenth century are the growth of domestic demand arising from growing agricultural productivity at home and the expansion of demand for exports and re-exports, the trans-Atlantic trade being particularly important. From around 1750 rising population and urbanisation added to the sources of domestic demand. They provided a favourable environment both for the improvement of transport and communications, and for the search for new ways of producing goods through mechanisation. Larger markets and better communications meant the possibilities of economies of scale, and this, in itself, irrespective of technical improvements, would raise productivity.

Out of growing markets at home and abroad came growing profits for firms able to produce for these markets. Profits were easily the most important source of capital investment during the eighteenth and early nineteenth centuries, and increasingly capital went into forms of fixed investment, such as factory buildings, machinery, canals, and railways.

Thus one explanation for Britain's ability to finance its industrial revolution was simply the fact that Britain was a rich country: profits and personal savings, coupled with social attitudes which encouraged thrift, all fostered investment. At the same time actual expenditures on early industrial plant and equipment were relatively small, and not beyond the resources of moderately well-off entrepreneurs.

Putting the industrial revolution in perspective, we must also emphasise that recent research has taken away much of its 'revolutionary' character. The overall growth rate of the economy (national income) and even the rate of industrial growth were much less spectacular than earlier writers had supposed. Indeed, in terms of growth rates, no marked acceleration occurred until around 1825, at the beginning of the railway age.

This should not lead us to underestimate the importance of the post-1780 changes, however. Those years saw major new industries and new technologies developed, while progress was seen far beyond industry, in agriculture, banking, internal trade, transport, overseas commerce, and many other areas of economic life. Moreover to achieve these changes while population was growing at an unprecedented rate was indeed a considerable feat.

A further perspective to emphasise is the narrow range of industries on which Britain's nineteenth century prosperity was developed. Nearly all these industries were based directly or indirectly on Britain's great natural resource, coal. It was coal which provided coke for iron smelting, and fuel for steam power. Steam power drove the mills, the railways, and the steamships. A major element in Britain's commercial superiority after 1860 rested on her monopoly of world steam shipping, and Britain continued to lead the world in shipping down to 1914.

Britain's great industries evolved on the basis of her natural advantages in raw materials and ocean-going shipping: coal, iron, and cheap supplies of raw cotton and other imported raw materials. But it was this narrowness which led ultimately to the disappointing performance of the late nineteenth century. In understanding this performance, again we should put matters in perspective. Britain's economy did **not** stop growing (except, perhaps, in the decade after 1900). Overall growth rates were not significantly slower in the last quarter of the nineteenth century than they had been in the third. Real wages increased considerably after 1875, and between 1875 and 1900 grew more quickly than they had done at any time previously.

In retrospect, though, Britain's economy does seem to have reached a turning point around the 1870s, even though phrases like 'great depression' are misleading. First, new countries, the United States and Germany, began to challenge Britain's hitherto unassailable economic lead. As these other economies grew they developed industries and forms of industrial organisation which Britain could not match. Secondly, Britain's export markets, though still growing, were not expanding with the same buoyancy which had marked the middle years of the nineteenth century. Thirdly, and related to this, industrial growth rates were lower after 1870 than before, leading to generally low profits, a low demand for new investment at home (and low interest rates), and talk of 'depression'.

Why was Britain's economy slow to adjust to the new environment? We must remember that not only particular industries, but also much of the supporting financial, distribution, and transport system had been developed as adjuncts to the great basic industries. Britain's economy was inflexible partly because it had been so successful, while new markets for the older industries, many in the underdeveloped areas of India and elsewhere, were still growing. Change was difficult: the pressures for change were often not overwhelming.

Yet was it really such a bad thing that Britain should have remained wedded to her traditional products, and should import manufactured goods produced more cheaply elsewhere? This was, after all, the logic of free trade which had served Britain so well in mid-Victorian times. If Britain in 1913 could produce and export coal and cottons cheaper than elsewhere, and in return bought electrical and other sophisticated goods from America and Germany, this was a process which maximised the real incomes of British people. The average Briton in 1900 enjoyed a living standard which had doubled since 1850, while total population had also roughly doubled. Earlier, the real wages of British workers may have doubled between 1820 and 1850. This achievement was not gained without considerable social stress and suffering, and it was not attained without incurring many costs which came inevitably from being the pioneer industrial nation. But it was, nevertheless, a remarkable achievement, and one which ushered in a new era not only for Britons but for peoples throughout the world.

Further Reading

There are a number of useful textbooks on British economic and social history for this period. One of the best and most comprehensive, though aimed at university level and not at all easy to digest, is Peter Mathias, *The First Industrial Nation, an Economic History of Britain, 1700-1914* (2nd edition, 1983). At a more elementary level, and dealing with a longer period, is J Walker (revised by C W Munn), *British Economic and Social History, 1700-1982* (Fourth edition, 1982). Students will probably find it more useful, though, to read on particular topics rather than consult a stream of textbooks. Here the excellent series published by Macmillan and The Economic History Society under the general title *Studies in Economic and Social History* is especially helpful. Among the best of these is S B Saul, *The Myth of the Great Depression, 1873-1896* (1969); R A Church, *The Great Victorian Boom, 1850-1873* (1975); E L Jones, *The Development of English Agriculture, 1815-1873* (1968); T R Gourvish, *Railways and the British Economy, 1830-1873* (1981); and P L Cottrell. *British Overseas Investment in the Nineteenth Century* (1975).

For industrial changes the best comprehensive work is A E Musson, *The Growth of British Industry* (1978). For agriculture, J D Chambers and G E Mingay, *The Agricultural Revolution, 1750-1880* (1966) is readable and reliable, though now somewhat out of date. The collected essays edited by P J Perry, *British Agriculture, 1875-1914* (1973) are excellent for the later period.

The development of transport and communications is well covered in P S Bagwell, *The Transport Revolution from 1770* (1973) and H J Dyos and D H Aldcroft, *British Transport: An Economic Survey from the Seventeenth Century to the Twentieth* (1969).

Social history has attracted a great deal of recent research, but unfortunately no single book covers the subject comprehensively. E J Evans, *The Forging of the Modern State, Industrial Britain, 1783-1870* (1983) is a fine, though rather advanced, study of the combination of politics and society. For particular topics the following are excellent: J Stevenson, *Popular Disturbances in England, 1700-1870* (1979); E H Hunt, *British Labour History* (1981); Jane Lewis, *Women in England, 1870-1950* (1984).

The best introduction to the Industrial Revolution is Phyllis Deane, *The First Industrial Revolution* (2nd edition, 1979). Eric Pawson, *The Early Industrial*

Revolution: Britain in the Eighteenth Century (1979) is particularly useful because it covers the often-neglected areas of Scotland, Wales and Ireland as well as England. On factories and the factory system the two volume collection of documents by J T Ward, *The Factory System* (1970), Vol 1, *Birth and Growth*, Vol 2, *The Factory System and Society*, is recommended because it combines an excellent selection of important documents with a helpful commentary on their significance. For technical developments in industry and other sectors see E R Chamberlin, *The Awakening Giant: Britain in the Industrial Revolution (1976)*, which has many useful pictures and diagrams. This can be supplemented with *L T C Rolt, Victorian Engineering* (1970), which has a lot of information on the lives of some of the pioneer engineers.

Index